Creative Dramatics

IN HOME, SCHOOL, AND COMMUNITY

Photograph by James O. Sneddon
Office of Public Information, University of Washington, Seattle

"And now, Cinderella . . ."

Creative Dramatics

IN HOME, SCHOOL, AND COMMUNITY

by Ruth Lease and Geraldine Brain Siks

HARPER & BROTHERS · PUBLISHERS
NEW YORK

CREATIVE DRAMATICS IN HOME, SCHOOL, AND COMMUNITY

Library of Congress catalog card number: 51-11933

To

Our Children

Mark and Jan Siks

Barbee and Alice Jean Lease

Your Children

and

Their Children

Contents

Contents

Foreword

THE MOST interesting thing in life is—and always has been—magic. Few human enterprises have thrived without magic at their core—that element which produces the wonderful result, by secret or supernatural means. Sometimes the secret can be shared with others without the wonder and the mystery being lost, but that is possible only when the magic is real, and not a trick.

Creative dramatics, as the readers of this book will discover, is real magic, and it is being shared. Its reality is based on the imagination of children, as firm a base as anyone could wish for, and the process of its sharing at present resembles nothing so much as a prairie fire.

Although it is entirely possible that several thousand years ago a cave-mama employed the principles of creative dramatics in the rearing of her cave-child, it appears to be certain that the first consciously organized application of these principles was carried out only a few years ago by Winifred Ward at Northwestern University. It is from Miss Ward's pioneering that creative dramatics has come to be an accepted technique.

The present book, despite its universal applicability and its international outlook, is primarily an elaboration of what in creative dramatics circles is known as "The Seattle Story." This story begins in 1941, when Ruth Lease (who had just moved with her husband and two daughters to Seattle from Montana) offered her services to the Seattle Public Library as a teller of stories for children. In this capacity, she felt, she could make her best contribution to the morale of a war-industry city.

Out of her story-telling, and out of the psychological needs of hundreds of assorted, and in some cases ill-adjusted, children in housing projects, grew the complex and fascinating experience which is here described.

By the end of the war Mrs. Lease and her associate volunteers had such an impressive record of accomplishment that Seattle Junior Programs Inc., recognized the importance of the program and gave assistance to it. Later, the Seattle Junior League adopted the city-wide program as a major project and provided funds for a professional creative dramatics supervisor. Shortly afterwards it became apparent that there must be a training course for future leaders in this rapidly expanding field, and Mrs. Lease naturally turned to the School of Drama at the University of Washington for assistance. The result of her appeal was that in the autumn of 1947 the School of Drama added to its curriculum a course in creative dramatics, and, in coöperation with the Seattle Junior League and the Extension Services of the University, brought Miss Agnes Haaga to Seattle to serve as instructor and supervisor. A year later the University assumed complete responsibility for the program, which now employs the talents of several highly trained young women—one of whom is Geraldine Siks, co-author of this book. Mrs. Siks was for a number of years associated with Winifred Ward in Evanston, Illinois, for four years as associate director of the Children's Theatre of Evanston, and for seven years as instructor in creative dramatics in the Evanston public schools. Her teaching is characterized by a remarkable spiritual quality and unusual sensitivity. One of her outstanding achievements has been her conducting of demonstration classes at the Seattle Art Museum, where through the medium of creative dramatics she has guided children to an understanding of arts and cultures of other countries. Mrs. Siks is also a skillful playwright, and her *Marco Polo* is a favorite with the younger generation.

As the innocent and rather unsuspecting bystander who became involved in the creative dramatics excitement, I am in a position to testify as to its inflammatory nature. It is true that, as executive director of the School of Drama, I am proud to be credited as the giver of academic standing to this new subject of instruction, but it is also true that there are times when I experience the sensation of having a lion by the tail. To change the metaphor, being godfather to thousands of children creates a special kind of fright which no one could accurately anticipate.

It is natural that a person with the vision of Ruth Lease should see creative dramatics as a partial solution to the problem of world unification. After all, the children of France have the same kind of imagination as the children of Kansas or Korea. Acting on this theory, Mrs. Lease (in company with Mrs. Raymond B. Allen) journeyed in 1947 to the San Francisco meeting of UNESCO, where the two inspired women pleaded their case. The next year in Boston they obtained before the same organization an approval of creative dramatics as a technique to be applied to the children of Europe, whose psychological problems are so challenging. Following up this interest, Mrs. Lease spent the summer of 1949 in Europe, where she made a survey of the Austrian youth program and was able to introduce creative dramatics. As a result of her activities, several European specialists are now on their way to America for training in creative dramatics.

Meanwhile, the College of Education of the University of Washington has decreed that every candidate for a teaching certificate in the elementary schools of the state must have at least one quarter's training in creative dramatics. This I consider to be a most significant decision.

It is a tempting subject, and I find it necessary to restrain myself. It is not my business to write the book. That job is in the hands of two experts, both of whom are mothers as well as instructors. Mrs. Siks has two sons and Mrs. Lease two daughters. What they have to say, therefore, is of domestic as well as dramatic and literary importance. Both of them assure me that creative dramatics is building audiences for the theatre—the theatre which has been dying. Perhaps they are right. The happiness of a child is pure gold, and pure gold does not change to brass.

GLENN HUGHES

University of Washington, Seattle

Preface

THIS BOOK is for parents, teachers, and community leaders who have faith in children. It is written for all adults who are wholeheartedly concerned with how boys and girls are growing up in the world today.

Creative dramatics is a way of teaching for adults—a way of learning for children. It is a dynamic activity program that has grown rapidly throughout the past quarter-century. It is educationally sound and has proved its worth. Not only does it appeal to children of all ages, but it contributes immeasurably to the social, emotional, intellectual, physical, and spiritual development of growing boys and girls.

Never before has it been so important for the people of the world to know each other as it is in this atomic age. Through creative dramatics children can learn to understand the cultures of other countries as well as their own. Creative dramatics encourages each child to make use of his gift of imagination so that he may live the lives of other people. Through continuous creative experiences children gradually develop a tolerance and an understanding of others that is strong and real.

Now as never before it is equally important for individuals to recognize creativeness within themselves. Creative dramatics is a group activity that respects each individual and encourages each child to release and develop his creative power. This activity keeps alive the creative spark of individuality. It encourages independent thinking. It develops awareness. It gives each individual something to live by.

Creative Dramatics in Home, School, and Community is a practical handbook that has been written in answer to the many questions that have been asked and continue to be asked about creative dramatics for children. This book is intended to interpret a practical philosophy and technique of creative teaching. First of all, we have made an attempt to explain what creative dramatics is, and to show why it is of real value to children. Secondly, we have shown how to introduce creative dramatics to children's groups from kindergarten through junior high school. Thirdly, we have explained how it may be used at home, at school, and in various phases of community living. And, finally, we have included useful bibliographies. In Appendix A we have listed rhymes, verse, and stories that have been enjoyed by children in creative dramatics experiences. In Appendix B we have given suggestions for rhythm and dramatic play and for a variety of pantomimes. In Appendix C we have included a bibliography of reading material that has proved useful to teachers, parents, and community leaders who have been concerned with creative teaching.

It is our hope that this book will serve a two-fold purpose. It has been designed for methodized reading and study as in college courses. It has been planned for individual reading, as in the case of parents, classroom teachers, librarians, recreation leaders, social workers, religious educators, and other youth leaders who may be working in small groups or alone. We have endeavored to make a helpful and specific guide for both beginning leaders and for those far-seeing adults who have been striving in their own ways to guide children into creative pathways.

Many people have helped with this book. It would not be possible to mention all the mothers, teachers, librarians, social workers, and friends who have contributed in various ways. To each one we are grateful.

For specific acknowledgment we first of all wish to thank Winifred Ward for many ideas, and for the inspiration she has always been to us. We are indebted to our good friend Glenn Hughes, who not only was the critic on this book, but who has enthusiastically lent his support to the cause of creative dramatics for children.

To Agnes Haaga we are grateful for the help she gave us in writing our chapter on recreation, for reading our manuscript, and for the outstanding contribution she has made to creative dramatics.

We appreciate the kindness of Dorothea Jackson for guiding us in our education chapters and for encouraging the use of creative dramatics in the public schools.

We wish to express our sincere appreciation to Alice Jean Lease, Virginia Morrison, and Robert D. Monroe, and we want to thank Hazel Dunnington and George B. Brain who read and criticized our manuscript and offered useful suggestions.

We are indebted to many community organizations in Seattle who recognized the values of creative dramatics in the community and guided the development of this children's program. We wish to express our appreciation to the organizations represented by the Seattle Children's Recreation Project Board including the Junior League, Public Library, Housing Authority, City Council, Public Schools, Junior Programs, Park Board, Art Museum, Council of Social Agencies, and the University of Washington.

Lastly, we wish to remember the hundreds of boys and girls who enjoyed working and playing together and whose creative experiences we share with you.

R.L.
G.B.S.

September, 1951

Creative Dramatics

IN HOME, SCHOOL, AND COMMUNITY

Chapter 1

WHAT IS CREATIVE DRAMATICS?

A little child shall lead them.

"It's sharing thoughts and stories, and it makes you feel so good inside!" Seven-year-old Judy was telling a group of her young friends about creative dramatics. "We act out stories and we get to *be* the characters and make up our own words. Today I was one of the mean sisters, and after a while I was the fairy godmother. It was fun!"

Judy's concept of creative dramatics was exceptionally accurate, for she had experienced the *sharing,* the *feeling,* the *thinking,* and the *being* that come from active participation in many creative dramatics group experiences. Judy had lived these delightful moments. Her enthusiasm came from the joy in creating a play with others of her own age.

Because boys and girls the world over enjoy playing at make-believe, creative dramatics is genuine fun for all children. It is an activity that approaches a child through the medium of play, but it does not stop there. It goes far beyond and reaches deeply into the hearts and minds of children.

1

CHILDREN'S DRAMA

In order to understand more clearly what is meant by the term creative dramatics, let us first consider the broad field of drama for children. A careful analysis reveals two marked divisions, namely, drama for the child audience and drama for the child participant.

Children's theatre is the term given to the form of drama which exists for the purpose of the child audience. In a children's theatre a play carefully presented by capable actors affects each individual child who sits in the audience and vicariously experiences enjoyable and breath-taking moments. In a children's theatre actors memorize the lines of a play written by a playwright and in turn are directed through the action and interpretation of the play by a qualified director. Staging and costuming are important considerations of a play which is to be presented to an audience, for product is the major emphasis in a theatre for children.

Creative dramatics is the term given to the form of drama which exists for the purpose of the child participant. It is *playing with purposeful group planning and significant evaluating,* and it affects each individual who actively participates in this art experience. Staging and costuming are of little concern, for it is the process rather than the product which is the region of emphasis in this activity. The process is the end in itself from the standpoint of child growth and development; however, to the children who are creating it, the play is vitally important. The teacher guides rather than directs the children through the process of creative playing. Creative dramatics is not concerned with training children to become actors, nor in creating plays for an audience. *It is aimed toward the development of the whole child, socially, emotionally, intellectually, physically, and spiritually.*

Winifred Ward, author of *Playmaking With Children* explains that creative dramatics is an expression "used interchangeably with *playmaking,* since it, too, is a general term meaning the activity in which informal drama is created by the players. *Informal drama* is not conventional. That is, its dialogue and action are extemporized rather than written and memorized."[1]

Creative dramatics is commonly referred to as *educational dramatics,* since it is characterized by spontaneous flexible drama, as distinguished from the more familiar formal type of drama which is rehearsed and produced for an audience. Creative dramatics and children's theatre work harmoniously together for the benefit of the child. They complement rather than conflict with each other. When a child who has worked through many creative dramatics experiences becomes a member of an audience in a children's theatre, his appreciation and interest are exceptionally strong. On the other hand, if a child first becomes interested in drama by seeing plays in a children's theatre, his understanding and enthusiasm generally lead him into making plays with other children of his own age.

Understanding the purpose behind creative dramatics we see that it may be defined as *a group activity in which meaningful experience is acted out by the participants as they create their own dialogue and action.*

AN OLD ART

Creative dramatics is not new. It is as old as the world. As far back as the days of the Greeks and the Romans, people acted out their feelings. The Greek word for action (δραμα) described this art, meaning "to act or to do." Formal drama characterized all known drama throughout the years. It developed and progressed widely, for there were people with ideas and feelings, people who had something to say. These people were the artists, the playwrights, who gave expression to their ideas in the form of drama.

Simultaneously with the development of formal drama came the development of informal drama, but it was not recognized as such.

---

[1] Winifred Ward, *Playmaking With Children*, D. Appleton-Century Co., Inc., 1947.

Informal drama was developed by the children of the day. Since the earliest days children have played and pretended, but for centuries their activity was dismissed by older people simply as play. Many children, growing up through the years, listened to wonderful tales of troubadours and traveling minstrels. They wondered about strange and far-away places, about the tales of pixies and pirates and plunderers. They wished that they might journey to castles and speak with kings. Now and then they wanted to be princes or princesses and eat delicious morsels from golden platters. Many of these children who felt like acting out their feelings did just that. Sometimes they played alone. Sometimes they played in groups. Sometimes they "put on a play" and invited friends and the family.

In some homes and in some places in these earlier years, it did not seem important when children had something to say. Grown-up people here and there said, "Children are to be seen and not heard." And in many of these places far too many children *were* seen and not heard. If a child living in one of these proper places started beating loudly upon his mother's saucepan and marched gaily around the kitchen like a drummer in a band, someone hurried to quiet him. His banging was annoying and disturbing. Many older people could not figure out why a child wanted to be a drummer and go banging with all his might. They could see neither rhyme nor reason for boys and girls to feel like kings or queens or cowboys. These people had definite ideas about raising children. Children were supposed to be quiet and by being quiet were supposed to grow up into fine ladies and gentlemen.

Fortunately for many of these children they did bang on saucepans later in the afternoon, or they released their feelings in other ways. When they were away from watchful eyes they ran into the garden, out to tall friendly trees, away to the big barn. Some of them tiptoed to the attic or closed themselves in their rooms. They found places that were far enough away from unsympathetic adults so they wouldn't be heard. There they talked or even yelled, and they said what they wanted to say. Some wrote in diaries. Some cried, which was all right too, for they were finding an outlet for a hurt feeling. Some of them acted out their feelings. They pretended to be their own mothers and fathers, doing the "bad" things they did, like scolding and lecturing and making children mind. Some of them pretended to be their own school teachers, walking and talking and teaching exactly as their school teachers walked and talked and taught. Unfortunately, there were other children who did not have a chance to work out these pent-up emotions. Innermost feelings buried themselves deep into hearts and minds. Sometimes miserable tensions were harbored for years which worked destructively within or forced their way into actions that were extreme or trying or dangerous.

Early in the twentieth century, when interest in child welfare spread widely throughout the country, more and more adults who were concerned with child growth and development saw the need for allowing children to express their innermost thoughts and feelings through legitimate channels. Psychologists studied the nature of child characteristics and child behavior. Educators recognized this knowledge as the basis for determining educational methods for the development of a wholesome child personality and for the development of well integrated citizens in a democratic society. New methods of learning were introduced in schools throughout the country. It was at this time that informal dramatics, which had always been a natural child activity, was recognized as a strong force in child development. When this idea came into its own as a powerful medium for child learning, it became known as creative dramatics.

DEVELOPMENT OF CREATIVE DRAMATICS

Winifred Ward, nationally known authority on children's drama and Professor of Dramatic Production at Northwestern University, led the way in pioneering in the field of creative dramatics in the elementary schools at Evanston, Illinois. Since that time, drama for the child participant has spread to children in many parts of the country. It has been introduced into outstanding school systems from kindergarten through junior high school, and many high schools offer creative dramatics as an elective class in the daily program.

Because creative dramatics is a worthy activity with a strong appeal for children, and because it is inexpensive and practical, it has been recognized by many communities as an ideal leisure-time program for children's groups. Many summer camps, vacation Bible schools, community park departments, Camp Fire and Scout organizations, museums, and public libraries have provided creative dramatics activities in their educational programs. Social workers, church-school leaders, and parents have also found creative dramatics helpful in working with children.

NATURE OF THE ACTIVITY ·

"In creative dramatics you can be anything you want to be. If you're fat you can be thin; if you're short you can be tall; if you're poor you can be rich. You don't have to say what the teacher says. You can say what you think to say." Such was the enthusiastic reply by a ten-year-old boy to a question asked by an adult in a demonstration group. From the point of view of a child, creative dramatics is a dynamic play activity. It is regarded by children as an opportunity to make up a play in which a part of the group becomes the characters and plays a scene while the remaining members of the group become the audience. The children in the audience know that they will become the characters in the following playings and, therefore, they watch the play with alert interest.

Nearly all children discover creative dramatics for themselves, but too often their playing follows the patterns and impressions they have gained from frightening moving pictures or from reading materials of low standard. Unless a child's dramatic playing is skillfully guided, his thinking is likely to become so colored by this mediocre activity that he will develop a strong desire to enter into daring and destructive experiences in reality. Adults who understand the philosophy and technique of creative dramatics will be in a position to guide children in their playmaking activities and will thereby be able to help them channel their thinking and their energy into richer and fuller playing and living. In the activity of creative dramatics the experiences which the children act out are carefully chosen by an understanding adult who recognizes the needs of the children with whom she works. She approaches them on their own level of thinking and gradually leads them into many and varied creative experiences which in turn influence their thinking.

It is in the great field of children's literature that a wealth of the very best experiences for children to act out creatively is found. Creative plays may be developed from a poem, a riddle, an object, an article, an experience from reality or an experience from the life of a well-known artist or composer or explorer or statesman. A group of children may want to create a play from a single word, from a letter they have received from a child in a far-away country, from a season of the year, from a storm, from a first snowfall.

Mother Goose rhymes, with their lively action and simple plots, provide excellent material for creative dramatics for children of all ages, particularly when the activity is first being introduced. Fairy tales, folk tales, ballads, legends, adventures, myths, and many of the modern stories provide vital material for dramatic playing. Happenings from everyday life have great value for many groups of children when they are relived through dramatic playing.

New situations which the child is going to encounter are springboards for satisfying creative experiences. A little boy who is going to the barber shop for the first time will enjoy meeting the barber and having his hair cut if he has played "barbershop" many times previously with his mother or father at home. Going to the dentist, shopping alone for the first time, introducing a distinguished speaker at an assembly program, and applying in person for an after-school position are only a few of the many situations which can be enjoyable experiences in reality if the child has been prepared for them in advance by acting them out creatively. Long-wished-for articles and long-dreamed-of experiences are delightful starting points around which children may create, for they satisfy in part the great desire to have some object or to be someone different from themselves.

VALUES TO THE INDIVIDUAL

Stimulation of Social Development.   Teamwork is at the very heart of creative dramatics activity, for in every experience children learn to work together for the purpose of creating a fine and satisfying play. In a group activity in which a friendly, stimulating atmosphere reigns, as each child is encouraged, he becomes eager to share his ideas with the others. By the very nature of creative expression, every experience is necessarily positive and harmonious, and children regard the activity as delightful play and fun. It may be the adventurous fun of "Tom Sawyer" or of "The Three Pigs" going out into the world to find themselves a home. It may be the rollicking fun of "The Bremen Town Musicians" and of "Epaminondas." Many times it is magic fun such as that of *Mary Poppins* and "The Three Wishes." Stories may bring exciting or quiet or fearful or many other kinds of satisfying experiences, but in addition to the delight of the story's coming alive comes the wholesome social enjoyment that children experience when they work and play harmoniously together.

There is social coöperation as children plan a scene together. There is a sharing of minds as each child expresses his ideas concerning how the play should begin and progress. There is a friendly give and take of ideas, a reaction and intercommunication among members of the group as they work together with real purpose. Social development takes place during the actual playing as well, for while a part of the group creates the scene, the remaining members become an active, listening audience. Each child grows in his ability to discriminate and evaluate as he participates in the discussion that comes after the scene is played each time. An evaluation of character from the standpoint of the play rather than from the standpoint of comparison of individual effort is always stressed. Both the teacher and the members of the group judiciously give praise and recognition to each child who contributes in his own particular way toward the development of the play.

Creative dramatics experiences provide many opportunities for the development of social skills and for satisfying "mutuality" needs within the individual child. In a second-grade group James was having considerable difficulty in learning to read until he gained a feeling of personal worth among the children by creating fine characters in the stories they played together. When the group played "Millions of Cats," Marlene, a leader among the others, commented, "It's all right if James isn't a good reader, because he's such a good cat. Why he can meow better than my kitty can."

Development of Creative Self-Expression. It recognizes that all children are individuals, each one with ideas that need to be expressed. It recognizes, too, the confidence that each child has in himself as a maker, a doer, a creator. It would be safe to say that every healthy, normal child, the world around, has at one time or another made a castle. To adults the structure may have been only a tower of blocks, but to children who *live* their playing, it was a very real castle, probably stately and beautiful.

In exercising their creative power young children are artists and poets and dreamers. They speak from the heart and they say what they feel like saying and they do what they feel like doing. Theirs is an honest and sincere expression from within.

Six-year-old Susan, who was playing in a make-believe toy shop with other first graders, captured the enthusiasm that comes from creative playing and gave it expression from her heart. She danced gaily around the shop with other children who were being dolls and clowns and trucks and trains. Then she bowed gracefully and stood very still for several seconds. When she was given an opportunity to tell how she felt while she was in the toy shop, she said, "I was a fairy, looking at a baby fairy, sleeping in a flower."

When children create characters they search deeply for words to express their feelings, and in so doing they exercise careful and independent thinking. They learn to think quickly, to communicate orally and freely in meaningful experiences with their peers. They recognize the need for increasing vocabularies and for using careful diction, for there is real purpose in having the right words for expression while they are in character and feel the importance of keeping the story going until "curtain" is called.

These values were clearly revealed as a group of nine- and ten-year-old children were playing the story of "Hansel and Gretel." When they came to the scene in which Hansel and Gretel were lost in the woods, the little girl who was Gretel exclaimed fearfully, "Hansel, we're lost! We must say our prayers." She drew on her past experience. She crossed herself, bowed her head, knelt down and quickly repeated all of "Hail Mary" and started through the "Litany of the Saints." Hansel listened intently for a few seconds. As he did so, he became curious and puzzled. Finally his independent thinking led him to resolve the desperate situation by reaching into his past. He threw his hands upward and cried out in a literal plea, "Please God, come down and save us from the wolves! Amen."

In creative dramatics situations the leader encourages each child to express his ideas and opinions. The leader endeavoring to draw the finest expression from the child provides many opportunities for real rather than surface thinking from each member of the group. An eight-year-old boy who had been a gay little elf in a creative play with other third graders explained to the group that he felt like leaping lightly because he was "dressed in cloth cut from a cloud."

"What color was your suit?" the leader inquired.

"Green," he answered quickly.

"Green, just green?" the leader continued as she endeavored to draw further expression from him.

"A soft, soft green of gooseberry juice," he replied after a few minutes of careful thinking.

Under the stimulation of active, creative play children become so interested in and moved by the enjoyment of the situation that the avenues for self-expression constantly open wider.

Wholesome Emotional Development. Emotion has to do with feelings. Psychologists are inclined to believe that emotional feeling in varying degrees pervades all thought and action. Strong inner feelings which are so often curbed in everyday living are brought out into the open and guided into healthy channels as children play strong and vigorous characters in the activity of creative drama. By being a wicked giant, by stamping and shouting and giving orders to others, a child may be doing the very thing he has been wanting to do in reality.

Vigorously chanting, "Fifteen men on a dead man's chest!" and being red-blooded pirates aboard the "Hispaniola" as they acted out rugged scenes from *Treasure Island* proved to be an exciting and stimulating experience for a group of junior high school boys who had previously directed their energies into playing mischievous pranks and tricks on people in their neighborhood. As pirates the boys carved swords and knives, and they made a sturdy crutch for Long John Silver. They wore kerchiefs for hoods, and many used grease paint to create weird pirate masques. This experience was challenging enough to satisfy the emotional needs of these lively youngsters, and at the same time it provided for growth in social adjustment and behavior.

Cinderella's selfish sisters, the witch in "Snow White," the Robber Chief and the thieves in "Ali Baba," Rumpelstiltskin, and other emotionally strong characters from children's literature provide excellent opportunities for children to work off what otherwise might be negative feelings in a forceful, yet controlled and positive way.

Group activities in creative dramatics are helpful to the emotional growth of the timid, sensitive, and self-conscious child. A child's sensitivity readily leads to a strong interest in wanting to join in the merriment, but he may be too shy to enter into the play-

ing. With a patient, understanding leader, a child will find his way
by degrees into the actual participation of the group activity. At the
outset a shy child experiences a feeling of importance as he is
chosen with others to become a member of the audience, for he
realizes that he is watching the play with the purpose of "making
it better." If he desires to comment on the playing an opportunity
is always provided for him to do so. If he is not ready to share his
ideas with the group, the leader does not insist, for she realizes that
he is still lacking in social and emotional bearing and will contribute
when he is ready. When the group is planning the characters for a
play, the leader carefully guides every child into active participation
by suggesting, "Let's all be bears walking through the forest while
our porridge cools." The timid child with a strong desire to belong
to the group and with a fear of being conspicuous by failing to participate generally enters into the playing and finds joy in the experience.

Being Queen Isabella in a play created from the story of Columbus was such a stirring experience for Helen, a ten-year-old girl
with a noticeable speech impediment, that it transformed her entire
personality. The class members chose her to be the queen for their
Columbus play on the afternoon when they had invited an audience.
Helen was so happy to realize that the other children wanted her
to be the queen that she seemed to forget her difficulty in speaking.
When the play started she was no longer her timid self but rather
the confident Queen Isabella. She was stately and dignified as she
led the procession into the courtroom, and when she spoke to
Columbus she spoke with conviction and power in spite of the
impediment. This experience gave Helen the feeling of belonging to
the group, and it increased her faith in herself. From that day on
she was content to be a villager or a page or a guard or a member
of the audience, for she had felt a long-desired approval and recognition by the boys and girls in this class; from then on she developed
an even greater confidence in herself.

The over-aggressive child and the child with tendencies for

leadership also benefit greatly as they participate in creative dramatics activities over a period of several months, for they learn to share responsibilities and ideas with others. A child quickly learns that he must first be a good member or follower in a group before he can be a successful leader. A bully type of youngster particularly benefits from actual democratic participation, for he sees the necessity of waiting one's turn, of accepting criticism without bitterness, and of accepting praise without swaggering.

Development of Fine Attitudes and Appreciations. Stories which are strong in fundamental truths provide excellent experiences in right and honest thinking as children identify themselves with noble characters and experience their worthy deeds and actions. Living through the trying experience of Sir Roland in "The Knights of the Silver Shield" is much more effective in teaching a child the importance of loyalty and obedience than many lectures would be. Being August in "The Nürnberg Stove" and experiencing his deep love for art and beauty make a strong impression on the heart and mind of each boy and girl who plays through this story.

Fourth graders playing the story of "Cinderella" in a creative dramatics class at school grew rapidly in their appreciation of good speech habits and correct word usage. A noticeable example occurred when they came to the scene in which the fairy godmother waved her wand and brought forth the pumpkin coach. A little girl who was being Cinderella called out, "A pumpkin coach! A golden coach! Ye gads, ye gads, it's beautiful!" When the scene was over the children commented on Cinderella's use of the term "ye gads." The girl, in defending herself, said, "That's just what I would say if I saw a coach made from a pumpkin." One of the boys commented quickly, "You might say it, but Cinderella never would." The teacher noted the conscious effort on the part of this girl and every other child, too, to avoid the use of this term during the remainder of the school year.

In evaluating their creative plays, children learn to give criticism fairly and in turn to accept criticism kindly. They develop a respect for the opinions of others, and they gradually develop finer discriminations in taste and judgment. They gain an understanding of the rightness of things and grow in their desire to learn that which is acceptable to society.

A group of older children in a beginning class acting out the old ballad, "The Barring of the Door," played the story with real spirit. One boy who was playing the old man became so absorbed in his character that before he realized what he was saying he called out sharply, "Good wife, get up and bar the door, or I'll kick you in the teeth." Immediately the children watching the scene giggled, for they were embarrassed by his bold comment. As the children and leader evaluated the scene, the leader purposely led the discussion away from the character of the old man. The next time the scene was played the good man called out, "Wife, wife, go at once and close the door." When the wife didn't stir, the old man grew angry, and, clapping his hand forcefully against his knee, he shouted, "Do you hear me? It's across my knee I'll take you if you don't get up and bar that door!" When the scene was over and the good man's character was discussed, the children made an evaluation between the two ways of expressing one's feeling. A constructive rather than destructive discussion followed, and the situation was forceful in driving home the importance of good judgment in all situations.

Desirable attitudes are cultivated in an atmosphere of friendly coöperation where each child is encouraged to express his opinions and ideas. As a child participates in many creative dramatics experiences and becomes many different characters, he begins to understand how other people think and feel, and he gains a better understanding not only of others but also of himself.

Development of Inner Security.   When a child is praised for contributing an idea or for creating a character exceptionally well, he gradually develops a faith in his own creative efforts. A child who has confidence in his ability to achieve frees himself for independent thinking. When a child thinks freely and independently, he draws on his inner resources of creative power. His thinking carries over into many fields of interest which are characterized by purpose and direction. A child who continues to think independently and who develops a good sense of taste and good judgment gradually finds his own worth in the scheme of things. He gains a security within himself and feels free to express himself.

VALUES TO THE HOME, SCHOOL, AND COMMUNITY

Creative dramatics not only benefits the children who participate in this activity, but it is valuable also in the home and in the community in which the children live. A community reflects the life of its people. Young people are always a vital factor in a consideration of the security of the community. When children enter into worthy activities and spend their time and energy in constructive thinking, the entire community benefits.

More Vital Recreational Programs for Children. A Sunday School room in a community church is an excellent place for Bible stories to come alive for boys and girls. As they act out the story of Noah and the Ark or encounter through vital playmaking such exciting experiences as the battle between the Philistines and King Saul's army, children become fascinated with Biblical literature. Going to Sunday School has real meaning for boys and girls when they are given an opportunity to participate actively in dynamic programs.

The public library takes on new significance for many children when they are invited to participate in delightful adventures with storybook characters such as Peter Pan and Wendy who dance out of the pages of a book and invite every child to join in their wonderful experiences.

City playgrounds and town parks become the meeting places for large groups when children of all ages work together to create a merry circus, a country fair, or perhaps a lively rodeo.

Historical museums and art galleries find creative dramatics helpful in enriching the cultural life of children and in encouraging a strong interest in the customs and cultures of people in other countries and earlier days. A child seeing a snuff box is one thing, but a child being an early American colonist making use of an imaginary snuff box as he lives the early history of the country is quite another thing. A music box that entertained colonists of a generation ago is a beautiful treasure to see, but think what it can do for boys and girls as they listen to its sprightly melodies and dance the Virginia reel, feeling that they are early colonists living and dancing long ago. Each treasure has a story or many stories behind it. First-hand material provides excellent motivation for leading children into unusual and dynamic creative dramatics adventures. Quill pens, shoebuckles, powder horns, arrow heads and tomahawks are only a few of the fascinating treasures handed down from one generation to the next that can make history live for children.

Social workers promote creative dramatics experiences for the purpose of gaining an insight into the needs of individual children. A child's home life, his attitudes and emotions, and his relationships with other members of his family are revealed as he acts out carefully chosen experiences. With the release of emotions, better adjustments are made. Children living in crowded city areas may be brought together for the activity of playmaking in neighborhood centers, in housing projects, in field houses, and on playgrounds.

After school and on Saturdays many children are unoccupied, and it is then that they look around the community for something exciting to do. Juvenile delinquency and vandalism can be lessened in communities everywhere if leisure-time youth programs are challenging enough to bring children from the streets. Creative dramatics offers an active program whereby children are given a chance to "blow off steam," where feelings are expressed rather than suppressed, and where boys and girls find pleasure working together.

NEED FOR CREATIVE EXPRESSION

Parents and teachers everywhere are conscientiously looking for ways of guiding boys and girls through important growing-up years. In our strong desire to help children through the formative years, we often destroy the very things we are striving to preserve. We impose patterns and prejudices. We dictate and direct. We make such an effort and struggle out of trying to help the child that we forget to understand him. We forget that he has strong feelings that must be reckoned with. We forget that a child's world is an active world with real people and real things all around him. Too many of us forget, in a few short years, how we thought and felt when we were young. Too often we suddenly check strong outbursts of emotional feeling instead of rechanneling them. Too often we discourage rather than encourage the creative impulse within a child. All too soon children begin to lock up disturbed feelings within their hearts and bury them deeply within, or they release their feelings in destructive ways. Without careful guidance and encouragement from adults children soon lose a desire to create. Many children become watchers instead of doers. They become passive rather than active, acceptors rather than creators.

CREATIVE EXPRESSION FOR THE CHILDREN OF THE WORLD

Children growing up today must be encouraged to think creatively, rather than to submit to a passive acceptance of things as they are. They must be guided in building a resourcefulness within themselves. They must experience the joy of accomplishment from their own creative efforts. As more children learn how to think independently, and as more children begin to feel free to express their opinions at home and at school, the community and the entire country benefit, for the level of thinking and action reaches a higher plane and a greater tolerance results.

The activity of creative dramatics can be a strong factor in helping to build international understanding. When children everywhere are guided and encouraged to speak and act from their hearts, they will gradually come to an understanding of themselves and others that will be far-reaching. Cultural forces are far more unifying than political ones. We should be ever mindful that the world's children are its greatest and strongest single resource, and we should start now to help the youth of the world to live good lives and thereby help to build a foundation for world peace.

Chapter II

HOW TO INTRODUCE DRAMATIC PLAY
ON THE LOWER ELEMENTARY LEVEL

And children's faces looking up
Holding wonder like a cup . . .
—Sara Teasdale

"Let's play house!" . . . "Let's play train!" . . . "Let's play cowboys!" . . . "Let's play boats!" . . . "Let's play butterflies!"
One has only to watch a group of young children at play to see
how universally they constantly pretend to be someone else. Make-
believe is the young child's very life, and as he plays he characterizes with his whole body. He uses dynamic energy, and he finds
real joy in motor activity when he uses big, fundamental muscles.
In the freedom of his play a five-year-old may at one moment be
a fire engine racing down a make-believe street, sounding his siren,
clanging his bell and chugging his motor, while the very next second
he may be the fireman climbing a make-believe ladder, swinging a
make-believe hose and working hard to put out a make-believe
fire.

The young child is an explorer, and with each new happening

19

his world stretches and grows. Dramatic play is a child's own way of "trying on life," of translating into action something that has interested him. The something may be a single impression he has gleaned from his environment, a person or thing that has tickled his imagination, something he wants to know better.

A six-year-old rides to school on a bus. He watches the bus driver. He wonders about him. He likes the way the driver makes the big yellow bus start and stop. He watches him put on the brakes, honk the horn, steer the wheel. When he gets to school that day, or perhaps several days later at home, he becomes a bus driver with a big yellow bus of his own. He may use a single box, a chair or a row of chairs. The six-year-old dramatizes the entire experience. His mind and his muscles and his emotions are set into action as he becomes this person whom he has admired. If he is not interrupted, he plays with his idea until he comes to understand a bus driver in his own way.

In emphasizing the importance of dramatic play, Arnold Gesell and Frances Ilg caution that "Dramatic expression must not be confused with rehearsed theatricals or formalized kindergarten play acting. It is a developmental form of self-expression, which must be evoked impromptu and by ingenious indirection."[1] They further state that the six-year-old "learns not by rote but by participation and a creative kind of self-activation."[2]

THE YOUNG CHILD

Before a leader meets a group of little children whom she has never seen before, she will find it helpful to consider for a time just what it is like to be five or six or seven years old.

Although every child is an individual in his own right, the young child may well be called a child of action. As he moves about he runs, he jumps, he skips, he hops, he dances. He bubbles over with

[1] Arnold Gesell and Frances L. Ilg, *The Child from Five to Ten*, Harper and Brothers, 1946.
[2] *Ibid.*

energy which he quickly transforms into play. His world at this time is a very real world, with his interests closely related to real people and real things. He spends much of his time playing with toys or with a friendly dog or a kitten.

Both little girls and little boys identify themselves with mother and with the many activities of the household. Likewise they identify themselves with father and grandfather, with truck-drivers, taxi-drivers, pilots, farmers, engineers and conductors. Most five- and six- and seven-year-olds have become acquainted with a milkman, a mailman, a grocer, a barber, a doctor, several next-door neighbors, and perhaps a Sunday School teacher.

The young child lives close to beauty and nature, much closer than we sometimes think. He likes the wind and the way it moves. He likes the rain and the snow and he wonders about the sun and the moon and the stars. He enjoys sunsets and clouds and birds and butterflies. Sometimes he talks to robins and caterpillars and ants. He likes the trees that are near his house, and he likes the grass and the earth and finds them good to play in.

GETTING STARTED

It is a Saturday morning. A creative dramatics class is just beginning for twenty little children who do not know each other. They are in a cheerful basement room of a community building seated in a large circle on the rug. The leader, who is friendly, attractive, and neatly dressed, is sitting with them. Three little boys are wearing cowboy shirts and one little girl is mothering a doll.

"Good morning!" the leader says in a cheery voice and with a friendly smile. "Everyone looks so happy today. It's going to be good to have so many new friends. As soon as we find out each other's names and what we like to do, we'll have a good time playing together."

Most of the children are six-year-olds, but there are a few who are five and a few who are seven. The seven-year-olds are in the second grade at school. Most of the six-year-olds have been to kindergarten for a year. To others, school is a brand new place.

"My name is Miss Brown," the leader continues, "and one of the things I like to do best of all is to go riding on a pony! Sometimes I like to walk along slowly, and sometimes I like to gallop like this."

The leader gallops around the circle being a very real and friendly pony. Smiles appear. The leader is speaking the children's language. One little boy in a cowboy shirt speaks up, "I have a pony, too. He's mine and Daddy's. His name is Prince!"

"Does Prince go fast?" the leader asks.

"Sure! Prince can gallop faster than your pony, I think."

The leader sees that the boy is a brave little fellow. "Do you want to show us how Prince goes?" she asks.

The boy gallops joyously around the room, not playing like a pony but being a pony, as he nods his head and gallops about.

"My, what a dandy pony! He's so frisky!" the leader exclaims as Prince comes to a stop. Then with a nod to the children she says, "Let's all be ponies prancing in this big barnyard." She indicates the entire room. "We'll follow Prince!"

Because little children understand and enjoy dramatic play they know just what to do, even though they have never played together before. In a minute they are up from the floor, each being a pony following the first little boy. The leader joins in with them, and as she does she chants in a gay trotting rhythm:

> Prancing pony light and gay,
> Frisking on this autumn day,
> Toss your head and swish your tail!
> Follow us and make a trail!

The children go around and around the room, moving gaily to the rhythm of the verse. Some of the ponies frisk about. Some toss their heads freely. Some whinny. Some seem to watch the others, but they go trotting along. The leader notices that two little girls are sitting on the floor. They had started to play but were not quite brave enough to go on with the others. "Two of our ponies are resting in the barnyard," the leader says in a friendly way. "Let's all rest now."

The ponies trot back to their places and quickly become boys and girls again. Most of them are laughing. They are eager. "This is fun!" "Let's do it again!" "I like to play like this!" "Let's . . ." Everyone speaks at once.

"So many fine thoughts!" the leader says, "but they all flew away! When a thought flies away sometimes it is gone forever. Do you think we can get back some good thoughts about our ponies so we can share them one at a time with each other? I liked the way each pony trotted in his own way! Who would like to tell about his pony?"

"My pony was black and he was named Beauty."

"My pony was white and shiny!"

"My pony was hungry." Everyone laughs.

"What nice thoughts," the leader says. "It's going to be nice to hear about *you*, too. I can hardly wait to find out who everybody is. Now here's somebody sitting right next to me and I don't even know her name. I wonder if it could be—let me see, maybe it's Susan."

The little girl laughs out loud. "No, I'm not Susan!"

Everyone guesses and has a good time. After a few minutes, when everyone gives up, the little girl tells them that her name is Meg.

"What a pretty name," the teacher says. "Do you like to ride a pony, Meg, or is there something you like very much to do when you're home with Mother?"

"I like to play with my dollies and I like to help my mamma."

"Good for you! What fine things to do!"

"I help my mother, too," another little girl says quietly.

"I do, too!" several of the others call out.

Meg turns to the leader. "I iron the handkerchiefs for Mamma," she says softly.

"Meg, how nice!" the leader praises, "but I don't think everyone heard you. Maybe you would like to tell us by *showing* us."

Meg nods eagerly. The leader speaks to the others. "Meg has a secret. She's going to *show* us how she helps mother. As soon as we know we'll raise our hands."

Meg starts ironing. Many hands go up quickly. "Would you like to choose someone to guess?" the leader asks as she touches Meg's arm gently.

Meg points to one of the boys. "Ironing," he says, and Meg nods.

"Let's all iron for mother," the leader suggests. "Let's iron a handkerchief or a dolly's dress or a cowboy kerchief or whatever we think of."

The children pantomime the action. Most of them use large movements, and they enjoy the fun. "Who can show us another way that we help mother?" the leader asks.

One little girl pushes her hands up and down. "I'm washing clothes," she says confidently.

Everyone washes clothes. "Now let's wring the clothes dry and hang them on a line," the leader suggests. The children laugh as they put the clothes on an imaginary line. Then they follow the leader who sits on the rug again.

As the children continue to get acquainted, they find that Jack likes to go fishing with his daddy, Julie likes to play with her baby sister, Billy and Stephen are the cowboys who like to ride ponies, Mark likes to have picnics, Tommy likes to go to the zoo, Sandra and many of the girls like to play with their dollies and help their mothers, too, Dick likes to go to the beach, and Mary Lou likes to go shopping.

When Mary Lou mentions shopping, the teacher asks, "Does everyone like to go shopping?"

The children nod their heads.

"What do you like to buy at a grocery store?"

The children are thinking but no one speaks out.

"Do you like to buy cookies and . . . candy and ice cream?" the leader asks as she makes each thing seem very special.

"Yes . . . yes . . . yes!"

"Suppose we go shopping right now with Mary Lou," the leader says eagerly. "I'll give each of you a penny, and you be thinking of what you'll buy."

"I'll buy candy," Mary Lou says, as the leader carefully hands her an imaginary penny.

"I will, too," Billy calls out as he gets his penny.

"So will I," several others say.

"All right, we'll all buy candy," the leader says as she finishes giving each one a penny. Then she goes to a far corner of the room. She sees a small table and pulls it in front of her. Then she becomes a storeman and calls in a jolly way, "Candy for sale! Candy for sale! Come and buy! Come and buy!" With a nod to the children who are watching her closely she adds merrily:

> "Hippity-hop to the barber shop to get a stick of candy,
> One for you and one for me and one for Jack-a-dandy."

She continues the lively rhyme until all the children have skipped to the store and back to their places. As the leader returns to the group, she enjoys eating her imaginary stick of candy. "I have a yellow candy stick," she says. "It tastes like lemon. What does yours taste like, Mary Lou?"

Mary Lou is taken by surprise. "Lemon," she says quickly.

"Lemon is tasty, isn't it?" the leader says as she sits by Mary Lou. "Who has a different flavor? Who has a red stick of candy?"

Billy speaks right up, "I have, and it tastes like raspberry!"

"Mine's chocolate candy," Meg says now, tasting it again to be sure.

"Mine's peppermint," Stephen says. "Peppermint's the kind I always buy."

The leader sees that one of the little girls who didn't want to be a pony is thoroughly enjoying her candy. "How does yours taste?" she asks in a friendly way.

The little girl smiles. "Good," she says softly.

DRAMATIC PLAY

This is dramatic play. It is a game of characterization and of make-believe. It begins and ends spontaneously. It is fragmentary and simple. It is full of delight and wonder. It works well with the young child because he understands it. It is his way of learning and growing.

Throughout all the grades the emphasis should always be on the playing rather than on a play, *and this is particularly true in the kindergarten and primary level.* Hence, little children should not be restricted by a stage but should be encouraged and should feel free to play all around the room. Neither should young children play for audiences other than an audience which is made up of a part of their group. The presence of adults and onlookers immediately inhibits many children, and when they feel that they are being watched they may either keep real thoughts and feelings hidden away or possibly become "show-offs" from overstimulation. An audience unconsciously expects to be entertained, and even parents are likely to laugh at something which has not appeared to be funny to the children at all. Parents may be invited occasionally when a group has played a story many times and has enjoyed making it into a delightful and artistic, but simple, play which the children are eager to share with others. In a situation of this kind a leader will always explain the nature and the values of creative dramatics to the adults before the children start to play.

Since one of the values of dramatic play is to stimulate a child's imagination, it would seem advisable not to use real properties; however, many leaders feel that suggestive bits of costume and scenery go far in helping children to lose themselves in character when they first begin to play. A discarded handbag or an appropriate headdress can often amazingly and magically transform a little girl into a dignified lady, and again something as simple as a crooked stick can help a little boy suddenly become an old grandfather walking with a cane. If a group seems to need or to want such help at the outset, there can certainly be no harm in allowing the children to make use of simple properties until they feel confident enough to play without them. The important thing for a leader to remember, however, is *to lead the children into stirring make-believe experiences without the help of such "crutches," so that the children will gradually develop imagination and resourcefulness through their play.*

When children have created a play and are planning to share it with an invited audience, an entirely different situation is at hand. The audience has come to see a play, and simplified pieces of scenery and appropriate costumes will add to the enjoyment of the occasion.

THE LEADER'S ROLE

Discovering Interests.   The very first half-hour that young children spend getting acquainted through dramatic play opens the way for delightful make-believe times together. The children find new friends. The leader finds all kinds of little doorways opening up. She finds cues to the children's interests. She gains an insight into each individual. She finds leaders. She finds followers. She finds children who are shy and emotionally tense. She finds children with imagination.

After a first day of getting started with dramatic play, what will a leader do to keep the activity going? How will she guide the children and keep them growing and moving ahead with wonderment? A leader working on the primary level guides the children into many different dramatic play experiences by *setting the mood, by playing with the children,* and by *recognizing and praising real thinking and feeling.*

Setting the Mood.   A leader quickly finds that she is the barometer of a group. She creates a friendly mood right away by getting the children started into the fun of a specific kind of dramatic play. She guides their imaginations and makes an experience so inviting that the children forget themselves and eagerly join in the fun of playing together. If the leader who was working with Meg and Billy and the other children on the first day had not recognized the little cowboy's interest in ponies she might have found it necessary to arouse their imaginations. She may have done this by describing specific experiences she had had with ponies, by drawing comments from the children about ponies they had seen, perhaps by showing pictures of ponies which she may have had on hand or possibly by tapping out a galloping rhythm which would have led to a strong interest in ponies or horses. In an ideal situation the motivation comes from the children themselves, but a leader cannot depend on this. She must always be prepared to lead the children into an experience which she has carefully planned with probable and possible lines of action.

Playing with the Children.   As children in the kindergarten and first and second grades are being introduced to dramatic play, a leader will find that she can do much to help them get started if she joins with them in their playing. She will not show them how to play or how to act out a rhyme, but she will become one of the group, being a pony or a policeman along with their ponies and policemen. When a leader plays with the children, she is in an ideal position to help them keep the action moving along so that they will have a feeling of accomplishment and enjoyment in their playing.

A leader watches for ways in which she can guide the children while she is in character. For instance, if the children are playing "Mistress Mary," and each child is being a tiny seed sleeping in the ground, she may become the sun who gently awakens each seed and starts him to growing into a cockle shell or a silver bell or a pretty little maid in a row. However, as soon as the children become confident enough to play without her help, a leader will encourage them to do so. She will not step in, neither will she interfere with their playing unless it is necessary or wise.

Recognizing Real Feeling and Praising. Amidst the laughter and joy of dramatic play, many children will be completely in character right from the start. Others may tend to imitate or to act like a character, rather than think strongly enough to become a character. A leader watches for children who are completely in character, and whenever she recognizes real thinking and feeling, she will call attention to these in such a way as to encourage all of the children to work from within. *She will do this largely by specific praise.* She will praise everyone as she says, possibly, "My, what fine spiders I see in Miss Muffet's garden."

Then she will turn to two or three children who have been so much in character that they have forgotten everyone else. "Here are some of the busiest spiders I've ever seen! Let's watch and see how they are working!"

As the children become spiders, crawling and spinning in true spider fashion, the leader says, "Aren't they busy little spiders? Why do you think they are such fine spiders?"

"Because they crawl like spiders," some of the children say.

"Yes! And they *feel* like spiders! When we feel like spiders we see how much fun it is to *be* spiders. Let's all feel like spiders and spin lacy webs in the garden before Miss Muffet comes out to eat her curds and whey."

HOW TO PROCEED

Begin with Rhythms. *In working with young children a leader begins with the simplest of rhythmic movements. She proceeds gradually to dramatic play and after several weeks guides the children to the place where they are ready to create a play from a verse or a story.* Since creativity comes as a result of rhythmic living, a leader strives to get each child in tune with himself.

Simple rhythmic experiences, such as jumping with make-believe jump ropes, bouncing make-believe balls, and rowing make-believe boats will be used in the very beginning. A leader will then guide the children through a variety of rhythmic experiences which are strong in character feeling. She will do this in somewhat the same way as the leader guided the children into being prancing ponies. Children enjoy being chugging trains, dancing raindrops, marching soldiers, spinning tops, bouncing balls, fluttering leaves, scampering squirrels, and countless other familiar moving things which they see in the world around them. Beginning experiences will always be kept simple and will provide for a variety of large bodily actions. Rhythmic playing will be done almost entirely in pantomime, but a child who is ready to express himself in words should certainly be encouraged. In a kindergarten class where the children were being raindrops for the first time, a five-year-old danced around in great ecstasy and sang an accompanying merry little tune, "Pitter-patter, pitter-patter, what's the matter, what's the matter?"

With Chanted Verse.   There are many ways in which a leader may make beginning experiences meaningful, enjoyable and lively. She may chant a rhyme or verse with a marked rhythm such as was done with "Hippity Hop" and "Prancing Pony." Or, if the children know the rhyme, a part of them may say it with the leader while the rest of the group plays. In either case the leader will know the verse well, and she will use a strong rhythmic beat which suggests the action involved and guides the children's thinking.

With Music and Other Rhythms.   For variety a leader may use piano accompaniment occasionally, or she may improvise music which provides a definite rhythm and stimulates imagination so that each child feels free to create from the music in his own way. Phonograph recordings of specific rhythms which have been simply arranged and which have been graded for different age levels will be useful in beginning work.

A small drum, blocks of wood, bells, or even a clapping of hands may be used to provide a rhythm that seems to be just right for a certain action. At the beginning of a school year when a patrol officer, complete with shining badge, leather leggings, and guns in his holsters, talked to a first-grade class about safety rules, the children were eager to identify themselves with this important person. When the teacher presented the following verse with a spirited rhythm and beat upon a table top, the children became policemen almost at once and marched around the room in a lively parade:

> Tramp! Tramp! Tramp! Tramp! Hear the marching feet!
> Policemen are parading up and down the street!
> Broom! Broom! Broom! Broom! Sounds the big bass drum!
> Tramp! Tramp! Tramp! Tramp! Here the policemen come!

With Nursery Rhymes. Mother Goose, not unlike Shakespeare, has proved her worth to the world. For years she has opened the first gateway to literature. Her rhymes, her jingles, her musical bits of poetry and nonsense which have been enjoyed for many generations have come down to us on their own merits of beauty, simplicity, and fitness. These priceless bits of primitive art are a part of every child's inheritance, and they have a fresh and new appeal for every generation of children. Boys and girls who have enjoyed listening to Mother Goose always find a special delight in playing many of these same rhymes.

Almost every little child enjoys jumping, and he finds a new kind of fun in jumping over an imaginary candlestick. A leader may begin by picking up an imaginary candle and asking with a twinkle in her eye, "Do you see this tall red candle in this pretty candlestick? It belongs to a friendly little fellow! I'm going to put it right here on the floor for him." As she pantomimes the action, she may inquire, "Does anyone know whose candlestick this is?" Someone is sure to guess. Then the leader may continue by suggesting, "Shall we take turns being Jack and each one jump over the candlestick?" When the children are ready she says in a gay, lilting rhythm:

> "Jack be nimble, Jack be quick!
> Jack jump over the candlestick!"

When the children have enjoyed jumping for some time and have stopped to rest a leader may ask, "Why do you think Jack is jumping over the candlestick?" and "Who do you think told him to jump over?" Even though the emphasis is largely on rhythmic experiencing at the outset, a leader invites expression from the very beginning, for expression goes far in stimulating a child's imagination.

Children who have enjoyed jumping over candlesticks always find it jolly to guess the old riddle and play,

> Little Nancy Etticoat, in a white petticoat,
> And a red nose;
> The longer she stands, the shorter she grows.

After a group has talked about candles a leader may suggest, "Wouldn't it be fine to be a tall Christmas candle or a tiny candle on a birthday cake? It might be even more fun to surprise us and be a very different kind of candle! Each one think of the kind of candle you would like to be, and then find a good place to stand."

As soon as each child becomes a candle in his own way, the leader may comment, "What lovely Nancy Etticoats! Tell me about your petticoats!" After each one has told what kind of candle he is, the leader may suggestively say, "Now let us see how each candle grows shorter and shorter in his own way."

The candles may grow shorter to music, or they may grow shorter as the leader repeats the rhyme several times in a quiet, swaying rhythm.

The children will enjoy "Jack and Jill," "Wee Willie Winkie," "Shoe the Horse," "Little Jack Horner," "The North Wind Doth Blow," and many of the other simple nursery rhymes played in a similar way.

Singing a song and rocking a baby to sleep is a joyous pastime for little children everywhere. The beauty and simplicity of "Rock-a-bye Baby" makes it one of the loveliest lullabies for playing. "How many have baby brothers or sisters at home?" a leader may ask, to set the children to thinking about babies. Many of the children will have or they will know of a little baby that they will be eager to tell about. After talking about babies the children will think of the loveliest ways to rock babies to sleep out in the yard or garden or maybe in a beautiful forest. If the children know the song, they may sing with the leader as each one rocks a baby to the rhythm of the lullaby.

DRAMATIC PLAY IN GROUPS

It isn't always necessary to use a rhyme or a verse for dramatic play. A leader will be aware of the children's interests and will use these frequently as motivation for lively group experiences.

On a warm afternoon a leader may invite the children to look out of the windows as she comments, "Isn't it beautiful today? What do you like to do on days like this?" Every child will have an idea. One may say that he likes to go to the beach. Another may think of a picnic. Perhaps one will want to go to the zoo. Someone may suggest that it is a good day for fishing. Perhaps one will wish he could go to the mountains or perhaps to a farm in the country.

Each suggestion has wonderful possibilities for dramatic play and may easily be expanded into thirty minutes of spontaneous group pantomime. "So many nice places to go!" a leader may say with much enthusiasm. "Suppose we skip away this very minute?"

Children are always eager and will be ready to go at once. "Since we can't go everywhere in one afternoon perhaps we had better choose just one place to go." The children may feel strongly about going to one place or another, or they may decide by voting.

After the children have planned where they will go, a leader will ask questions to stimulate their thinking. If a group wants to go to the beach, she will comment enthusiastically, "Going to the beach is always fun! There are so many good things to do! What do you like to do best of all when you go to the beach?"

This one question may draw many suggestions from the children, such as digging in the sand, wading in the water, picking up shells, building sand castles, sailing boats, swimming, splashing, digging for clams, and finding pretty rocks. After a group has thought of many ideas a leader will guide them into pantomime. "What a nice sandy beach!" she may say, indicating a large open space in the room. "Doesn't the sand feel warm? Now that we're here suppose each one does just what he likes to do best!"

After the children have played freely for a few minutes a leader will guide them into a variety of pantomimes by commenting in somewhat this way, "Here's someone who has made a big mountain of sand! Let's all pile the sand high," or "Let's be ever so quiet while Mary listens to the pretty shell she has found," and then, perhaps, "Let's all look for a pretty shell. Maybe we can hear a shell singing too." While everyone is listening, the leader may ask in a quiet voice, "Who would like to tell us what he hears?" In a relaxed, happy atmosphere, children will enjoy having a wonderful time at the beach through such dramatic play.

Make-believe picnics can be almost as much fun as real ones. A single question, such as, "Why is picnicking so much fun?" may bring so many eager replies from the children that they will be quickly led into picnic merrymaking. As a group plays in pantomime each child may fix his own lunch, carry his picnic basket to the woods, eat sandwiches and other goodies which he has brought as surprises, peel an orange, build a bonfire, roast and eat marshmallows, wash sticky fingers, skip a rope, toss a ball, pick wild flowers, chase butterflies, and sit on the soft grass or on an autumn leaf and talk about how beautiful the woods or the park is.

Children enjoy being animals. It's quite a natural thing for many young children to pretend that they are animals before they begin to identify themselves with other human beings. When little children get down on all fours and exercise big muscles as they crawl about, they find real pleasure not only in becoming cows, horses, sheep, dogs, kittens, pigs and goats, but in making the characteristic sounds of each animal. Playing farm is always merry for young groups. Each child is encouraged to be the kind of animal he would like to be, while the leader and one or two of the other children become the farmers who feed and care for the animals.

A kindergarten class that had attended a county fair decided to have a farm parade of prize-winning livestock. They made a purple ribbon for the grand champion animal, blue ribbons for the first prize winners, and red ribbons for the second prizes. The teacher became the farmer who led his fine animals in a long parade in front of the grandstand. The boys and girls who were sitting in the grandstand benches were the judges, and they decided which animals were to receive the prizes. For many weeks this group played "County Fair." In the beginning the children played entirely in pantomime, but after several weeks the five-year-old judges enjoyed giving speeches telling the farmer why they had chosen the big, red steer to be the champion winner. As hard as the other animals would try, it seemed the steer would always win the purple ribbon.

Being forest animals, jungle animals, and animals at a zoo affords similar enjoyment for children, and the experience of being many different kinds of animals allows imaginations to flourish freely.

Day after day a leader will provide dramatic play experiences which grow out of the children's interests and activities. She will watch for unexpected happenings which may invite dramatic action. She will be alert for suggestions which come from the children and which will lead to group play. If a little girl should skip into the room before school starts for the day and call out eagerly, "I swept the kitchen for Mamma this morning," a leader will recognize the opportunity to use the little girl's interest for leading the group into pantomiming household activities. Children enjoy this kind of dramatic play. They ask to play it often. A leader may keep them reaching and lead them on into new panto-mime by asking, "I wonder if someone might show how he helps Daddy too?" On other days a group may decide to help Grand-father or a farmer or the milkman, the postman, or even the Easter bunny and Santa Claus. Second-grade groups enjoy playing this type of pantomime in the manner of charades. Many times they choose actions which require exceedingly careful thinking, such as polishing the silver, turning pancakes, drying glasses, and cleaning a bird cage.

On a bright autumn day when the wind is blowing, children like to be leaves falling from the trees, ever so lightly at first and then perhaps quite gaily as they flutter and scurry about. There are rainy days when young children enjoy being raindrops and windy days when they find real joy in feeling that they are the wind in its many different moods.

Little children like to be clouds, too. A first-grade class that had watched billowy, white clouds floating in a bright blue sky soon became the kind of clouds they had seen. For several minutes they enjoyed floating around in quiet, cloud-like ways. When they stopped to rest the teacher asked, "Would anyone like to tell us about his cloud?" Some said they were fairies. Some were lambs. Some were airplanes. One little girl who had danced about in a rhythmic pattern of circles piped up, "I was a flying saucer."

"I was a ship with white sails flying," another said.

"I was a shepherd," the youngest boy in the group said solemnly.

"I was an angel with my eyes open—swinging," a little girl with bright red hair volunteered.

When a second-grade teacher shared Carl Sandburg's "Fog" with her class on a cold, foggy morning and then suggested that each one "come in on little cat feet" and be fog in his own way, the children responded beautifully. Some tiptoed lightly. Some crawled quietly like cats. Some moved about in a ghostly fashion. The enjoyment and appreciation were so great that the children asked to play "Fog" whenever it became slightly overcast. *Quiet playing many times brings a deeper aesthetic experience than many leaders may realize until they see how eager children are to return to an experience which has been particularly beautiful and soul-stirring.*

There will be endless opportunity for dramatic play throughout the child's day as soon as a leader becomes aware of how to weave it into daily activities. When it is time for children to go home, a leader will find that instead of saying, "Make a straight line. Walk quietly; don't run," it is far friendlier and much more stimulating for children when she says, "All aboard! The streamliner is leaving from track Number one!" or "Who wants to join our policeman parade?" or "The wild geese are getting ready to fly in a straight line across the sky," or if she asks, "Who can think of a good way for us to go home today?"

PANTOMIMING RHYME AND VERSE

Individual Characters Within a Group.   After considerable experience in group playing the children will be ready to become individual characters within a group. For instance, in playing "Humpty Dumpty," one child will be chosen to be Humpty Dumpty, several children will become the king's horses, and several others will be chosen to be the king's men.

"Humpty Dumpty" is a favorite for young groups. Since most young children enjoy being ponies, possibly a leader decides to approach the rhyme in this way. After the ponies have galloped freely a leader praises generously, "What fine ponies! You were fine enough for a king! Has anyone ever heard of king's horses?"

Someone is sure to remember "all the king's horses and all the king's men," and the group will no doubt enjoy saying the rhyme with the leader. While the enthusiasm is strong the leader will then set the children to thinking about the characters. She may begin by asking, "Poor Humpty, why couldn't they put him together again? What kind of person is he? What does he look like before he falls off the wall? How do you think he feels while he is sitting on the wall?" Questions such as these will lead into a lively discussion which will stimulate independent thinking. *A leader will use care in not having primary groups spend too long a time in planning, for little children are naturally active and are more eager to be the* characters *than to talk about them.* A leader arouses imagination as she guides the children into the fun of characterization by suggesting, for instance, "Here is a long bench that looks very much like a castle wall. Let's all be happy Humpty Dumptys walking in the castle garden."

When they have enjoyed being Humpty Dumpty they may be guided into further experiencing of the same character as a leader suggests, "Now let's be Humpty Dumpty sitting on the wall and feeling so good before anything happens!" and then, "Would you like to be Humpty Dumpty falling from the wall?"

While the children are resting from this activity a leader helps them to think of the other characters by asking, "Who comes to help Humpty Dumpty after he falls? What do you think the king's men look like? How do they feel as they march along?" As soon as the leader feels that the children have an understanding of the king's men she will suggest, "Suppose each one finds a partner, and we will be king's men marching along together. Let's wear bright uniforms! Does each one have his sword ready? Left! Right! Left! Right! Forward march!"

The leader may clap her hands to beat out the rhythm as she leads the parade of king's men and strives to make this experience a stirring one. When characterization is fun and real for a child, the experience reaches within and is of great value to him.

Kindergarten children may be content to play only the characters in a rhyme, whereas first- and second-grade groups may want to play the rhyme from beginning to end. Little children should not be expected to do very much planning, for they tend to organize their thinking as they play. One or two guiding questions will be sufficient to help young children plan the action for a short rhyme such as this one. For instance, a leader may ask, "Why do you think Humpty Dumpty fell off the wall?" This question will bring many individual reactions and will lead directly into the action of the rhyme. One first-grade class decided that Humpty Dumpty was a little boy who had climbed on the wall to watch the king's horses parading. A group of second-graders decided that Humpty Dumpty was chasing a butterfly and was such a fat little boy that he fell from the wall.

When children have decided what their Humpty Dumpty will do, they will be ready to play the rhyme in their own way. *A leader will do well always to emphasize character feeling rather than to spend too much time on having the children discuss what to do, for when children are thinking and feeling in character, the action will be spontaneous.*

"The Butterbean Tent." For further experiencing in individual characterization young children delight in playing "The Butterbean Tent." Grieg's "Morning" from *Peer Gynt* provides an appropriate background for this verse and helps children to feel this peaceful mood of the outdoor world as they create tiny creatures. Since little children live very close to nature, just a suggestion or two will get them started talking about their gardens and about curious bugs and insects. After they have talked about vegetable gardens they enjoy hearing the verse:

> All through the garden I went and went,
> And I walked in under the butterbean tent.
> The poles leaned up like a big tepee
> And made a nice little house for me.
> I had a hard brown clod for a seat,
> And all outside was a cool green street.
> A little green worm and a butterfly
> And a cricket-like thing that could hop went by.
> Hidden away there were flocks and flocks
> Of bugs that could go like little clocks.
> Such a good day it was when I spent
> A long, long while in the butterbean tent.[3]

Making butterbean tents is jolly fun for children. They like to work in groups of three or four, and each group always makes a

---

[3] Reprinted from *Under the Tree* by Elizabeth Madox Roberts. Copyright 1922 by B. W. Huebsch, Inc., 1950 by Ivor S. Roberts. Reprinted by permission of The Viking Press, Inc., New York.

tepee in a different way with the children themselves becoming the poles. After a group decides which tent it will use, the children are led into a discussion of little green worms and how they crawl through the grass. When the music starts each one becomes a worm and moves about in his own way. Then in turn the children become butterflies, crickets, bugs, and other insects which fascinate them. Little children always enjoy talking about the kind of person who will be walking through the gardens, and most groups decide to have a little girl or a little boy just as old as most of them are. The primary children generally want to follow the verse rather closely and prefer to have one little worm, one butterfly, one cricket, and flocks and flocks of bugs hiding behind the tent.

"People."   Lois Lenski's "People" is another good verse to use when children are ready to individualize character. "People" is excellent, too, for leading boys and girls into the ecstasy and dignity they always experience when they become grown-up ladies and gentlemen.

> Tall people, short people,
> Thin people, fat,
> Ladies so dainty
> Wearing a hat.
> Straight people, dumpy people,
> Man dressed in brown;
> Baby in a buggy,
> —These make a Town![4]

"Shall we make a little town of our very own—a town with all kinds of different people?" A question such as this will open the way for a discussion of people. The children's thinking may be further stimulated by leading questions: "Whom shall we have in our town? Have you ever thought of all the people who live right around us? Have you ever watched the people walking along your street? Can you tell how people *feel* by the way they move about?

---

[4] Reprinted from *Skipping Village* by Lois Lenski, published by J. B. Lippincott Co., 1927. Used by permission of the author.

Does anyone know someone who is quite old? How do you think it feels to be old? Who would like to be an old grandmother and an old grandfather walking down to the corner to catch a bus?"

After several children have enjoyed being old people, a leader may suggest, "Now let's all be old people out for a walk around the block. When we think we are old we make others feel that we are old. To be old we have to feel old inside, don't we?"

In a similar way the children will be led into the jollity of being tall people, thin people, fat people, dumpy people, dainty ladies all dressed up, and happy young mothers pushing baby buggies. Then it is great fun for each child to become the kind of character he wants to be and to walk many different places in a make-believe town. Grown-up people may enjoy going to a city park on a warm afternoon and resting on park benches or perhaps walking to a corner mailbox after dark to post an important letter. There is a special elation that comes from being grown-up people dressed in Sunday clothes and walking to church in the early morning as the church bells ring and quite a different feeling that comes from being grown-up people hurrying home from a grocery store with groceries for dinner.

Children always enjoy being postmen, organ-grinders, ice-cream men, policemen, and other fascinating people from the town. They like to play the old nursery rhyme, "Christmas Is Coming," in which one person becomes an old beggarman and the others become Christmas shoppers or villagers walking by.

USE OF DIALOGUE

A little child expresses much more of his emotional feeling through bodily movement than through words, for his vocabulary is somewhat limited at this early age. When a six-year-old child is happy he may dance or skip or jump up and down spontaneously without finding it necessary to utter a single word. *A leader will not introduce dialogue as such to young children, but she will encourage them to speak gradually and naturally from the begin-*

ning. When a child speaks in character a leader will recognize the expression and call attention to his use of words by praising in somewhat this way, "Wasn't it exciting when Humpty Dumpty called, 'Help! help!'? It's always nice to *hear* what is happening as well as to see." And again, "All of the king's men were strong, and I liked the way one man said, 'We can't put Humpty Dumpty together so we will take him to the hospital!' " Praise is the very best way of encouraging each child to speak as he plays.

If a group has been quite content to play almost entirely in pantomime, and if the leader feels that the children are ready to express themselves through conversation but seem to be holding back from talking aloud, she may find that a make-believe tea party works wonders in getting children to speak freely in character. A leader may begin in a friendly way, "Do you like parties? Last night I read the finest tea-party poem! I could hardly wait until today so that I might share it with you." If she has been sincere and enthusiastic the children will be eager to listen.

THE TEA PARTY
In the pleasant green Garden
We sat down to tea;
"Do you take sugar?" And
"Do you take milk?"
She'd got a new gown on—
A smart one of silk.
We all were as happy
As happy could be,
On that bright Summer's day
When she asked us to tea.[5]

"Didn't they have a happy time? What was nice about their party?" When the response is strong a leader may suggest, "Do you suppose we might have a garden party just as they did? Who has a good idea where our garden might be? What shall we use for a

---

[5] Reprinted from *Marigold Garden* by Kate Greenaway; Frederick Warne & Co., Ltd., 1910.

garden gate? Who would like to be the one who invites the rest of us to come to tea?"

If several children are eager, a leader will choose a child who will be capable of carrying the action through. The leader will then become one of the guests along with the rest of the children. As they go to a far end of the room she may put on a pretty hat in pantomime and say eagerly, "Suppose each one wears his finest clothes to Mary's party. I see someone dressed in velvet, and I see fine neckties and gloves!"

When everyone is ready the leader starts the action by suggesting, "Shall we go to the tea party now? Who wants to knock on the garden gate?"

As the young hostess greets the guests the leader will carry on a friendly conversation with her as a means of stimulating everyone to talk freely. The first playing will be kept very simple. At the second playing the leader may choose to be the hostess, realizing that this character puts her in an ideal position to ask direct questions and in this way to help the children use dialogue more freely. Many groups enjoy playing tea-party again and again, and while a group is enjoying tea the leader guides conversation into new channels each time. The children may enjoy talking about the flowers, about the clothes each one is wearing, about the weather, or as grown-ups about the news of the town and other topics of grown-up interest.

"The Animal Store."   Another jolly verse which gives beginning groups an opportunity for using dialogue is Rachel Field's "Animal Store." Since almost all children like animals and like to spend money, too, the situation set forth in this verse provides a real incentive for speaking. A crisp one-dollar bill or a shiny silver dollar will capture a prompt interest in almost every group of children. "If you had one hundred dollars just like this one what do you think you would buy?" a leader asks to arouse a lively discussion. When each child has told what he would like to buy,

a leader may go directly into the verse by telling them in the
friendliest way:

> If I had a hundred dollars to spend,
>   Or maybe a little more,
> I'd hurry as fast as my legs would go
>   Straight to the animal store.
>
> I wouldn't say, "How much for this or that?"
>   "What kind of a dog is he?"
> I'd buy as many as rolled an eye,
>   Or wagged a tail at me!
>
> I'd take the hound with the drooping ears
>   That sits by himself alone;
> Cockers and Cairns and wobbly pups
>   For to be my very own.
>
> I might buy a parrot all red and green,
>   And the monkey I saw before,
> If I had a hundred dollars to spend,
>   Or maybe a little more.[6]

"Isn't that a dandy way to spend one hundred dollars?" the
leader exclaims. "Wouldn't it be fun to go to an animal store
today? Do you think we might be the animals and have an animal
store right here? What kind of animals would you like to have
in our store?"

Each child may decide what kind of an animal he would like to
be and surprise the others by showing them his animal in pantomime. Or a leader may guide the entire group into becoming
different kinds of animals such as dogs, parrots, monkeys, canaries,
and other pets which the children suggest.

"What kind of storekeeper shall we have?" a leader questions
as she leads the group into planning this merry character. "What
will he look like? How will he feel toward his animals? How will

---

[6] Reprinted from *Taxis and Toadstools* by Rachel Field. Copyright 1926
by Doubleday & Company, Inc.

the animals feel toward him? How do you think the storekeeper will feel when someone comes to spend one hundred dollars in his shop?"

Before children start to play a verse they always pantomime the main characters in order that they will understand them better. "Suppose we all become a friendly storekeeper walking down the street on his way to the shop," a leader guides. "Let's see how happy he feels as he thinks about his animals."

When the children are familiar with the characters and have decided who will come to buy the animals and where their cages will be, they will be ready to play the entire verse. They may need help in getting the action started. If so, a leader creates a strong mood to help each child get into character. "What fine animals I see in the Animal Store! Some of them are sleeping. Some of them are hungry. It is early in the morning and I see the shopkeeper coming to feed his animals and to open his shop for the day. Ready? Begin!"

This verse is easy enough for first- and second-grade children to play in one short scene. A leader should not expect the children to carry on lengthy conversations in character the first time they play a verse. It is quite likely that a child may say nothing more than "I'll take this and this," as he points to the different animals he wants to buy. This will be a beginning, however, and should be commended. *A leader always praises the children for what they have done and encourages them to play the same material many times, for as the children become acquainted with the characters, they enjoy speaking for them.*

TRANSITION INTO STORIES

Again we go back to the old folk tales for material which is rich in dramatic action. Search as one will it is difficult to find such priceless stories for young children to play as "The Three Bears," "The Three Billy-Goats Gruff," "The Three Little Pigs," "Henny-

Penny," "Teeny-Tiny," "The Elves and the Shoemaker," and other traditional tales which have long been classics in literature.

"The Three Bears" is unequaled for providing a nearly perfect transition from the playing of verse to the playing of a story. The characters are strong, the action is clear, the dialogue is humorous and rhythmic, and the suspense is just right for young children. Since the story is familiar to most six- and seven-year-olds, they may want to play it as it happened, starting at the beginning of the story and playing it straight through to the end. When a leader recognizes a desire such as this she will know that a group is ready for story dramatization, and she will guide them into joyous experiences in real creative drama.

Chapter III

HOW TO INTRODUCE CREATIVE DRAMATICS
ON THE UPPER ELEMENTARY LEVEL

Just as the twig is bent, the tree's inclined.
—ALEXANDER POPE

"My name is Johnnie Jones and I came from Nebraska. My father was a barber in Omaha—a *good* barber, too!"

This was nine-year-old Johnnie's way of telling about himself to a group of children whom he had never seen before. The seven boys and girls were sitting along a housing project street during the war. They were children of defense workers, and they were all young newcomers to an industrial area on the west coast. A leader who had joined the group had told the children about herself, where she had lived and what she had enjoyed doing when she was nine years old. Her enthusiasm and sincerity set a friendly tone, and as the children listened to her they became eager to speak. After Johnnie introduced himself all of the children began telling about themselves and about their families. While they were getting acquainted they were surprised to find that each one's family had

47

come from a different city or town or little village across the country. "Shall we take a trip around the United States this afternoon and see where everyone lived?" the leader asked. "Maybe we can see all our fathers at work! Would you like to go right now?"

The children were interested but puzzled by her question.

"How *can* we go?" one of the boys asked.

"Oh there are many ways! We can go by plane or by train or by horseback, or we can go this very minute with seven-league boots!"

With laughter and fun the children quickly responded to the idea of a make-believe trip. They pulled on seven-league boots in pantomime, and after several giant steps up the street they soon found themselves in Omaha where they *became* Johnnie's father. Each one enjoyed being a barber, and they took turns in giving imaginary haircuts to each other. From Nebraska the children went to a coal mine in Pennsylvania where for the first time in their lives they went underground and mined coal with imaginary picks and shovels. When they came up the shaft, they strode across the country by going to a vacant lot at the end of the block. There they stopped at a small Colorado town in the Rocky Mountains and became bakers mixing cakes and kneading bread and eating cookies. During the afternoon they were farmworkers pitching heavy bundles of grain in the wheat fields of Montana, and they were taxidrivers weaving in and out of the traffic along Chicago's Michigan avenue.

At the end of the first afternoon Johnnie and all of the others were so enthusiastic about this kind of playing that they went to their homes with the promise that they could wear their seven-league boots the next day and take a trip around the world.

STIMULATING CURIOSITY

Bringing a group of children together may be comparatively easy, or it may prove to be the most challenging part of organizing a class in creative dramatics. This leader who worked with Johnnie

Jones and the other children in the housing projects started many children's groups in the same area during the war, and she began each class in a different way. Because of the insecurity and frustration of many of the housing project children who had been uprooted from homes all over the country, they refused to meet together in groups. After many unsuccessful attempts to reach the children in auditoriums, the leader found that it was necessary to approach them in their home areas and on their own levels of interest, and there and then to arouse their curiosities and imaginations.

A make-believe circus proved to be the magic which brought one group of eight-, nine-, and ten-year-olds together. One afternoon when the leader was working in one of the projects, she saw two boys going down a street on their scooters.

"Where are you going?" she called after them.

"No place," one of them called as he continued on his way.

"Wouldn't you like to go to a circus?"

"A circus? Where?" they shouted as they came scooting back. "Where's the circus?"

"It's a secret," she whispered in fun. "Join my parade and I'll take you there!"

The two boys joined her parade and as they went down the housing project street in single file they called to all the children they met, "Come on, come on, join on, join on! We're off to a circus!"

As they paraded up and down the street, eight more boys and four girls joined the merry group. The leader pretended then that the auditorium in one of the community buildings was the big circus tent, and she led the children inside. There they had a gay circus with the children being trained elephants, talking seals, galloping ponies, ferocious lions, tight-rope walkers, and tumbling clowns. The leader was the circus barker, and she announced each act with vivid descriptions which helped the children to become convincing animals and confident performers. The news of the circus spread throughout the project, and in a few weeks many other children had joined the classes.

ORGANIZING A GROUP

Space for Playing.   In planning a class in creative dramatics, one of the first considerations will be that of securing a room or a place for the children to meet. This room may be an auditorium, a gymnasium, a classroom, a basement, or a recreation room. Ideally, it should be a space large enough for a group of twenty children to move about with ease. When children are planning characters they need room in which to pantomime freely. It isn't easy to be in airplanes or magic carpets whisking through the air when the space for flying is limited to a few feet. Indians and pioneers, too, need space in which to move about freely if they are to lose themselves completely in character.

If the children are meeting in a large gymnasium, however, a leader will find it wise to limit the playing area, for too much space tends to decrease the friendliness and intimacy which is needed for group work in creative drama. Children must be able to see and hear each other, and this may be difficult to manage if boys and girls are scattered around a large gymnasium. Placing the chairs or benches in a circle has proved to be the most satisfactory arrangement for quickly establishing unity among a new group.

If it is necessary for the group to work in a small classroom, the teacher should make the best of a crowded situation. If the desks are not fastened down to the floor, she may ask the children to move the first three or four rows to the back or to the sides of the room. Children will enjoy doing the moving in character of janitors, custodians, or stage managers, and as such will do this in a businesslike way, quickly and quietly.

If the desks cannot be moved, the group will use the largest remaining space for the playing area. While each child is planning his character he may use the space near his desk for his pantomime, or groups of children may move up and down the aisles. In a situation of little space a large part of the group will be the audience each time, and by taking turns in their playing each child will be able to play at least once and perhaps oftener during each class period.

Size of Group. Fifteen or twenty boys and girls make up an ideal beginning group in the elementary grades. This is not an absolute number, for a group may include many more or may be started with as few as four or five children. In a schoolroom or a Sunday School or in a situation where a group has already been formed and the children know each other, creative dramatics may be introduced where there are as many as thirty or thirty-five children in a group.

If fifty or sixty children respond to an invitation to join a new class, it is important that the leader divide the children into three groups according to their age levels. If a new group is limited to twenty members, there is more opportunity for individual participation and for a feeling of rapport to be more quickly and more soundly established. A child must feel comfortable in a group before he will allow himself the freedom he needs in order to think creatively.

Length of Class Period. Thirty minutes of spirited dramatic play will be of great value to a third-grade class at school, particularly if the class meets for two or three periods each week. If third-grade children meet once a week on a Saturday morning, they may enjoy playing for forty-five minutes or even an hour. Fourth-, fifth-, and sixth-grade classes should be planned for forty-five minutes or an hour. If the classes are scheduled in the school program, a teacher will find that the children will gain much more from two or three thirty-minute periods each week than they will if they play for one longer period only once during the week.

UNDERSTANDING THE CHILD

Children create best when their interest is high. The story or experience from which they are creating must have an appeal which is strong enough to capture and hold their attention. In order to determine specific interests, a leader always looks to the individuals with whom she is working, for each group of children and each child within the group is different; however, a leader who is thoroughly aware of the unique and delightful nature of the pre-adolescent child will recognize specific interests immediately.

What Kind of Child Is He?   Eight-year-olds are in a stage of transition. They are beginning to grow away from their everyday worlds and are venturing forth into regions of fantasy. Most third-grade children enjoy fairy stories and are fascinated with pixies and brownies and goblins and witches. Eight-year-olds are exceedingly imaginative. They are impressed with giants, ogres, and fairy god-mothers, and they like to identify themselves with kings and queens and princes and princesses. Some nine-year-olds dwell for a time in this make-believe world, and they too are intrigued by magic and wishes, by charms and incantations.

Ten- and eleven-year-olds are young individualists. Many nine-year-olds may be noticeably confident, too, for they may already have reached the glorious age when childhood is in full bloom. In the pre-adolescent years there is a time when every girl and boy comes into his own as an individual, and whether he outwardly declares it or secretly feels it each child makes his debut among his contemporaries. He is no longer content to be himself. He wants to be something more than just an ordinary person. He wants to be Jimmy Smith, the third baseman on the school team, or Billy Jones, the best newsboy in town, or Jane Clark, president of the girls' club, or Milly Brown, the best reader in the room.

Nine-, ten-, and eleven-year-olds are quite concerned with what they are going to be when they are grown up. Many of them assume the responsibilities of young executives during these years, and they work with zest on business ventures. They set up lemonade counters and flower stands. They get paper routes or jobs of their own.

The elementary age is an age of adventure. It is a time of heroes and heroines. Both girls and boys are interested in sports, in club work, and in gangs, and most children of this age have strong hobbies, strong interests in reading and in radio and movie programs. They are enthusiastic about pioneering and exploring, going on overnight hikes and sleeping, not in comfortable cabins, but "roughing it" and camping out. This age likes mysteries, secrets, excitement, magic, inventions, and wonder. They are curious about discoveries and are eager to push beyond the horizons of their own worlds and to investigate worlds larger than their own.

Freedom vs. Control. How much freedom does a child need in order to be creative? *A creative child is a thinking child.* He does not need the kind of freedom which allows him to run wildly and carelessly about, following his every whim and fancy, but rather the freedom which comes from putting forth his best efforts and working together with a group. One experienced leader wisely asks the children to make their rules the first day. "We need rules in all living," she tells the children. "We have stop lights and go lights and caution lights in everything we do. Suppose we make our own rules for creative dramatics." In this way she draws from the children the importance of having only one person speaking at a time, the necessity of everyone being both a good listener and a good thinker, and she helps them to recognize the need for teamwork as they plan and play together. In this way the children discipline their thinking from the very start.

Another leader has an effective way of guiding each new group by telling them at the first meeting about two "magic words." She explains that these words are "good audience," and she asks the children what they think a good audience means. She helps them to understand that people in a good audience *listen, think,* and *sit quietly* while they are planning a play and while they are watching others. To help the children see how the magic works she suggests that they get up and move about the room. Then she calls "good audience" in a quiet voice, and the children enjoy hurrying back to their places.

STARTING A GROUP

There are as many ways of bringing children together and firing their imaginations as there are children in the group. The first few weeks or meetings will be spent in pantomime, in characterization and in the use of dialogue. These experiences should be lively and should be based on the interests of the children within the group.

Each leader will discover her own best way of starting a new class, but in most instances she will spend a few minutes at the very outset in having the children get acquainted with each other. She will first introduce herself by telling not only her name but something about herself that shows the children what kind of person she is. If the class is beginning in September she may tell them about an experience she has enjoyed during the summer, or she may tell them about her hobbies or her favorite sports.

Specific suggestions and questions such as the following have been used with children in the elementary grades and have not only aroused lively discussions on a first day, but have brought out strong group and individual interests:

Let's pretend that this is a magic carpet that sails away to far-away places. Of all the places in the world, where would you like best to go on a magic carpet?

Here is a rare crystal ball. You can look into it and see ahead for ten years. Look in now and tell us—what kind of person will you be ten years from today?

What is your favorite hobby, and how did you become interested in it?

Think of the many experiences you have had. What is the most exciting thing that ever happened to you in your life?

What did you do during vacation that you enjoyed most of all?

If you were to find yourself alone—shipwrecked on an island for a year and a day—what two books would you like most to have with you?

PANTOMIME

Large Action. Children enjoy pantomime, for it is something that they already know. They have probably not regarded their playing as pantomime but have thought of it as pretending or perhaps as a guessing game. Since it is familiar to them they may be led into jolly pantomimes immediately, in somewhat the same way that Johnnie Jones and the other children pantomimed the occupations of their fathers as they went on a make-believe trip.

Or, a leader may prefer to give the children a reason for pantomiming by explaining in somewhat this way, "Whenever we meet together we are going to make up plays. We are going to *be* the characters and *do* the things they do. We can wave magic wands by imagining that we have magic wands, and we can dig for buried treasure with make-believe shovels. We don't need real properties when we use our imaginations! See if you can guess what I am doing right now."

The leader will then do an easy pantomime using large free movements. She may base her pantomime on the children's interests and ride a bicycle around the room, or she may wave a magic wand, dig for treasure, or sweep the floor of the room in which they are meeting.

As soon as the children have guessed what she is doing, she will invite all of them to do the same pantomime. She may encourage them to use the entire playing area and to move about freely in different directions. She may prefer to have them work from one side of the room to the other with each child moving in the same direction, or she may suggest, "Let's make a big circle. As we move around to the right, let's each try to forget everyone else. Each one sweep in his own way."

While the children are enjoying their first pantomime the leader will praise their efforts enthusiastically, "What fine sweepers! I see many different kinds of brooms. You make me feel that you are sweeping with real brooms and that you are getting the floor clean!"

If a part of the group has been watching, she will draw comments from them by asking, "What did you see that was interesting?" or "What did you like?"

Once the children have caught the joy of pantomiming the leader will guide them through many simple actions which use large muscular movements. These may be chosen at random, such as raking leaves, mowing a lawn, spading a garden, beating a drum, kicking a football, playing tennis, or they may be centered around a single theme.

"Who can show us something he did this summer?" is a question which will lead the group into such familiar pantomimes as rowing, swimming, fishing, hiking, camping, picnicking, and other experiences which the children will recall. If a child mentions camping or a picnic, a leader will immediately recognize the opportunities for spirited pantomimes and will quickly suggest, "Today is just made for camping! Let's roll up our packs and hike to the woods right now!" For the next thirty minutes the children will be entranced as they chop wood, build bonfires, whittle sticks, roast and eat wieners, wash and fish in cold mountain streams, and do countless other things which are dear to the hearts of young adventurers.

Beginning pantomimes should be kept simple. They should be so spontaneous and so much fun for the children that they will begin to think of specific things to do. These the leader will always encourage. She will help the children to see many possibilities for elaborating on a single pantomime. She will keep them reaching for new ideas by offering suggestions such as these, "Now that we've caught fresh mountain trout, who can show us how to catch a twenty-pound salmon?" or "Who would like to catch a different kind of fish while the rest of us guess what kind it is?" or "Who would like to show us how to cast?"

Make-believe trips always afford jolly fun for pantomime. City children enjoy going to the country, while children in the country consider it a special occasion to go to the city. It may take only a suggestion to arouse a group into action. "This is a busy time of the year for the farmers. Would you like to go out to the country and help on the farm? Who knows how to rope a steer with a lariat?" After each one has shown his skill at throwing a noose and roping imaginary cattle or fence-posts, the children will enjoy climbing into haymows, pitching hay, sacking grain, milking cows, turning separators, feeding chickens, hoeing gardens, and pitching horseshoes.

Seasonal activities provide excellent material for leading children into a variety of large actions. Spring, summer, fall, and winter each holds special interests which may be enjoyed throughout the year in creative dramatics activity. On a warm spring or summer afternoon children will find delight in pantomiming winter sports. A suggestion such as "Let's take a backward trip to last December and think of the good times we had in the snow!" may set the mood for making snowballs and having a snowball fight, which is one of the liveliest experiences for beginning pantomime. Rolling large snowballs, building snowmen and snowforts, skating, skiing, and shoveling pathways provide for vigorous action and are enjoyed by children everywhere.

If a new class is beginning in the fall of the year, children living in rural areas find a keen interest in showing how they pick apples, carry large pumpkins in from a field, dig potatoes, cut cornstalks and shock them, and catch Thanksgiving turkeys. Children living in the city will find a similar interest in showing everyday activities such as mowing a lawn, raking the yard, sweeping sidewalks, bringing in logs for a fireplace, carrying groceries, rowing a boat, riding bicycles, and pantomiming a television show.

Small Action.   Whenever the leader feels that the members of a group are ready, she will lead them into pantomimes which use smaller movements. Again these will be based on familiar actions such as brushing teeth, combing hair, drinking water from a glass, eating a sandwich, answering a telephone, threading a needle and sewing, playing a violin, picking flowers, beating an egg, turning pancakes, and opening a letter. A leader will soon discover how easy it is to expand each pantomime as, for example, that of eating a sandwich. After the group has enjoyed this pantomime the leader may ask, "Who would like to eat something quite different from a sandwich? What did you eat for breakfast or for lunch that would be interesting to pantomime?" Eating a banana, an olive, a marshmallow, soup, ice-cream, toast, popcorn, meat, a candy bar, and an orange provide for a variety of experiences in the use of fine coordinations, and children always enjoy pantomimes which have to do with food.

New fun and liveliness in playing can come from dividing the children into groups occasionally and having the groups guess what another group is pantomiming.

CHARACTERIZATION

"Now we are going to *be* characters," a leader says as she guides the children into the next step. "Since we've learned how to pantomime so that we can pick make-believe cherries from make-believe trees and eat imaginary sandwiches, let us see how easy it is to be someone different from ourselves."

Characters from Reality. The leader will then do a characterization entirely in pantomime, and she will ask the children to see if they can guess who she is and what she is doing. She may become a familiar person from everyday life, such as a friendly policeman, a streetsweeper with his broom and cart, a friendly flower lady who sells bouquets of violets on a nearby street corner, a postman delivering letters, a jolly organ grinder, or a messenger boy riding a bicycle and delivering a message which he carries in his hat.

After the children have guessed what character the leader has pantomimed, she will encourage them to discuss the characterization. Let us say that the leader has been a policeman directing traffic at a busy intersection. As she leads the discussion, she may ask, "How did you know the character was a policeman? What kind of policeman was he? What did he look like? How did he feel while he was on duty?" A leader will not expect the children to analyze a character too closely, for fourth- and fifth-graders are largely concerned with the enjoyment of being characters; moreover, they should never be made aware of technique but rather of the thinking and feeling which are necessary for strong characterization.

While the enthusiasm is strong, the children will be led into doing the same characterization. "If we are going to be policemen, we must think and feel like policemen. Who can think of a good word that describes a policeman?" A beginning class of fourth graders thought of the following words: straight, strong, brave, helpful, neat, businesslike, definite, fair, honest, firm, friendly, and Irish.

Characterization should always be pleasant, and it should be fun for the children. Keeping this in mind, a leader may ask, "Does each one have his blue uniform and his cap on? Are your shoes shined? Are your guns and badges ready?"

When a leader feels that the children are enjoying the characterization, she will lead them into pantomime by suggesting, "Now that our police force is ready to go on duty, suppose each policeman finds his station." When the children have assembled themselves around the room, the leader may encourage further thinking by commenting in somewhat this way, "My, the traffic is heavy tonight, but we have fine policemen ready to direct it. I like the way each one is being a policeman in his own way. Ready? In character! Begin!"

Praise is vital to individual growth. Commenting on specific pantomimes and characterizations is the best way to keep each child striving for his best efforts. "What fine policemen!" a leader may exclaim as soon as the children have finished their first characterization. "You made me feel that you were really on duty. I saw one policeman blowing a whistle. I saw one giving directions to a motorist who stopped to ask a question."

If there has been considerable giggling and breaking of character a leader will find it wise to use a positive approach in her comments and at the same time to stress the need for thinking in character. "Most of the policemen directed traffic well. The directions were fairly clear but I wonder if everyone really felt like a policeman? Is a policeman needed in the city? How do you think a policeman feels toward his work? Let's try again and see if we can be the best police force in the city!"

When a group is working on characterizations, a leader will watch for children who are thinking completely in character. "Let us watch these policemen," she may suggest. "Why do you think they are such strong characters?" In this way she emphasizes from the very beginning the need for thinking and feeling, and she helps the children to see how they may create convincing characters.

Making a game of characterization has a strong appeal for eight- and nine- and some ten-year-olds. A leader may interest them in characterization by asking,

> "This morning as I came down the street
> Whom do you think I chanced to meet?"

She will then proceed to show them through pantomime, and in this way she will lead them into being familiar townspeople such as a milkman, a postman, a doctor, a minister, a secretary, a baker, a nurse, a beggarman, a salesman, a banker, an artist, a farmer, a merchant, and other grown-up people from the world of reality.

Characters from Make-Believe and Mother Goose.   There is no better way for leading third-graders into characterization than having them become make-believe characters from fairyland. It is truly a thrilling experience for eight-year-olds to become sly old witches, mischievous goblins, wicked kings, dancing fairies, bold giants, stately princes and princesses, and other fairy tale folk. If children learn how to get under the skin of a new character from the very first meeting, they will always put forth their best creative efforts.

Mother Goose provides excellent and delightful material for beginning work in creative drama, for the characters are well known to almost every child, and the action is strong and definite. Many leaders consider Mother Goose the very best material to be found for characterization, and they use the nursery rhymes with every new group of children rather than beginning with characters from reality. Some of the favorite characterizations which are interesting to both boys and girls are these:

A crooked man walking down a crooked street.
Old Mother Hubbard going to her cupboard and looking for a bone.
The king in his counting house, counting out his money.
The queen in the parlor, eating bread and honey.
The maid in the garden, hanging out the clothes.
The Knave of Hearts stealing the Queen's tarts.
Old King Cole coming merrily into his court room.
Doctor Foster walking to Glo'ster in a shower of rain.

These characterizations will be discussed in much the same way as that of the policeman characterization. For instance, if the children were going to pantomime "Old Mother Hubbard," a leader would ask questions similar to these: "Who has an idea of how Old Mother Hubbard looks? How does she feel toward her dog? What kind of house does she live in? How will she feel when she finds the cupboard empty?"

CHARACTERIZATIONS IN SITUATIONS

When the children have enjoyed being many different kinds of characters, they will then be ready to pantomime situations which involve more than one character. Up to this time the children will have worked on the same kind of characterization within a group; that is, each one will have been a crooked man, or Mother Hubbard, or a policeman at the same time. They will now be ready for individual characterization in which, for example, one child will be chosen to be a policeman directing traffic, while the rest of the group become pedestrians. Each child will be encouraged to create his own characterization of a pedestrian.

"Be the kind of person you feel like being," a leader will suggest, as the pedestrians wait to cross the street according to the policeman's orders. "Perhaps you will be old or young or maybe middle-aged. Perhaps you will be someone you know, like your grand-father or a neighbor."

A leader will keep the children working for strong character feeling as she suggests for succeeding pantomimes that they be pedestrians going to work early in the morning, tired pedestrians at the end of the day, eager pedestrians hurrying to see a parade, shoppers carrying packages and bundles, and pedestrians caught in a sudden downpour of rain or in a windstorm.

Situations such as the following provide for a *variety of emotional feelings* and have proved to be excellent for fourth-, fifth-, and sixth-grade groups to pantomime:

A jolly ice-cream man pushes his cart down the street. Children and grown-ups come from every direction hurrying to buy.

An excited newsboy sells "extras" on a street corner. The news is alarming to the townspeople. What do the headlines say?

A cross old gardener discovers schoolboys in his berry patch.

Tired pirates dig for treasure. They are weary and disheartened. They decide to abandon camp when one pirate suddenly strikes something. What is it?

A champion baseball player is up to bat. The score is tied. His teammates stand near by. He misses the first two strikes. He strikes the third time. It is good.

School children are waiting for a school bus when a dog starts across the street in front of a fast-moving car. Screeching wheels and brakes are heard, and the car comes to a stop. The children wait anxiously. When the car moves on they see that the dog is safe.

Need for Variety.   Children need variety in everything they do. This is vitally important in all creative arts, for each new experience stimulates a child in a different way. Mother Goose Rhymes are rich in group situations and offer splendid variety for character pantomimes. A leader will soon find that throughout the elementary grades nursery rhymes are invaluable for creative playing, and she will look to them often when groups are first beginning. Among the delightful group experiences which appeal to children in these grades are the following, which experienced leaders have used again and again:

Hark, hark, the dogs do bark, the beggars are coming to town.

Polly putting the kettle on and greeting her friends who drop in for tea.

Four and twenty tailors going out to kill a snail.

The King of France marching with his twenty thousand men.

The three fiddlers playing a merry tune for Old King Cole.

Four and twenty blackbirds flying out of the pie when it is opened for the king.

Pantomimes from Verse.   Since adventure holds a singular place in the lives of children at this age, they enjoy experiences which satisfy the adventuresome spirit. Modern verse and story-telling rhymes may provide excellent material for characterization when a group expresses a specific interest, such as that of wanting to be pirates or gypsies. Rachel Field's "Gypsies," and Mildred Plew Merryman's "Pirate Don Durk," have proved to be favorites for satisfying these urges.

When children come under a magical spell, there is nothing quite so fine as Rachel Field's "Roads":

> A road might lead to anywhere—
>   To harbor towns and quays,
> Or to a witch's pointed house
>   Hidden by bristly trees.
> It might lead past the tailor's door,
>   Where he sews with needle and thread,
> Or by Miss Pim the milliner's,
>   With hats for every head.
> It might be a road to a great, dark cave
>   With treasure and gold piled high,

Or a road with a mountain tied to its end,
Blue-humped against the sky.
Oh, a road might lead you anywhere—
To Mexico or Maine.
But then, it might just fool you, and—
Lead you back home again![1]

"What kind of road shall *we* have?" is a question which opens the way for a friendly discussion. "We can make our road exciting or wonderful or beautiful or any way that we would like a road to be. Who begins to picture a road in his mind? What kind of road do you see?"

Most groups enjoy making a very unusual road that begins at the waterfront and winds fantastically past the witch's, the tailor's, the milliner's, past the treasure cave which is likely to be inhabited by robbers or pirates or an old miser, and a road which almost always ends with an enchanted mountain.

If the leader feels that the children are ready to work in groups, each group may plan a pantomime for a certain part of the road and surprise the others. If not, the entire group may work together. "Who has a good idea of how we can show a harbor?" a leader questions to start the group thinking. Suggestions of ferry-boats, motor boats, passengers sailing out of the harbor, boat whistles, and sea gulls generally come readily from children who are familiar with harbor towns; with leading questions all children will have many appropriate suggestions.

One fifth-grade class decided to have a single person be a fog horn down at the harbor; then at the end of the road this group had six girls form a rainbow under which a quaint little dwarf counted gold pieces which he dropped into large crocks.

Some groups are content to have the activity take place quietly and simultaneously along the road, while others feel that it is very important to have someone traveling down the road to see each of

---

[1] Reprinted from *Pointed People* by Rachel Field. Copyright 1924 by Yale University Press.

the happenings. The questions concerning who the person might be and why he is venturing down this particular roadway always invite an alert discussion.

TRANSITION INTO DIALOGUE

For how long a time should a group work on characterizations? How many class meetings should be spent in pantomime? These questions are often asked by beginning leaders, and they can best be answered by the leader herself. If the class is organized for a three-month period in which the children meet once each week, a leader will probably devote three or four meetings to pantomime. On the other hand, if the children meet once each week during a school year, a leader will find that six or eight meetings spent on characterizations in pantomime will give the children a strong foundation for creative work.

A leader who listens to the children's comments will recognize the right time for making the transition from pantomime into the use of dialogue. "May we please use words this time?" "When do we get to talk out loud like the characters?" "When I was Mother Hubbard I wanted to tell my dog how sorry I was when I couldn't find a bone for him."

Expression comes as a result of having something to say; when children are completely in character, they will speak freely and spontaneously. The leader reminds the children often, "When we are really *being* a character we find that it is easy to speak for the character. We don't worry about what to say. We become the character, and we say what the character thinks to say."

Speaking in a Group. An ideal transition from pantomime to the use of words is their use in a simple situation in which each character speaks at the same time. We have found that children are much freer in expressing themselves when they begin in a group situation, for the attention is not focused on an individual child at the outset. This does not mean that the group speaks in unison —far from it, for each child is always encouraged to speak in a natural way, and there are very few occasions in reality when people speak in unison.

In beginning work the children may become criers on the streets of London, and each one in his own way and at the same time will call, "Old chairs to mend," or "Old clothes to sell," or "Hot cross buns!"

Again the entire group may become newsboys selling "extras" on a busy street in a large city, and each one will be encouraged to call out the headlines in his own way.

Situations which are favorites with this age group are carnival barkers calling along the midway at a county fair and market vendors selling their wares in a public market. A leader never tells the children what to say, but she asks leading questions which help them to understand how a character thinks and feels. To help the children see that market vendors are good, hard-working people, a leader may ask such questions as these: "What kind of people are market vendors? Is this their only means of earning a living? Does it matter to them whether they sell their produce while it is fresh? How does each one feel when he sees a customer coming? What might a vendor say to interest a customer in his vegetables? How do the vendors feel toward each other?"

When the children have a good understanding of the vendors, the leader becomes a single customer and walks down the market aisle while each one calls out his wares and tries his best to get her to buy. Some of the vendors may speak out freely. Others may say nothing more than "Carrots for sale!" Praise should be given for sincere and real effort. If the children speak softly, the leader will encourage them to speak out, "Let us see if we can really *sell* vegetables this time! We are hard-working vendors. We must sell tomatoes, lettuce, radishes, and onions before we go home tonight!"

The leader will keep the children working until they really become market vendors and feel quite pleased with their brisk market scene. As soon as children enjoy speaking in character, they may go a step further and play A. A. Milne's "Market Square," which affords a direct carry-over for the venders to speak in dialogue with the little boy who comes to buy a rabbit.

Speaking in Dialogue. After considerable experience with speaking in groups, children should be ready for conversation between two people. The first few experiences will be kept simple and natural and between two persons, in order that a child will be able to think and to express his thoughts clearly at the outset.

"Old Mother Hubbard" and other nursery rhymes such as "Jack Spratt" and "Old King Cole" are excellent when groups are using dialogue for the first time. In a third-grade class where the children planned that Mother Hubbard would be a kind and sweet grandmother and would be forgetful and friendly to her dog, one little girl was so eager to be Mother Hubbard for the first time that the others wanted her to be this important character, too. When she was chosen she immediately became old and started knitting. When Tippy, her dog, started barking and whining, Old Mother Hubbard stopped her knitting and watched him closely. Finally she rose from her chair. "Goodness sakes alive, Tippy!" she said, clasping her hands together. "It's nearly noon and I haven't given you your breakfast!" The dog whined, and Mother Hubbard hurried to the cupboard. Finding it bare, she turned away sadly. "Poor Tippy," she said, "there isn't a thing to eat. We're all out of groceries! Well, we'll just go to the butcher's right now, and I'll get you a bone and a wiener to make up for it!"

This little girl was ready for dialogue, and, what is even more important, she understood the character. A leader will soon find that *when the emphasis is placed on the joy of being a character, the action and conversation will largely take care of themselves.* Children will be far more creative if time is spent in getting acquainted with a new character—in talking about how the character thinks and feels, rather than spending too much time on having the children discuss action for action's sake or dialogue for dialogue's sake. The latter method tends to thwart spontaneous, individual interpretation and can quickly defeat the purpose of creative dramatics.

Conversation in Situations. Beginning with simple dialogue, the children will find real pleasure in adding conversation to many of the situations which they have already done in pantomime, such as the scenes with the ice-cream man, the pirates, the baseball team, and the boys in the berry patch. They will enjoy playing "Roads" again and bringing it alive with conversation. Another of Rachel Field's fine poems, "General Store," provides excellent motivation for leading children into the friendly and familiar experience of playing store. Once a group has decided where their store will be and what kind of storekeeper they will have, each child likes to figure out what kind of character he will be, and he decides for himself just what he will buy when he comes to the store.

TRANSITION INTO STORIES

To move the children on a step further, a leader may use a short story with a simple plot. She will choose a story which is strong in characterization, yet easy enough for the children to do with satisfaction. Stories which appear almost too easy for the children from the standpoint of reading will be challenging enough from the standpoint of playing for beginning groups. It is one thing to read the old fable, "The Shepherd Boy Who Called Wolf," and yet to become excited villagers hurrying to the hilltop in answer to the boy's cries is quite a different thing. Fables and old folk tales are rich in simple plot material for beginning groups. "The Bremen Town Musicians," "The Three Wishes," "Pandora's Box," and "The Wise Men of Gotham" are excellent to use in the elementary grades when children are being introduced to story dramatization. One of the very best of modern stories is "Mrs. Mallaby's Birthday," by Helen Earle Gilbert, which was written for younger children. Yet it is a story which appeals to older children and gives them an opportunity to be many of the familiar townspeople who come to see Mrs. Mallaby for the purpose of wishing her a happy one-hundredth birthday.

Animal tales such as "The Town Mouse and the Country Mouse" and Uncle Remus's "Tar Baby" and Kipling's "The Elephant's Child" are splendid to use when children show a strong interest in being animal characters.

When a class has worked through a good many short stories, they will be ready to proceed to the dramatization of longer stories with more involved plots, such as "Cinderella," "Rumpelstiltskin," "Jack and the Beanstalk," "Sleeping Beauty," "Pinocchio," "The King of the Golden River," "The Nürnberg Stove," "The Knights of the Silver Shield," "The Emperor's New Clothes," "Why the Chimes Rang," "Old Pipes and the Dryad," and many episodes from "The Adventures of Tom Sawyer." A leader will strive always to keep the children reaching upward through creative experiences which are carefully chosen, yet she will use care in keeping these experiences within the children's reach. She will choose material challenging in the way of characterization but still on the children's level of appreciation and interest.

Chapter IV

HOW TO INTRODUCE CREATIVE DRAMATICS
ON THE JUNIOR HIGH SCHOOL LEVEL

What liberty a loosened spirit brings.
—EMILY DICKINSON

Creative dramatics is of tremendous value to junior high school students, and if it can be offered at only one grade level in a school curriculum, it should be planned definitely for the early adolescent years. During this period of rapid development and great adjustment, each child experiences a surging need to express and assert himself. Even though a child may not outwardly reveal the complexities of his feelings, he may be experiencing terrific inner tensions which greatly need to be released and legitimately channeled. As a child projects himself into the roles of many different people, he carries his emotional problems into his characterizations, and as he does so he begins to have a better understanding of his own disturbing thoughts and feelings. Creative dramatics introduces a child to strong and worthy characters from literature, and as he

70

lives through dynamic dramatic experiences, new horizons and lofty vistas are opened to him which gradually help him to become a confident individual in his own right.

NEED FOR EXPRESSION

Although the need for expression is strong in junior high school, many young adolescents are too sensitive and self-conscious to enter wholeheartedly into this activity without the right kind of stimulation. Many youngsters may want very much to participate but will hold back unless they come under friendly and understanding guidance.

During the past war, a leader tried in many different ways to bring a group of junior high school students together for creative dramatics in an after-school program. The class was widely publicized, and invitations were sent to many children who were new in the community and who were living in housing projects. When there was no outward evidence of interest being shown in such a class, the leader found by questioning an individual here and one there that the children were confused and disturbed both by the war and by the readjustments that they had had to make in living conditions. Then the leader was even more desirous to introduce creative dramatics to them, for she realized the values of such a program in helping emotionally disturbed children. One afternoon she noticed a group of young teen-age boys in a vacant lot behind a grocery store. The evening before, the city baseball team had won an exciting league game in a last-minute home-run play. As the leader saw the boys, she recalled the baseball game. She broke a rule of rhetoric for a purpose and spoke to them in a friendly yet straight-from-the-shoulder manner, "Say, did any of you guys see the game last night?"

"Sure we did, what do you know about it?" was the quick reply from the largest boy in the group.

"Boy, did you see Speed Jensen hit that homer!" the leader continued triumphantly.

Because every one of the boys had seen the game from a rooftop or a board fence, and because all of them had lived that heroic moment, they were on their feet in a second and eager to tell exactly what they had seen. At first they started to describe the play, then in their enthusiasm they started showing what had happened. They were doing creative dramatics without knowing it. They were being Speed Jensen, walking heroically up to home plate and swinging an imaginary bat with tremendous power to strike a home run. The leader suggested that each one be a key player in this dramatic scene and that they use the open space of the outdoor lot for the baseball diamond. The boys were intrigued with the idea of playing without a ball or a bat, and they entered into this new game with great spirit. When the leader saw the good time they had acting out the ball game, she asked if they would like to share their game with some of the other children on the following week. They were not wholeheartedly receptive to the idea at first, but the leader persuaded them through wise and tactful praise until they finally agreed to play this new kind of baseball in the auditorium for some of the neighborhood children.

A week later they went to a large community building, and they relived the baseball game with spirit and enthusiasm. Several other boys and girls who had been cajoled into coming to the auditorium to see a play were waiting when the baseball boys arrived. When Speed Jensen went up to bat he flexed his knees and danced on his toes, and he swung his imaginary bat sharply, trying out his swing and making certain of his grip. When the pitcher threw the perfect strike, he hit the imaginary ball with all his might and struck the famous homer. The outfielders disappeared from the stage looking for the ball, and Speed Jensen ran so fast around the diamond that when he reached third base he slid off the stage into the auditorium. The audience laughed and shouted. With all the grandeur of Speed Jensen, the boy jumped up and finished his heroic play.

The players and the audience had such a good time at the pantomimed ball game that the leader asked if they would like to come back on the following Thursday.

"What will we do next time?" one of the older boys asked.

"Why don't you plan a surprise?" the leader suggested. "If you plan something, I'll plan something, too."

A week later many of the children came back again. Their surprise was a play which they had made up and wanted to act out on the stage. It was a tragedy from beginning to end, and there were three acts in all. It began with a tremendous firing of weapons, and the first act ended with twelve killings. Machine guns with fearful sound-effects ripped through excited crowds of villagers, and people fell helplessly to the street, screaming and wailing in agony. The children play-acted the killing with real feeling. They played their wild story for nearly an hour, until every boy and a good many of the girls had manned the machine guns. As they played they expressed strong feelings of hate, and they gradually worked these bitter feelings out of their systems. The hostility which they felt so keenly as they started to play had somewhat spent itself through its very expression, and when the children had had enough of this ugliness they seemed to be ready for the leader's surprise. She was ready with a vigorous telling of Norse tales, which proved to be a good substitute for the excitement which they had experienced.

CHARACTERISTICS OF ADOLESCENCE

By the time boys and girls reach junior high school, they are going beyond the realm of childhood and are coming face to face with reality. As a result of all the physical and emotional changes that are taking place, many adolescents hardly know themselves. They grow so fast and experience so many complex feelings that their attention is likely to be drawn almost completely unto themselves. Many adolescents have a tendency to be self-conscious, to worry about any little defects they may have, to get distorted ideas about themselves, and to exaggerate and magnify experiences which have been embarrassing, trying, confusing, or pleasant. They experience difficult periods of physical and emotional awkwardness as they try to gain control of new bodies and new feelings. They weigh and measure new ideas in relation to themselves as they have never done before. They become greatly concerned with a sense of their individual worth.

A girl in junior high school is likely to be a year or even two years ahead of the average boy in physical development; however, she is apt to be very unstable in her emotional feelings and in her interests. She may be very touchy and may become upset easily. At one moment she may feel quite grown up and will want everyone, including her friends, her family, and her teachers, to treat her as such, while at the very next moment she is likely to feel and to act very much like a child again and will want to be considered as such. An adolescent boy experiences similar feelings of instability and irritability which are noticeable in many different ways. Probably the most evident physical aspect affecting embarrassment is the way in which his voice keeps breaking down and up as he speaks.

Adolescence brings an age of realism and idealism. Each young adolescent is in constant search for ideals. He has high interests in philosophical, ethical, romantic, and spiritual problems. He finds new and absorbing interests in his immediate environment, and he gradually becomes aware of the complexities of society and of the world. He pursues knowledge with increased earnestness. He is sensitive to beauty, even though he may conceal it from others. He strives to conform to society. Intellectually and emotionally, each individual in his adolescent years experiences a gradual broadening and deepening in his capacity to think and to feel. He respects adult guidance which is kindly and sincerely given, and he resents imposition of authority in realms in which he feels secure.

During this period boys and girls secretly try to put themselves in the place of others whom they admire. A child may change his style of hairdress, his way of laughing, his stance, his manner of dress, in order that he may be more like someone he idolizes. He may lock himself in his room and secretly strut in front of a mirror, imagining himself to be an adult hero or heroine. He identifies himself not only with people from reality, but very often with characters he finds in books and in moving pictures.

STARTING CREATIVE DRAMATICS IN JUNIOR HIGH SCHOOL

Beginnings are important. A first day of school or a first meeting of a new class makes a strong impression on children of all ages, and this is particularly true in regard to sensitive adolescents. Above all a leader will be prepared and will have carefully planned the procedure of the entire meeting. By her friendly manner, her pleasing appearance, her enthusiasm, and knowledge of this art she can win a respect for creative dramatics immediately. She will have taken care of such details of organization as were considered by the leader in the elementary grades. In a junior high school a creative dramatics class will most likely be scheduled for three forty-five minute periods each week, whereas in an after-school program in which the children meet only once each week, the class will be planned for either an hour or an hour and a half.

As soon as a group is assembled for a first meeting, a leader will introduce herself in a friendly manner and through her introduction will endeavor to set an interesting mood which will make it easy for each student to introduce himself in a similar way. In addition to learning each other's names the students may enjoy hearing about each one's hobbies, or they may find it interesting to learn where each one was born. If the students are already acquainted with each other, a leader may find that a thought-provoking question, such as one of the following, will arouse real interest among a group and will provide valuable insights into individual personalities and furnish clues to specific interests:

If you had an hour in which you could do anything you wished, what would you choose to do?

Of all the interesting places in the world where one might travel, where would you like most to go?

In thinking back over the past ten years, what do you consider the finest, the most exciting, or the most wonderful experience you have had in your life?

What is your favorite book, your favorite radio or television program, and your favorite moving picture?

While the children are introducing themselves, the leader will not only check the class roll, but she will strive to identify each child with specific associations in order that she will remember his name and something about him from the first day. A child is not only honored, but he has a great respect for a leader who is able to call him by name at a second meeting.

As soon as everyone is acquainted, a leader will give the children an enthusiastic introduction to creative dramatics, explaining it in relation to themselves. She may arouse an interesting discussion concerning dramatics in general in which she will encourage the students to tell about different plays they have seen or perhaps have been in. Thus, by approaching the subject in terms of drama which is familiar to them, she will be able to help the students see that in creative dramatics they are to make up their own plays and to speak for the characters, rather than to memorize lines which have been written by a playwright. She will describe with enthusiasm the genuine fun which comes from creative dramatics when each person really thinks and feels like the character he is creating, and she will emphasize, too, how much more enjoyment each student will gain from the entire experience if he puts forth his best efforts. From the first day she will help the students feel that the class is largely their own and that she is there to help them have a good time creating plays which will perhaps be stronger or better because of her help. She will then draw from the children suggestions of stories which they would like to make into plays.

If a leader has been dynamic and sincere in introducing her

subject, she may find that the students are eager to create a play right then and there. It is at this point that inexperienced leaders should be cautioned against the danger of allowing the students to proceed so rapidly that they do not have time to build a solid foundation for dramatic work. Leaders who guide beginning students into the dramatization of a story at a first or second meeting cannot hope for much more than superficial playing. Until students first learn to pantomime and to characterize gradually in a variety of comparatively simple situations, they cannot be expected to stay in character and keep a story going with any degree of success. Because of the idealistic nature of adolescents, seventh- and eighth-grade students prefer to learn how to use the tools of dramatic work or to start at the bottom of the ladder, so to speak, when they realize how much finer their plays can be once they have learned how to create convincing characters. When students understand that they are to use no costumes and very few properties in their plays, they readily see the importance of strong characterization and are not only content but eager to learn how to pantomime and to characterize well.

GROUP PANTOMIME

There are many possible variations in the way in which a leader may introduce pantomime to junior high school students. She may begin in somewhat the same way as the leader did with the teen-aged boys who were interested in baseball; that is, she may use a strong group interest as the medium for lively pantomimes. Or, she may begin with pantomimes which have to do with strong emotional feeling. Or, if she prefers, she may begin immediately with characterization. There is no exact order in which a leader introduces these basic elements which are fundamental to creative drama, and each leader will proceed in the way in which she feels most confident.

Because of the shyness which adolescents feel toward each other, it is advisable to have the entire class work together for the first few meetings. When working in a group there is less attention called to each individual, and each child benefits from many different experiences during a single class period. A sensitive child feels much more at ease when he is working with many others than he does when he is working entirely alone, and consequently he feels freer in expressing himself. However, a leader is careful to encourage individual interpretation within a group rather than allowing the children to resort to imitation.

Large Action.   A brief explanation of pantomime by the leader followed by a skillful demonstration will immediately prepare the way for group pantomime, particularly if she chooses an action which has a strong appeal for the group. Since sports are universally enjoyed by both boys and girls in junior high school, let us say that a leader decides to pitch a baseball for a first pantomime. As soon as the students guess what she was pantomiming, she will suggest that everyone pitch a softball over home plate. She will indicate an imaginary home plate at one end of the room and she will build up a friendly mood for playing by commenting enthusiastically about baseball and pitching.

The laughter and fun which come from pitching an imaginary ball will lead to many further baseball pantomimes, such as pitching curves, catching fast balls, catching fly balls, batting, striking out, and other actions which baseball enthusiasts will suggest. While the students are pantomiming, a leader will watch for action which is clean-cut and clear, and she will praise pantomimes which are definite. Other sports, such as tennis, badminton, football, golf, rowing, skiing, skating, and hockey may motivate interesting pantomimes when a group shows a particular enthusiasm for certain sports. Many of the pantomimes which are used in the elementary grades can readily be adapted to seventh- or eighth-grade classes when creative dramatics is first being introduced. Pantomimes which have had to do with playing musical instruments, with outdoor activities, and with various occupations have been enjoyed by beginning groups in junior high school.

Small Action. If children are plunged too quickly into story dramatization without having first built up a gradual foundation for disciplined thinking, they will not understand how to pantomime fine details of action. Consequently, a child who does not know how to make his pantomime clear will be satisfied with careless action, and he will never know the thrilling experience of skillfully co-ordinating the muscles of his body with his imagination. On the other hand, if he is able to think clearly through an action, not only will his pantomime be easily understood by others, but the experience will be satisfying and stimulating to him.

Pantomimes which are concerned with eating never fail to stir up an immediate interest among hungry adolescents. The suggestion of eating hamburger sandwiches immediately arouses a jolly mood among most junior high school groups and indirectly leads into pantomimes of fine detail. "Would anyone care for a tender, juicy hamburger sandwich?" a leader may ask in a friendly way to motivate group thinking. "Suppose we each have one right now," she continues while the enthusiasm is strong. "We will use these hot buns and these sizzling hamburgers here on the griddle. Each one may fix his sandwich in the way he likes it best."

A leader indicates the imaginary food as she speaks, and she encourages the students to make sandwiches and then to eat them. After the boys and girls have finished eating sandwiches, she may suggest that they eat chicken drumsticks. She will encourage them to show the difference between these two pantomimes, and she will call attention to actions which are distinct and precisely done.

Junior high school students work with zest on material which challenges their thinking. They will find great satisfaction in showing the difference between peeling an orange and peeling a banana, in eating soup and eating spaghetti, in drying a plate and drying a glass, in picking violets and picking sunflowers, in vacuuming a rug and using a carpet sweeper, in winding a wrist watch and winding an alarm clock, and in tying a knot with thread and tying one with rope.

Emotional Feeling. Many leaders prefer to begin with pantomimes which make use of basic emotions, since this kind of pantomiming introduces children to unified body action from the very beginning. Since each child must discover his own power of expression, he can do this best by participating in many experiences which encourage him to work from within. A leader may explain to the students how necessary it is for a character to show outwardly how he is feeling within. She may illustrate by doing several pantomimes for them, showing how she enters a room when she is joyous, when she is fearful, when she is sad, and when she is cross.

Or, she may begin by suggesting, "Now we are going to use our imaginations in quite a different way. We are going to imagine ourselves in many different situations. Let us suppose that school has been dismissed for a championship football game, and we are going out to cheer for our team. How would you feel about this?"

After a few minutes of lively discussion, she will encourage the entire group to walk briskly around the room or to a designated place as she joins with them and perhaps leads the way in order to get them started. *Above all, the leader will see that the students enjoy this beginning step in creative dramatics, for it is through the medium of imaginative play that each child forgets his fears and frees himself for his best thinking.*

When a group has worked through an initial pantomime, a leader will guide its members in a similar way into many pantomimes which provide for a variety of strong emotional experiences. The children may suggest pantomimes which they would like to do, and these will be encouraged if they are neither too complex nor too difficult for beginning work. The pantomimes listed below have proved to be interesting in junior high school and are particularly useful for beginning students, since each pantomime not only provides an emotional experience but has to do with *walking*, which serves to get the children on their feet and accustoms each one to unified body expression:

You are walking home from a school football game. Your team won the city championship!

You are walking home from the same game. Your team lost the city championship.

You are hurrying after a fire engine which has just gone down the block where you live. You fear that your house or a neighbor's might be burning.

You are walking home from school. You have your report card with you. Your grades are much lower than you expected them to be. You are upset and angry.

You are walking home from church on Sunday morning. You have just learned of the sudden death of a respected and beloved citizen in the community. You are deeply shocked and moved.

Change in Emotional Feeling. A leader will move a group ahead as quickly or as slowly as she feels is best for the growth of the individuals within the group. From pantomimes which were strong in emotional feeling she will lead them a step further into pantomimes which make use of a change of emotional feeling.

"Our pantomimes are going to be even more interesting this time!" a leader says to arouse a positive attitude and a stronger challenge. "We will show one kind of feeling when our pantomime starts and an entirely different feeling when it ends. Let us suppose that we are hiking through the woods. We've been on a picnic, and we're feeling good as we tramp along. Suddenly we come to an open place among the trees. We stop in our tracks, for there above us on a mountain ledge is a mother bear and her two young cubs. In our minds we will see the bears and we will hear the mother bear growl sharply. How do you think you would feel when you suddenly notice the bears? What do you think you would be most likely to do?"

A few minutes of dynamic discussion will set the mood for strong feeling. "Let's try this pantomime together for the first time. Let us see if we can *show* a sudden change from feeling pleasant to feeling fearful. Each of you think about it and do it in your own way. Ready? We've been picnicking! We're hiking through the woods, and how good we feel!" Thus the leader starts the group.

While the students are working through the pantomime, a leader will watch for boys and girls who are showing strong emotional feeling. She will choose five or six of them to do the same pantomime a second time, while the rest of the group watches.

A leader always praises worthy effort, and she helps the students to recognize what is good. After a small group has finished a pantomime, a leader may comment, "Well done! You certainly made us feel that the bears were after you!" Then, speaking to the children who were watching, she will ask, "What did you like about the pantomime? How did Bill show that he enjoyed hiking? How did we know Margaret was frightened when she saw the bears? What strong feeling did Jim show when he turned on his heels and ran?"

Following such group pantomime, a class may be divided into two or three groups, and each one will plan a different pantomime. A spirit of friendly competition always arises from this kind of play and adds spontaneity in thinking and feeling. Pantomimes with a change of emotional feeling such as the following have a strong appeal for young adolescents:

You are at an airport waiting anxiously for an airplane that is two hours overdue. Your father is on the plane. You scan the sky anxiously as you wait. Suddenly you hear the humming of motors, and at last you see the plane coming in for a landing.

You are watching tight-rope walkers at a circus. They are performing daring acts high in the air. One performer nearly loses his balance. At last the act is over. The band strikes up a lively march as tumbling clowns hurry into the sawdust ring.

You are hurrying home from school. You are hungry, but you have no money with you. You pass a bakery shop. You stop and linger as you feast your eyes on the goodies in the window.

You are at a railroad station pacing up and down waiting for your younger sister. You are greatly irritated by her slowness, for the train which is to take you both to the country for the week end is scheduled to leave soon. Two minutes before train time your sister arrives.

You are hiking through the woods and come into a clearing. You stop suddenly, for there before you is the most beautiful sunset you have ever seen.

CHARACTERIZATION

Use of Balladry. Balladry is ideal for characterization. It is not too advanced nor too elementary in substance to challenge junior high school students. Its material, so varied, so vigorous, so charming in simplicity and romantic spirit, seems tuned to the hearts of young adolescents. Some ballads are robust, others romantic, some are joyous, others plaintive, while many are animated with mystery, trickery, or chivalry. This form of literature closely reflects the life of yesteryear, for traveling minstrels and ballad makers of medieval days wove vigorous tales and romantic verse about the people of their times. As minstrels and troubadours wandered from castles to cottages and mingled with the rich and the poor alike, many were the tales and adventures which they heard. Such is the substance from which the old ballads sprang. Growing out of humble folk life as well as from the tales of crusaders and from legends of the sea, medieval ballads are characterized by superstitious beliefs, naïve conceptions of royalty, and eager delights in sensational bravery and wrongdoing.

When ballads are presented to growing youth with a colloquial freshness they hold their interest with a firm insistence, for this material of medieval life is thrilling and sensational yet ethically and artistically sound. When a leader interests thirteen- and fourteen-year-olds in balladry, she brings them into a rich heritage which is rightfully theirs, and at the same time she satisfies their forcible demand for realities.

Enthusiasm is contagious. A leader who thoroughly understands and appreciates the greatness of balladry will honor this form of literature with more than an ordinary introduction. She may find it necessary to reinforce her background by reading from John Hampden's *Ballads and Ballad-Plays*, from *Old Ballads in Prose*, by Eva March Tappan, or to consult the picturesque descriptions in *Medieval Days and Ways*, by Gertrude Hartman.

A paragraph from Miss Hartman's book will immediately convince a leader of the wealth of possibilities for dramatic playing:

> Although the lives of the peasants were hard and monotonous there were some bright spots to relieve their ceaseless round of toil. Sometimes there was a fair at a neighboring town which they were permitted to attend. Sometimes a group of jugglers on their way to a castle stopped at a village and showed their tricks. There was occasionally a strolling minstrel for the common people too. He wandered about, dressed in his bright-hued jacket with a long peacock's feather stuck in his cap and a viol slung on his back. At a village green he would unsling his viol and begin strumming the strings, and soon the peasants would be crowding about to hear him sing some well-known ballad. After the performance he would collect offerings from his audience. Then he would start off again, perhaps to a near-by fair, where the merrymakers would flock about him. It was a carefree, roving life.[1]

What does a leader do to interest a group of modern youngsters in medieval living? *She begins a dramatic campaign in behalf of balladry.* She gives stirring accounts of jugglers, mountebanks, acrobats, and sleight-of-hand performers. In essence she "barnstorms" them with ideas from the past. Nothing is commonplace, but everything is treated with a sense of real adventure. She gives vivid descriptions of life in the days before there were newspapers, moving pictures, radios, or television. She reviews with picturesque clarity the ways in which both the nobility and the peasantry lived and were entertained. A lusty "build-up" to balladry will kindle an interest among the most modern-minded youth, and the first responsibility of a junior high school leader is to become so enthusiastic about balladry herself that she can sell this worthy interest to twentieth century teen-agers.

When a leader feels that a group is sufficiently excited about medieval life, she indirectly leads them into characterization by

---

[1] Gertrude Hartman, *Medieval Days and Ways*, the Macmillan Co., 1940.

becoming a strolling minstrel strumming on an imaginary lute, or a jolly juggler performing tricks for the pleasure of the nobility. *She then leads everyone into being the same character and works for a spirit of fun rather than clarity in early characterizations.* The leader encourages the students to come into the playing area by suggesting, "Let us see the minstrels approaching the lord's castle along this roadway. Perhaps we will see minstrels who are young, old, gay, weary, eager, or merry. How do you think a minstrel will feel as he approaches a castle? Each one be a minstrel in his own way. Ready? In character! Let's be wandering minstrels!"

If a leader feels that it will be helpful to a group, she may become a minstrel along with them or if the students seem confident, she will get them started and then watch closely for strong character feeling. If a leader finds that a beginning group does not seem to understand how to characterize, or if several of the children are self-conscious and are inclined to laugh at themselves rather than to think in character, a leader will bring the group together for a discussion of characterization. She will explain how necessary it is *to think and to feel like a character in order to become whatever character one is creating.* She may do further characterizations, analyzing each one in order that the students will gain a better understanding of how to characterize for themselves. She may create an interesting characterization of a hungry old tramp stopping along a highway to eat a lunch that he has just begged from a nearby farm house, or she may become a gay young peddler carrying a heavy pack. She may find it interesting to the girls in the class if she becomes a wealthy young noblewoman sitting in a castle garden weaving a garland of flowers as she anticipates a forthcoming tournament. Whatever characterizations she does she will invite the children to create similar ones by using their own ideas rather than following hers too closely.

Importance of Audience. Listening, observing, and evaluating are vital aspects in a creative dramatics program. *One of the best ways for a child to grow through characterization is for him to* *learn to observe others, for awareness is the strongest motivation for creation.* A leader encourages each new class to watch many different people as they move about in everyday life. She asks them to watch people at home, people at school, people on the streets, and to observe the many different reactions of people when they are exhilarated, worried, cross, fearful, alarmed, tired, excited, surprised, or experiencing other strong feelings.

"Now we are ready for an audience," a leader explains as she introduces a class to the importance of observation. "Part of the class will be an audience that watches while the others play. In this way each one will have an opportunity to *see* characters as well as *be* characters. A good audience can always tell how a character is thinking and feeling even when he is playing in pantomime, depending, of course, on the player's ability to create a convincing character. Let us see if our audience can discover what kind of characters we have and also tell exactly what they are doing."

After a part of the group has participated as members of an audience watching others pantomime, a leader will guide them into evaluation by commenting favorably, "Good work! There were many excellent pantomimes!" Then she will draw specific comments from the audience members by asking, "What did you see that you liked? What did you feel was particularly well done? What unusual ideas were used in some of the pantomimes?"

The students may work in groups of four or five, and although they will work on the same characterization at the same time, each student will be encouraged to work independently of the others. Characterizations based on medieval life should be planned with variety and interest. The following have proved to be popular with junior high school groups:

A proud herald reading a proclamation from a scroll.

An old scribe carefully writing a manuscript with a goose quill pen.

A jolly, rotund servant bearing a great tray of pastries to a banquet hall.

A pleasant young noblewoman embroidering an altar cloth.

A slow-witted servant struggling with a huge log which he is bringing into a castle hall.

A weary peasant woman flailing grain.

A trumpeter sounding a blast on his trumpet to start tournament festivities.

Modern day characterizations which offer a sharp contrast to medieval living are thoroughly enjoyed by students when they have learned how to characterize with some degree of satisfaction. Characterizations such as the following have a strong appeal for seventh- and eighth-grade students:

A conservative, middle-aged gentleman turning on a radio to listen to a "world series" broadcast.

A young artist sketching a mountain scene at sunrise.

A friendly clerk at a drug store counter preparing an ice cream soda.

A college gridiron hero entering a football game at a crucial moment.

A fussy maiden lady sitting for a photograph.

A stern public stenographer typewriting a documentary report.

A radio celebrity conducting an orchestra at a fashionable resort.

Working in Pairs. As students grow in their ability to characterize, they find a keen satisfaction in having their fellow students as an appreciative audience to observe and praise their efforts. When a child has gradually built up confidence in himself by playing first in a large group and then in a smaller group, he will look forward to the challenging experience of playing with one other person. Or, an occasional student may express a desire to create a characterization entirely by himself. If a child is eager to work alone he should be given an opportunity to do so, and his efforts be evaluated fairly, but care should be taken in seeing that he does not monopolize too much of the playing time from the rest of the group.

Pantomimes for two people may be treated in a manner similar to that of charades. After the students have organized themselves into partners, each couple will be given a slip of paper suggesting characterizations from which they may plan a surprise pantomime for the others. Increased interest both for the players and the audience always comes when pantomimes are to be guessed. Medieval characterizations such as the following may be suggested to motivate ideas:

A stern shoemaker instructing a young apprentice in the art of cobbling.

An exacting guild judge weighing loaves of bread which have been made by an honest, humble baker.

A kind peasant wife showing a young peasant maid how to draw water from a well.

A young squire arming his knight as he prepares for a tournament.

Two serving women slyly gossiping about happenings at the castle while they are busily engaged in carding wool and spinning.

A pleasant young noblewoman learning the art of needlework from the gracious lady of the castle.

A hungry kitchen scullion stealing a roast chicken and being caught in the act by the angry master cook.

A humble serf receiving orders from his haughty overseer.

A poor and weary wayfarer seeking rest at a monastery where a gentle monk welcomes him.

Junior high school students will be encouraged to create original pantomimes based on actual experiences as well. If some of the boys and girls seem to need help in planning further characterizations, the following suggestions may lead them to think of pantomimes of their own:

A particular lady trying on hats in a millinery shop while a patient clerk tries hard to please her.

A nervous mother trying hard to thread a needle in a hurry while her young son waits impatiently to get a button on his shirt.

An eager salesman endeavoring to sell his wares to a stern house-wife.

A traffic patrolman escorting an elderly gentleman across a busy street.

A cross maid hanging out clothes and ignoring a pleasant gardener who is mowing grass nearby.

PANTOMIMING RHYME AND VERSE

Strong in Character Interest. By the time the students have worked through a variety of characterizations, they will be ready and eager to work on pantomimes which tell a short story. The students may find pleasure in working on improvisations, or they may prefer to pantomime a rhyme or a verse in which the plot is clear and definite.

Several of the old rhymes, when introduced as an outgrowth of medieval characterization, are stimulating and challenging to beginning junior high school groups. "The Queen of Hearts," "The Old Market Woman," and "Old King Cole" offer excellent material when a class is making a transition from single characterizations into pantomimes which are based on a simple plot.

Old King Cole. Since ceremony and ritual hold a strong appeal for adolescents, "Old King Cole" with its jolly court festivity has proved to be a favorite, particularly when it is presented in its original setting. After a class has become enthusiastic about medieval life, a leader may motivate an interest in this rhyme in many different ways. She may read an imaginary proclamation from King Cole requesting the presence of the nobility (the members of the class) at his castle for feasting. Or, a leader may enrich the students' background with descriptions of life within a castle, or she may find that a discussion of various musical instruments of the day will indirectly motivate a desire to become court fiddlers entertaining King Cole.

Even though the students may be familiar with the rhyme, a leader will always refresh the material from which a class is to create, as she presents it with zest and enthusiasm.

In guiding a group through a dramatization, a leader will be of greatest help by stressing characterization, for *when the students have a thorough understanding of the characters, they feel free to create the action set forth by the rhyme or verse.* A leader will begin by asking guide questions: "What kind of person is King Cole? Who has a good idea of how the king looks? How old do you think he is? How does he feel toward his courtiers? Is he always merry?"

After a discussion stimulated by questioning, the students will be guided into pantomiming the character as a group. "Create the character in your own way. Be the kind of king you feel Old King Cole would be," a leader will suggest, to encourage originality and to stimulate imagination. Music which represents the mood of the rhyme may help to vitalize the experience and to get the students started in a free interpretation of the character. A gay processional or a recording of Wagner's "Festival March" from *Tannhauser* may go far in helping each one to feel the impressiveness of the ceremony and thus to become a convincing king.

"What merry kings! What gayety!" a leader praises after the students have worked on this characterization. "Suppose we watch these kings," she suggests, as she chooses several students from among the group who were completely in character. After these students have pantomimed the characterization, a leader will draw favorable comments from the others who were watching.

To encourage independent thinking and to give the students the feeling that the play is entirely of their own making, a leader will ask, "How shall we begin our play? Will King Cole be in his court room? Will he be feasting in the castle hall? Who has an idea for an interesting beginning?"

After a class decides how the play will start, the leader will continue to emphasize characters which are necessary to the playing of the scene. If a group decides that King Cole will enter his court room in a gay procession, a leader will help them plan the order of the procession. She may find it necessary to explain that a herald generally leads a procession, followed by trumpeters who sound a gay fanfare for a king's entrance. The king may be attended by few or many servants, and he will be followed by courtiers, knights, and lords and ladies who honor him.

A few guide questions, such as: "What kind of herald do you think King Cole would have in his court? How would the herald feel as he leads the king's procession?" will perhaps be sufficient to give the children an understanding of the herald without finding it necessary to have the entire group pantomime his character, unless, however, all seem to want to identify themselves with the importance of the herald's position.

"Let's be trumpeters sounding fanfares to announce the king!" a leader may suggest with enthusiasm. "Let us hear how differently each trumpet sounds!"

After the merriment which comes from sounding imaginary trumpets, the leader will guide a class into planning other characters such as a Keeper of the Pipe, a Keeper of the Bowl, Three Court Fiddlers, and a Page. Each character may be discussed in detail and pantomimed, or the students may feel confident in creating original characterizations without spending too long a time in group planning.

Before the students are ready to start their play, one or two questions will be asked to help them visualize the throne room necessary for playing this rhyme. Stage managers will be chosen to arrange a throne from chairs or benches and to provide an entrance in whatever way they feel will best suggest a castle doorway.

When the characters have been chosen, a leader will make it clear to the players just how far they are to play for the first time. That is, she will be definite in stating that they will play only to the place where the court is assembled, or to the place where King Cole calls for his pipe.

Then, to add to the significance of the experience, the leader will create a strong mood as she gives a spirited announcement: "It is a festive day in Old King Cole's court! The king is ready to lead a merry procession into his spacious court room. His courtiers are elaborately dressed, and everyone is eager to please his royal majesty. We go now to King Cole's court!"

During a first playing, a leader can tell whether a group is confident and thoroughly enjoying the experience, or whether its members need further help in analyzing characters before they play again. If the enthusiasm is strong, and if the students have remained in character throughout the playing, a second cast may be chosen immediately. In a rhyme such as this one, in which the action is clear and strong, a second cast may pantomime the rhyme through to the end.

TRANSITION INTO DIALOGUE

When a class has been inspired by seeing a rhyme come alive through action, the desire to use words will be exceedingly great, and thus the transition into the use of dialogue becomes natural and direct. When the students are familiar with the characters and with the sequence of action in a rhyme which they have pantomimed, they may be ready to create dialogue immediately. If they appear to be enthusiastic about speaking for the characters, a cast will be chosen immediately and the dialogue left entirely to the children's imagination and creation.

If, however, a leader senses a timidity or a self-conscious attitude among a group at the suggestion of using dialogue, she may ask a few specific questions: "How do you think the herald feels as he announces King Cole? Does he respect and honor the king? What do you think he might say to make the king feel pleased as he enters the court room? Is this a merry or a serious occasion?"

The children will no doubt think of several different ideas, or a leader may find it necessary to suggest such announcements as: "His Majesty, King Cole; Make Way for the King; King Cole

Comes; or King Cole and His Royal Court." Then, to add to the jollity of speaking and to break down emotional barriers, a leader will suggest that each one become a royal herald and announce King Cole at the same time and in his own way.

Further general questions may help a beginning group to see the need for respecting court language and courtesy: "How will the page show respect as he answers King Cole's requests? Do you think a page will simply say 'yes,' or do you feel that he might be more honorable as he addresses his royal majesty? Do you think the Keeper of the Pipe will be pleased that the king has requested the pipe? What might he say about the royal pipe that would please the king?"

A leader will avoid having the students analyze the dialogue of each character too closely, for if children are made too conscious of exact conversations, their dialogue is likely to become stilted, for they will be striving to imitate rather than to create their own ways of expression.

After a leader has chosen a cast that she feels is capable of creating dialogue, she will give its members further security before they begin to play by reassuring them in somewhat this way: "Now we are going to hear the rhyme as well as see it. Each character will speak in his own way, for there is really no exact way of playing the rhyme. The way we play it is best for us. Let us see what a merry time everyone has at King Cole's court. Ready? Curtain!"

Praise will be given immediately for sincere effort and for spontaneous dialogue. A leader will praise good thinking, regardless of how small a contribution a child may have made, since by such acknowledgment a child knows that his efforts have been approved and appreciated. Since adolescents long for approval by fellow classmates, a leader will draw favorable comments from the students who were in the audience, as well.

A beginning group should play a rhyme several times before proceeding to new material, for as children become better acquainted with the characters they enjoy more the creating of spon-

taneous dialogue. A leader will motivate a strong interest in each repeated playing, however, by guiding a group toward a specific goal each time. For instance, in one playing the children may work toward building a stronger climax, another time they may strive for more ceremony in the procession and throughout the procedure at court, while in another playing they may introduce a court jester, and again they may elaborate on the dialogue by planning for the action to take place on a special day in Old King Cole's court. One seventh-grade class created a lively scene by planning the action around King Cole's fiftieth birthday, while another group of seventh graders decided that King Cole's festivities occurred during an elaborate banquet following a tournament in which one of the king's knights, who had broken the most lances, was being honored.

An eighth-grade class found great enjoyment in creating a scene wherein King Cole was celebrating in honor of a lady whom he had chosen to be the new Queen. The Piper, the Bowler and the Three Fiddlers became musicians who entertained the court, preceding a wedding which the class created as well.

If a leader feels that students need more experience in using dialogue freely before they proceed to further dramatizations, she may lead them into creating lively situations which provide for the use of simple dialogue. These scenes should be based on experiences which are familiar and may be planned around an information booth in a railway station where many different travelers inquire for specific travel information, or around a lost and found department in a large hotel at the time of a national convention, or, perhaps, at a parcel post window in a post office where a long line of people are waiting to mail Christmas packages. In each scene the leader will be the central figure who will speak freely to the characters by asking questions in character and encouraging each child to speak naturally.

TRANSITION INTO STORIES

Beginning groups should spend considerable time on short plot material which is strong in dramatic action before proceeding into longer stories. This is particularly necessary for classes which meet only once or perhaps twice during the week. "The Old Market Woman" offers splendid beginning material and may be played satisfactorily during a single class period. Herein the possibilities for creative characterizations are many. In addition to the old woman, the sly Pedlar Stout, and the woman's little dog, a class may be guided into introducing many peasant folk trudging along the highway to and from the market.

"The Old Woman and the Tramp," an old folk tale, is another favorite with seventh- and eighth-grade groups when it is treated in a humorous manner. Again, many peasant characters may be readily added to heighten the curiosity caused when the sly tramp not only tricks the stingy peasant woman into believing he can make tasty soup from a rare stone, but sets about to do it.

An old ballad from the North, "Get Up and Bar the Door," has an earthy flavor and broad humor which certainly appeal to almost every junior high school class. It is particularly fine to use when a group enjoys creating dialogue readily. The action takes place in a peasant hut on the eve of a feast day and is concerned with a stern old man and his good wife who get into a strong argument over which one is to close the door. Because neither will give in to the other, they make a pact between them that they will remain silent, and whoever speaks first will have to bar the door. In the silence which follows the fire burns low, the cottage becomes bitterly cold, and the anger between the two grows stronger. Two hungry robbers enter the cottage, eat the freshly boiled puddings, and jest about shaving off the old man's beard and kissing the good wife. When it appears that the robbers intend to carry out their plan, the old man breaks the pact, and in so doing brings the story to a sudden and surprise ending.

Other ballads, including "The Enchanted Shirt" and "The Raggle Taggle Gypsies," and narrative verse, such as Leigh Hunt's "Abou Ben Adhem" and "The Glove and the Lions," offer challenging experiences for beginning groups.

When a class is ready to create a play from a longer story, a leader will ask the students to choose from among several appropriate stories which she has selected. Many of the *Robin Hood Tales* may appeal to a seventh-grade class. "Robin Hood and the Widow's Three Sons," "Robin Hood and the Old Woman," "Robin Hood and Little John," and "The Shooting Match at Nottingham" are among the most popular, and each tale readily lends itself to creative playing. A parable-like story, "The Rabbi and the Diadem," which is characterized by suspense and mystery and is interwoven with idealism has been thoroughly enjoyed by both seventh- and eighth-grade groups. "King John and the Abbot of Canterbury" and "King Henry and the Miller of Mansfield" have proved popular largely because of the intrigue of mistaken identity in each of them. Many groups have found "Rip Van Winkle" a challenging story for an early dramatization and other junior high school classes have gained genuine pleasure from "Aladdin," "Ali Baba and the Forty Thieves," and other *Arabian Nights' Tales.*

A leader will guide a beginning class through story dramatization with deliberate thoroughness. She will keep the students reaching for new viewpoints, and she will stimulate imaginations as she helps the children put forth their best creative effort on each small scene and incident, rather than allowing them to rush through an experience. When the groundwork in characterization has been soundly and gradually developed, students will respond with enthusiasm to the challenge of working on such splendid material as that to be found in "Lochinvar," "Paul Revere's Ride," "What Men Live By," "The Legend of the Moor's Legacy," and episodes from King Arthur stories, *The Canterbury Tales,* the Nativity, *Little Women, The Prince and the Pauper, Treasure Island,* and *A Christmas Carol.*

Use of Shakespeare's Plays.   When seventh- or eighth-grade students have participated in creative dramatics experiences during an entire school year, they may be ready to create short scenes from some of Shakespeare's comedies as they continue creative dramatics during the following year. The artisan scenes from *A Midsummer*

Night's Dream have proved unusually satisfying for mixed groups of junior high school students. Nick Bottom, Peter Quince, Snug, Snout, and the other Athenian artisans offer attractive characterizations in a rollicking yet substantial manner, and the characteristics displayed by each one are the characteristics of the rank and file of ordinary people, entirely comprehensible to young teen-agers. If a class is made up largely of girls, they may find genuine pleasure in the fantasy of the fairy scenes from this comedy. The scenes between the lovers should not be attempted, however.

If a leader has a strong appreciation for Shakespeare, she will immediately recognize the excellent opportunities for creative playing in *The Taming of the Shrew*. Several of the broad comedy scenes will be thoroughly enjoyed by eighth- and ninth-grade students. A class may begin with the scene in which Petruchio and his man Grumio arrive at Padua, continue with the scene between Katherine and Bianca in Act II, and work on the several episodes between Katherine and Petruchio, particularly the scene in which they first meet and the vigorous "home-coming" and "beef and mustard" scenes.

When students have participated in creative dramatics during the elementary grades, they may look forward with keen interest to the experience of working on scenes from some of Shakespeare's tragedies when they reach junior high school. The witch's scenes from *Macbeth*, the opening scene from *King Lear*, which is commonly referred to as the dower scene, and the quarrel and funeral scenes from *Julius Caesar* will offer rich experiences for creative interpretation.

Shakespeare, like balladry, should be introduced by an enthusiastic and appreciative leader. She will begin by giving a vivid description of Elizabethan living, including accounts of Shakespeare's life and of the theatre of his day. Several meetings may be devoted to enriching the children's background for this study, particularly when Shakespeare is to be the project for the entire year or a semester. Motion pictures, costume plates, theatre designs, and other illustrative material will add considerably to a student's understanding of this colorful period.

In presenting a Shakespearean play to junior high school students, a leader will always tell it first in narrative form. *The Shakespeare Story Book,* by Mary McLeod, will be of real value in preparing one of Shakespeare's plays for telling. After a class has heard the entire story and discussed it, the leader will read several scenes of the play from the text. She will find this reading of value in helping students to gain a flavor of Shakespearean language and, also, in setting a guide for the dialogue which they will create when they start to play.

When the play is clear in mind and the students are enthusiastic about working on it, a leader will proceed as she does with other dramatizations. She will strive to keep the experience vivid and zestful. When boys and girls thoroughly enjoy dramatizing scenes from Shakespeare's plays, they unconsciously reach an appreciation for his works that can hardly be gained in any other way.

Chapter V

HOW TO GUIDE CHILDREN IN CREATIVE DRAMATICS

Art is more godlike than science,
Science discovers—art creates.
—Plato

Children are the world's freest creators. They create best when their enthusiasm and interest have been fired to the place where they are ready—almost impatient—to give way to their own expression. *After a group of children has been introduced to creative playing, and a good foundation has been laid in which each child has experienced and enjoyed being many different characters, the group is ready for experiences in real creative drama.*

The process which is used in leading children through this creative art is similar for all age groups; that is, a leader will guide young children through a dramatization in much the same way that she will lead an older group. However, she *always keeps the experience within the child's level of interest.* Young children will enjoy making a play from the Nativity story, and older students will work with interest on the same material, but each group will create from the same material in a different manner.

99

How does a leader guide a group of children through an experience in creative drama? How does she go about making each creative play an artistic, enjoyable experience for each child? There is no set rule, no rigid technique, but there is a creative process which a leader follows in guiding children to artistic heights. The way in which a leader works is in itself creative, and for this reason her process must always remain free and flexible. *She does not direct but rather indirectly guides both individual thinking and group enthusiasm.* "Ingenious indirection" is the skill for which every good leader strives, and in order to attain this she uses her creative imagination constantly. She gives considerable thought and preparation to the entire experience, for careful preparation on her part pays off in rich creative effort from those with whom she works. If a leader gives much, she will get much in return. If she gives little, she will get little. The way of the leader determines to a great extent the creative way of the children. A leader who succeeds in getting sensitive and unusual creative results from every group of children with whom she works is one who is so well prepared that the entire experience is dynamic and alive.

The process which the leader follows in creative drama consists of *motivating, presenting, planning, playing,* and *evaluating.* We shall consider each phase carefully in order that a leader will understand how to proceed.

MOTIVATING

Stirring a child's imagination and arousing his curiosity are the first important factors in leading him into creative dramatic experiences. This is done by means of motivation. A good motivating force serves to awaken a tingle of excitement and to kindle an immediate interest among a group of children. It arouses independent thinking on a limited, concentrated field, narrowing down many interests to one specific area. The time spent in motivating the material is a necessary "warming-up" period in which each child gradually gets his heart and mind in tune with the material with which he is to work. As Natalie Cole so forcefully points out in referring to all creative arts, "Children cannot create out of a vacuum. They must have something to say and be fired to say it."[1]

If a leader says to a group of children, "I am going to tell you a story, and then we are going to play it," she will get a similar response from the children. Their thinking will lack the fire and spirit that it might have had, had she spent a few minutes in setting the mood for the story. A leader will quickly learn that this approach is too ordinary, too usual, too uninteresting to appeal to a child's imagination. It is too abrupt and too direct, for it requires voluntary thinking. It compels rather than attracts attention. A good motivation is one that *involuntarily* captures a child's interest. It "sneaks up" on him, catches him unaware, and carries him into the enthusiasm of group discussion without his realizing it. It may take only a few minutes to channel the thinking of the group, but it is one of the most important considerations of the leader. During this time a friendly atmosphere is built up, rapport is established, barriers disappear, and the group becomes psychologically and socially ready for the activity which follows.

How does a leader plan a good motivation? *She considers the children, and she considers the material. She attempts to find a natural and a delightful way of bringing the two together.* She looks for strong elements within the story or experience which will have a fresh interest for the children. She searches for specific clues that will appeal to a child's emotion or to his intellect. *She analyzes the story to find its theme and strong appeal. She determines the kind of receptive mood that must be created for the specific story that is to be told.* A leader may find that it is necessary to enrich a child's appreciation for a certain story by giving him interesting information and background material.

A single question may serve as a thought-provoking motivation. For instance, a leader may ask, "If a small dryad or a tiny fairy

---

[1] Natalie Cole, *The Arts in the Classroom*, John Day, 1940.

were to appear this very minute and grant you one wish, what would you wish for?" This question or a similar one would arouse a discussion that would prepare the way for "The Three Wishes," "Cinderella," or for other fairy stories in which wishes are important.

Appealing to a child's senses stimulates imagination and may provide strong motivation for specific material. Listening to a recording of Haydn's "Eighteenth Century Dance" or Boccherini's "Minuet" would arouse a discussion about court dancing which could lead indirectly to an interest in Cinderella's ball or the story of "The Twelve Dancing Princesses." Whistles, bells, drums, trumpets, echoes, tip-toeing and other sounds have a strong appeal for children, and a carefully planned sound may be used to awaken an interest that will lead to a specific story theme.

Looking at interesting objects and being allowed to touch them may draw forth a child's best ideas on a given subject and indirectly prepare the way for a story which the leader plans to use. Examining an interesting pair of shoes, such as those which are worn in India or Japan, or looking at a small antique glass slipper would be another effective way of motivating an interest in "Cinderella." Colored pictures or sound films have been used to stimulate interest in a similar way. In a second-grade class an outstanding creative playing of "Little Boy Blue" developed as a result of the discussion aroused by a cow's horn which was brought to school by one of the children. When a leader recognized a strong interest in archery among a group of teen-aged junior high school students who were meeting on a city playground, she encouraged an archery contest which set the mood for a vigorous playing of "William Tell."

Activities within a community, such as a pet show, a county fair, a rodeo, or a community celebration may serve as spring-boards for leading into creative playing.

Many leaders are alert to *seasonal motivation* for stirring up group interest. On a morning after a first snowfall a leader may quickly set the mood for winter stories or poetry by asking, "How did you feel this morning when you first looked out of the window?" Or again, it may be that rain or wind or fog provides a perfect stimulation for special poems and stories. An imaginative leader could very well use a real pumpkin to motivate the playing of "Cinderella." The pumpkin would arouse interest and lead to group discussion. The leader would guide the discussion toward the *theme of the story* and would indirectly set a mood that would prepare the way for Cinderella's strong desire to go to the ball. Or, a leader might find that such a question as "Have you ever wished and wished that you could go to a special place?" would serve to arouse an immediate discussion without the use of a pumpkin.

An appreciatively aware leader will find a wealth of material in the *world of nature* for arousing an immediate interest among children and in leading them to significant creative playing. When a group of five-year-olds became frightened when they discovered a spider spinning a web in a corner of their kindergarten room, the teacher made use of this opportunity for leading the entire class into a delightful playing of "Little Miss Muffet." Real creative thinking comes when the time is ripe for playing; that is, when a readiness and an identity of self with character are strongly established. In the spring of the year when young children become aware of the early daffodils, a leader will find it quite easy to interest both boys and girls in playing A. A. Milne's "Daffodowndilly." The time for making up a play about a rainbow is not the last fifteen minutes of a school day, but rather when a rainbow appears in the sky and can be seen from the classroom window.

Variety and delight are vital considerations in planning a good motivation. A skillful leader will make use of the special delights of holidays, such as using carols, evergreen trees, or candlelight to set the mood for certain Christmas stories. Occasionally she may begin with a game, a riddle, a joke, a secret, or a surprise, if *it functions in motivating specific material.* Appealing to a child's imagination by the use of make-believe may set just the right mood for fantasy.

A beginning leader should be warned against entertaining children without stimulating their imaginations as she strives to motivate an interest in a specific story. If a leader overwhelms the children's thinking by using an abundance of material, she may satisfy them so completely that she will fail to challenge their thinking. Such was the situation encountered by a conscientious young leader when she planned an elaborate motivation to interest her class of eight- and nine-year-olds in a Hawaiian legend. Before the children came to the library room where the class was meeting, the leader arranged the stage with flower blossoms and bamboo place mats. Trays of shredded coconut, pineapple, and bananas added to the impressiveness of the setting. When the children arrived, a recording of Hawaiian music was softly playing, and the leader, dressed in authentic Hawaiian costume, greeted each child as he entered. The children were naturally delighted, but little was left to their imaginations, and they spent a good part of the period eating the food and listening to further recordings. The leader could not understand why the children were not wholeheartedly interested in hearing the legend which had been the real purpose of her extensive preparations. Her motivation had not fired the children's imaginations, nor had it required them to think sufficiently. Had the leader used a single element—perhaps the music, the bamboo, the pineapple, or the costume—as an immediate point of focus, she would probably have been able to arouse a lively discussion through guide questions which would have led to a real interest in hearing the legend. The abundance of material served to enrich the experience for the children, but it did not fire their imaginations sufficiently.

A leader will always examine her motivation before using it. Does it capture the theme or "heartbeat" of the story? Will it challenge the children's thinking? Will it invite group discussion and allow for self-expression? Is it interesting enough to appeal to every child? Will it function in leading the children to the material in a delightful way? Will it set the desired mood?

PRESENTING MATERIAL

Once the mood has been established, the leader will sustain the same zestful feeling as she shares the material with the children. The manner in which the material is presented governs to a great degree the quality of creativity that comes from the children. To be effective, the material must connect—it must penetrate and get "inside" a child before he can create from it.

In presenting material for dramatization, whether it be a short nursery rhyme or a long story in book form, the leader will strive to make the material crystal clear. She will not memorize a story but rather will strive to know it as an experience. In order thoroughly to enjoy sharing a story with others, a leader must first of all like the story herself. If she does not find real pleasure in the *Uncle Remus* stories, for instance, it will be difficult for her to tell them with any degree of conviction. If a leader does not enjoy a particular story, it is far wiser for her to choose a story which she does like, rather than attempting to tell one which holds no real appeal for her. When a leader becomes enthusiastic about a certain story, she will familiarize herself with the material until she makes it her own, and when she knows it well she will not want to read it but will be ready to make it live for others as a vivid experience that is very real to her.

If children are to recapture the feeling of a story and become the characters involved in a story experience, they must thoroughly understand the characters, the action, and the tone of the story. When a story is well told, children are able to visualize it as a moving picture taking place in their mind's eye. This requires careful preparation on the part of a leader, but it does not mean that she will set about learning the story word for word. Ruth Sawyer, a superb storyteller in her own right, feels that "the true significance of storytelling is lost or never discovered" if one attempts to memorize or learn a story by rote. In her belief, "it means there is never a knowing of the untold joy of the artist in taking substance, giving it form and color, blowing the breath of life into it, and then watching it take on life for others."[2]

How then does a leader go about preparing a story for dramatization? She first reads a story carefully. If it is an old traditional tale, such as "Cinderella," it is helpful to read several versions and to compare the different ways in which incidents and characters may have been treated. A leader will then adapt the story for dramatization. The point of attack, or the event at which the story opens, is an important consideration in preparing a story which children are going to play. For instance, some versions of "Cinderella" open with long descriptive passages of the wedding ceremony in which Cinderella's father is marrying for a second time, whereas other versions open dramatically at a much later point in the story where Cinderella is helping her stepmother and stepsisters prepare for the Prince's ball. If a story opens late enough to allow children to plan their action within three or four scenes, they will not grow tired of the same material before they have created a satisfying play.

Equally as important as a dramatic opening, for a story from which children are going to create, is an economy in the number of incidents which take place during the time set forth by the story. If the incidents are repetitious they may not offer enough challenge for the children to put forth their best creative efforts, and it is therefore wise for a leader to cut down on the number of incidents, if this does not essentially affect the plot of the story. In the case of "Cinderella," many of the versions describe three successive evenings at the ball, whereas other versions heighten the action considerably by having Cinderella lose her glass slipper on the first evening when she attends the ball.

In adapting a story, a leader may find that it is helpful, in some instances, to expand an incident or to elaborate on a characterization. She will use care, however, in not interfering with the author's

---

[2] Ruth Sawyer, *The Way of the Storyteller*, Viking Press, 1947.

original intention but endeavoring to heighten the creative possibilities of incidents or characterizations so that the children will recognize them more readily. For instance, in telling the story of "Cinderella" to a large group of children, a leader may emphasize the importance of the court musicians by adding significance to these minor characters as she elaborates slightly on the lines from the story which simply say, "Everyone left off dancing, and the violins ceased to play."

Thus, by adapting a long story so that the characters are clear and the action dramatic, a leader will help to make the creative experience more enjoyable for the children. However, she will recognize that many stories will not require adaptation in any way but will be ready to use just as they are.

When a leader feels that a story is ready for her specific use, she will give considerable thought to it in its entirety. She will think, meditate, and reflect on the story as a whole. She will discover the rhythm, the feel, and the story tone, and she will attempt to capture this quality in her telling. This will be achieved largely through a leader's understanding of the story. One leader may tell the story of "Cinderella" with such warmth that a group of listeners will fairly see everything happening, while another leader may tell the story in all its exactness yet fail to capture the romantic spirit and human heartbeat that bring "Cinderella" to life.

After a leader finds out what it is that gives a specific story its singular vitality, she will become acquainted with the characters. She will regard them as living beings and will attempt to picture them in her mind. She will discover character attitudes and reactions and will learn how the characters feel toward one another. When a leader feels that she knows the characters as people, she will inquire into their story experience. She will find out what they do, what happens to them, what problems or pleasures they encounter, and she will make certain that she knows exactly how each problem is resolved.

With the characters and action well in mind, a leader will begin to tell the story aloud for her own benefit in preparation. If the images and incidents are clear to her, she will be able to explain exactly what she sees happening, and as she weaves the story aloud she will speak for the characters. She will tell the story several times and will no doubt find it necessary to read again certain parts of the story in order to clarify incidents and dialogue in her mind. She will keep the dialogue simple and direct but will always retain the artistry of the original tale. In order to do this well a leader may find it necessary to live with the material over a long period of time and to identify herself strongly with the characters. After a leader has told the story aloud several times to herself, she will probably be ready to share it with a group of children. If she does not feel that she is ready, it will be advisable for her to read parts or all of it, for it is essential that the material be clear to the children. A good reading of a story is far better than a poor telling, but a good telling goes far in firing the flames of creative thinking. When a conscientious leader stops to consider how ineffective most sermons and lectures are when they are read rather than delivered with straightforward sincerity, she will realize at once the values which are to be gained from listening to a story that is vividly told. A leader who is intently interested in making each creative experience worthwhile will see to it that she begins early enough in preparing a story so that she will feel confident in telling rather than reading it to children.

PLANNING ACTION AND CHARACTERS

Action follows interest. If the story has reached into the hearts and minds of the children, they will be eager to play it immediately. With a beginning group a leader may find it necessary to suggest that they dramatize it by asking, "Would you like to play the story?" or "Wouldn't it be fun to be a little gray mouse and suddenly change into a prancing steed?" or "Shall we make the story into a play?" After a few satisfying experiences in creative drama, the response will come directly from the group.

During a summer program a leader told the story of "The Elephant's Child" to a group of children whom she had never met before. In her telling she retained the humor and charm of Kipling so well that when she finished, the children called out, "Tell it again! Please tell it again!"

"All right," the leader said cheerfully. "We'll tell it again, but this time we'll all tell it. Who can think of a way that will be even finer, a way by which we can see the story as well as hear it?" In this way the leader brought from the children the desire to play this delightful tale.

Young children may not want to spend a very long time planning. They may prefer to play the story immediately. If a leader finds this to be the case when she is working with five- or six-year-olds, she will guide them in much the same way that she did in their dramatic play, encouraging them to play the part of the story that they like best again and again.

As soon as a leader finds that children are interested in the form that their play takes, she will guide them in planning the scenes, the characters, and the setting.

Planning Scenes. The order in which the planning is done remains flexible and is determined largely by the children's reaction. To draw forth a discussion from the children, a leader may ask several questions as soon as she has finished telling a story: "What did you like about the story? What part did you think was best? What characters did you find most interesting?" These questions will serve to indicate the children's reaction to the story and will give them an opportunity to talk and to laugh about incidents which were particularly pleasing or amusing.

"How shall we begin our play? What do you think will make a fine opening when curtain is called? What is the first thing you would like to see happening when our play starts?" Questions such as these stimulate thinking, and it is the leader's responsibility to keep the children searching and reaching for good ideas. If a child should suggest that their play of "Cinderella" begin just as the stepmother and the stepsisters are leaving for the ball, a leader will see the need for stimulating further thinking in her comments. If a leader is entirely satisfied with the first idea a child gives, the rest of the children may be content with this suggestion and will think no further. However, realizing the value which comes from encouraging each child to express his ideas, the leader may reply, "Fine! That is one good way of beginning. Can anyone think of a different way in which we might start our play? Does anyone feel that it is important for us to see how the stepsisters and the step-mother treat Cinderella, and in turn to see how kindly she treats them before they go to the ball? Let us get everyone's ideas about this."

When many suggestions have been given and each one has been considered, a leader combines the suggestions and states clearly the different beginnings. She then encourages the children to vote on the idea which they feel will make the finest opening. If a leader sees that a group unanimously favors one of the suggestions, there will be no need for voting, for she always makes the children feel that the entire play is of their own making. If a class decides that they will begin their play by having Cinderella clean the house while the stepsisters mock and jeer at her while they are busily engaged in final preparations for the ball, a leader will move them on in their planning by asking, "As soon as the stepmother and the stepsisters leave, what do you want to happen next? What action will take place after that?" Through questions and suggestions a leader helps the children plan the action of the fairy godmother scene, in which mice are changed into horses, a rat into a coachman, lizards into footmen, a pumpkin into a coach, and Cinderella's ragged clothing into a beautiful gown decked with jewels and the prettiest pair of glass slippers in all the world.

When children are creating a play from a story, they are encouraged to follow the action set forth by the story rather than being allowed to distort the material by creating something entirely different. The leader becomes a moderator who guides the children into a natural and free interpretation, in order that they may be creative in their thinking without misconstruing the original intention of the story. A leader strives consciously to keep a planning period moving along with spirit, avoiding the tendency of the children to get lost in planning details or of spending too much time on an incident of minor importance. When a leader has the action well in mind, she will be able to help the children plan clearly without imposing her ideas on them.

"Where will our second act take place? How will it begin? When will it end?" These questions will be considered briefly when a class is making a general over-all plan for a story but will be regarded in detail when they set to work on the second act specifically. In a similar manner the leader will guide the children into completing their plan. "Does anyone see where our third act will be most likely to take place? Do you feel that the Prince will accompany the courtier who has been sent to try the glass slipper on every maiden's foot? Will our play come to an ending here, or do you wish to plan a wedding at the castle?"

When a tentative plan of action has been considered by the children, the leader will return to the opening scene and will help them to become acquainted with the characters.

Planning Characters. It would be quite an easy thing for a leader to explain to the children the dominant character traits of the main characters and to direct them into the action of the play, but in so doing she would defeat the entire purpose of creative work. *A leader guides rather than directs the children's planning* by asking questions, by expanding ideas which are suggested by the children, and by arousing an interest in new viewpoints.

In the story of "Cinderella," a leader may start a discussion of characters by asking, "Who has an idea of how Cinderella looks? What kind of person is she? How old do you think she is? How does she feel toward her stepmother and her stepsisters? How do they feel toward her? Why do you think the fairy godmother came to help her?"

When the children have a good understanding of a character, the leader guides them into pantomiming the character as a group. She may use a situation directly from the story, or she may plan an imaginary one by suggesting, "Now let us be Cinderella on the afternoon in which the invitation has come from the castle inviting every maiden to the ball. Cinderella will be cleaning the house and hoping that she, too, may go to the great ball. Each one will be Cinderella in her own way. Cinderella may be brushing the cinders from the fireplace, sweeping or scrubbing the floor, dusting, ironing the stepmother's dress, sewing ruffles on a petticoat, or doing any number of different things to tidy up the house while she dreams about seeing the prince. Each one think about how you will feel and then find a good place in the room in which you will be free to pantomime your characterization. Ready? In character. Begin!"

The leader may join in the pantomiming, or she may prefer to watch the children and to praise their efforts as a means of encouragement. "What fine Cinderellas! Each one seemed gentle and kind. I saw one Cinderella who looked from the window and gave the feeling that she was thinking about the castle. Another Cinderella showed that she was dreaming about going to the ball and was so completely lost in her dream that she forgot entirely about scrubbing the floor."

After a first pantomime, a leader may choose a part of the group to be the same character in the same situation for a second time; and whenever she feels that the class has a good idea of the characterization, she may ask for a volunteer to pantomime the characterization entirely alone.

Other characters necessary to the playing of a first short scene will be considered in a similar way. Rather than asking directly, "What kind of stepmother shall we have?" a leader will encourage the children to think for themselves as she asks, "What other characters do we need to begin our play?" or "Is there another character that you think we need to plan?" Since the stepmother and stepsisters will each be mean and haughty, a leader will guide the children into creating each one with individual characteristics. A single question, such as, "How can we make each of these three characters entirely different?" may result in having the older sister tall and slender, while the younger one will be short and fat and the stepmother will be a middle-aged combination of both her daughters.

"What will each character be doing as she enters?" will be a necessary question to ask in considering the characters in almost every play. "In what ways may the sisters need help as they dress for the ball? What might they ask Cinderella to do for them at the very last minute? How will they feel as they enter?"

If the story version which the leader uses does not indicate many of the fashions of Cinderella's day, it will be helpful for the children to know about various modes and manners, such as the importance of curtsying properly, of wearing a fashionable manteau or a stomacher, of dressing one's hair in an elegant manner, and of conducting oneself with proper civilities and etiquette at all times. When the children have decided what each character will be doing as she enters, it will be helpful for them to work out each characterization in pantomime before they play a short scene. This is particularly true when children are getting acquainted with entirely new characters.

Planning a Setting. "What do we need on our stage to help tell the story? In addition to the entrance leading to the outdoors and the stairway entrance to the sisters' bedrooms, what other entrances will we need? Where do you think they should be? Who has an idea of where the pumpkin will be changed into a coach?" Such questions will lead to a discussion of the setting and will help the children to visualize the stage picture. Two or three children will be chosen to be stage managers, and they will set the stage in accordance with the plan made by the group. A group may wish to set the play in the center of the room, using the theatre-in-the-round idea both for the audience and for the playing.

In creative drama a setting is not needed unless it functions in the action of the play. For this reason a leader will use great care in guiding the children through the important considerations of the setting for a specific story, for otherwise they may spend too much time on needless details. One leader has found a skillful way of disciplining the children's thinking in regard to planning a setting by asking, "Who can think of a good stage picture for our play that requires only three properties?"

PLAYING

"The play's the thing" wherein the children's ideas take wing! With a plan in mind a child is free to create a character with all the ingenuity he can muster. He does not become bound by the plan but rather has a guide and is free to follow it. The leader's enthusiasm and vitality will go far in establishing a strong spirit of playing and will invite eagerness on the part of the children as they volunteer to play the different characters. The leader will choose a cast not only from the children who raise their hands but from those who seem to want to play but who hesitate to raise their hands. She will watch for little indications, perhaps a new light on a child's face or a twinkle in someone's eyes that shows an eagerness.

In a formal play a director casts the most capable and best-suited individuals to play the important character parts, whereas in creative dramatics a leader chooses individuals because of the value that the experience brings to each one. Occasionally a girl is chosen to play a boy's part, and now and then a boy will ask to play a girl's part, such as that of a fairy grandmother, a witch, or a beggarwoman. *The leader will keep in mind that in all creative art the child is the first consideration.* She will always remember that the children's playing is far more important than the plays they create, but at the same time she will realize that the standard of playing must be kept high. If the children do not have the feeling of accomplishment in their play, they will gain very little from the experience.

How does a leader include every child in the activity and yet keep the playing on a high plane? Since the first playing of a scene is very likely to set a standard for the entire play, a leader chooses a first cast with special care. She will always choose children who she feels are confident enough to carry a first scene through with moderate success. A leader may choose the characters in the order of their importance in the story; that is, in this play she may choose Cinderella first, or she may reverse the procedure and choose the minor characters first. By stressing the importance of every character, a leader will build a strong feeling of teamwork and will indirectly strengthen the playing. She may suggest, "We need a fine coachman to call for the stepmother and the stepsisters. Who would like to be the family coachman who informs them that the carriage has been ready and waiting for several hours?"

A leader stimulates imagination as she casts by using variety in the way she chooses the characters. Rather than asking, "Who wants to be a stepsister?" a leader may arouse an eagerness by suggesting, "We need three people for a proud and haughty family. Who would enjoy being mean and selfish sisters? We will choose three people, and you may decide for yourselves which member of the family each one will be."

After a first playing, a leader will choose both confident and timid children to play together in the same scene for the mutual benefit of all the players. She will use great care in not allowing the confident members to dominate the playing. "Who hasn't played today?" or "Who has played only once?" will be questions a leader will do well to remember, and to ask after a second or third playing during each class period. Allowing the entire class to choose the characters for a scene many times stimulates interest and generally results in spirited playing. A leader may ask, "Who do you think would make a lovely Cinderella?"

When a cast has been chosen the children remaining in the group form the audience, and they are made to feel equally important as they are encouraged to watch the play for the purpose of evaluating it. From time to time a leader may choose the audience before she chooses the characters, in order to give the children who are watching a feeling of importance and responsibility. "We need a good audience to help our play grow," a leader may say with a friendliness and a conviction that impress the group with the importance of observation. "We need good listeners as well as good players. Who would like to be a member of the audience this time?"

After a cast has been chosen, a leader may help the children review the sequence of action in a scene by asking, "As soon as our play starts and we see Cinderella brushing the hearth, what will happen next?" and "What action takes place after that?" If a group understands just what they are to do before they are ready to play a scene, they will enjoy rather than worry about playing it. A leader always makes it clear to a cast how far they are to proceed in the playing of each small part: "This time we will play to the place where the cross stepmother enters and scolds Cinderella for not having called the coachman."

When a leader feels that the action has been clearly planned, she will be ready to get the cast on stage or into the playing area. She will do this with enthusiasm as she says, "Characters in their places," or "Cast on stage." While each character goes to the place where he needs to be when the play begins, the leader will include the audience by commenting, "What a fine audience we have," or "Our audience is ready and waiting for the play to begin."

A brief introduction to set the mood for the play may be given by the leader or by one of the children who will be chosen to be an announcer. As soon as the introduction has been given, the leader or one of the stage managers will call, "Curtain!" which will indicate to the players that it is time for the play to start. If a stage is being used and a curtain is available, it may be used, but an imaginary curtain adds to the delight and stirs imagination. Or a child may *be* a curtain in his make-believe way.

Once the play begins, the children must realize that they must remain in character and carry the action through to the place where they have decided to play. The leader is careful never to interrupt the playing once it gets under way but rather to insist that the cast keep the story going until they finish whatever scene they set out to do. Children do their best creative work when they take only a small part of the action at a time and develop it carefully before going further. Working on small units of the story allows for more children to participate and at the same time draws forth the children's best ideas on a small incident or on a detailed piece of action.

"Curtain" will be called again to bring the scene to an end, and the children will soon learn that it is time for the players to go quietly back to their places among the audience.

If a leader finds that a first cast is fearful or at a complete loss for words when they start to play a story, she may call them back for further planning or suggest that they play a scene for the first time entirely in pantomime. When children clearly understand how the characters think and feel, and when they are given an opportunity to pantomime the action of a scene, they are more confident and free when they begin to add words to their playing.

EVALUATION

"Fine work!" "Well done!" "What an interesting scene!" Such positive exclamations from the leader as soon as a scene is finished will immediately set the mood for favorable comments and will lead the children to an enthusiastic evaluation of their playing. *Evaluation is vitally important in the process of creative drama, for only by learning to evaluate their efforts fairly will children be able to get fine and worthy results in the plays they create.*

Sincere praise is the finest tool for spurring a child on toward exercising his native ability. Praise from the leader and praise from the children will be the strongest single factor in giving a child a strong faith within himself and in stimulating each child to tenacious effort and high achievement.

"What made our play so fine? Why was it interesting? What

was particularly good about the way we played it?" Questions such as these will open the way for constructive comments which should always be given first. These questions will be expanded as the leader guides the children through an evaluation of the most important aspects of their playing, which will include characterization, action, story, dialogue, and cooperation.

Characterization.   The children should be encouraged to evaluate characters rather than individuals and to use the names of the characters from the very beginning. This tends to keep the criticism impersonal, and it requires more thinking for children to figure out how the characters contributed to the play than it does simply to observe that Jack and Billy and Susan were good. As a group considers the characters, a leader may ask, "Were the characters in our play thinking and feeling like the characters in the story? Were they convincing? How did they make you feel that they were real? Did everyone stay in character throughout the entire scene? Although some of the characters did not speak, what did they do to help the play and to make it interesting? How did the characters feel toward each other? Did the characters react to one another?"

Action.   In emphasizing the action and the tempo of the story, the leader will arouse such thoughts as these: "Was the play interesting to watch? If we had played the scene in pantomime, would the action have been clear? If you didn't know the story, could you tell what was happening? Was the action strong enough to make the play interesting? Was the action free with large movements, or did the characters seem to use small action? Did we keep the story going? Did it move along in an interesting way? How do you think we might help it to move along a little faster?"

Story.   Children will soon learn to evaluate their play from the standpoint of plot, climax, and grouping as they analyze the story with guide questions similar to these: "Did the scene have the right 'feel' to it? Was it exciting and interesting, or did it seem too ordinary? Did our play tell the story? Did we make the climax of this scene strong? Did you like our stage picture? Did we make use of all the stage, or did we crowd the characters into one small space?"

Dialogue. As the children discuss the dialogue used in their play, the leader will indirectly emphasize the importance of good voice and diction and of speaking in order that one can be heard. "Could you hear the story as well as see it? Did the dialogue help to move the story along, or did the characters talk about something that was not needed in the play? How did the characters help each other to keep the dialogue going? Did the dialogue seem to stop sometimes? When the characters spoke, did their dialogue seem real? Did you notice any particularly fine way of speaking that helped to make the play interesting?"

Coöperation. Since the personal-social development which takes place in the process of creative dramatics is one of the major reasons for its existence, a leader constantly keeps before the children the importance of "togetherness" as each child contributes to the play. "Did we all work together to create this scene? How did the audience help? How did the stage managers help? How did the characters who were off stage part of the time coöperate for the good of the play? Did any character call attention to himself rather than help to make the play important? Was there a good spirit of team play among the cast? How did the players help each other? Do you think we did our very best?"

When the children have figured out for themselves why the play was good, the leader will help them to see how they can improve their playing. She will ask for suggestions as to how they can make the play more interesting, and she will keep before the children new possibilities for strengthening it. If a leader is too easily satisfied with the standard of playing, the children, too, will be satisfied and will not challenge their creative imaginations for new and better ideas. A leader praises judiciously, for with her praise she makes the children feel that they have done well but that they are capable of doing better. She may say, "Cinderella made us feel that she wanted to go to the ball when we first saw her, but do you think that she would let her sisters know how much she longed to go?" Again, she may praise with a purpose as she comments, "The stepmother was excellent when she first entered, but did she remain middle-aged throughout the scene? Did she make us feel that she was the mother of the two stepsisters?"

Occasionally, but not often, a leader may stir the children's thinking by becoming a character and playing a small part of a scene with them. By suggesting better work, rather than spending time in talking about what was poorly done, the leader influences the attitude of the group, for she soon realizes that positive thinking is essential to creative thinking.

When a child makes a comment, his opinion is considered according to its worthiness. It may be an idea which is worth developing. It may be a suggestion which has already been given. It may be an idea which should be disposed of quickly unless it has a direct bearing on the play. If a child says, "We couldn't hear Cinderella," the leader may say, "Next time let us see if each character can speak so that he will be heard." If a child says, "The play dragged," the leader may say, "Let us see if we can figure out why it was so slow, and we may be able to make it move faster next time." If a child says, "The stepmother can give Cinderella a lot of extra work to do just as she is leaving," a leader may say, "That's possible! It shows that John is thinking. What are some of the tasks that she might think of to keep Cinderella busy?"

As long as a leader sees new opportunities in a creative play and indirectly points them out to the children, she keeps the class keenly interested in a certain scene. When children are enthusiastic about making a scene better, they will work again and again on the same material, and in so doing they gradually develop discriminating attitudes toward high standards of work and toward drama as well. When the children have new and specific goals in mind a new cast is chosen, and they set to work to play again and to make their play stronger.

Each new part of a story is approached in a similar way, and a group works on small units until an entire scene is gradually created. In dramatizing a long story each scene is developed carefully, and when the children are satisfied with their efforts, the scenes are put together into one continuous play. It is quite possible for a class to create a play from a poem during a single class period, but if the group is working on a story or an experience that is rich in creative material, it will be advisable to develop the play over a longer period of time. Several weeks may be devoted to a long story if it merits this consideration from the standpoint of worthiness and if the children are enjoying this particular experience in creative drama.

Chapter VI

LEARNING THROUGH CREATIVE DRAMATICS

> Happy is the man that findeth wisdom
> And that getteth understanding.

Creative dramatics should be a part of every child's education, since it provides dynamic experiences for child growth and is basic in building understanding. Creative dramatics is an activity program that can be vital in motivating learning in the primary, elementary, and secondary schools. Today, more than ever before, education recognizes its responsibility in providing methods of teaching children in such a way that learning is significant and effective. In the words of Fay Adams, "The purpose of education will not be achieved until we understand and envision the thorough integration of the child in his environment, and build principles and practices in conformity with such an understanding. Neither personal nor social education alone will aid us in achieving our goal; we must have a unitary personal-social concept of the child which squares with reality, and which permeates and directs our educational thinking and planning."[1]

---

[1] Fay Adams, *Educating America's Children*, The Ronald Press, 1946.

In considering educational procedures in the schools, we must keep in mind that the way we teach governs to a great degree how children learn. Creative dramatics is one method of teaching that can strengthen every school program. It can serve as strong motivating force in guiding children into "unified learning" experiences. It should be made clear at the outset that creative dramatics is one way of teaching, not the only way, but an activity way that is helpful to the teacher in promoting good teaching. A teacher must first understand creative dramatics in relation to the learning process before she can make use of its specific techniques in fostering child growth day after day.

TRENDS IN EDUCATION

"The Century of the Child" is the term often used by psychologists and educators in referring to the twentieth century. Previously children had been regarded as adults in miniature, and educational methods were devised for the purpose of preparing the child for adulthood. Schools were set up on a "pouring in and giving out" procedure, with the acquisition of knowledge of prime importance. At the beginning of the twentieth century, psychologists began to study the child first-hand in order to determine his growth and development. It was a revealing fact, to educators particularly, that no two children were found to be exactly alike. Basically they appeared to be very much the same, but intensive studies revealed that each individual developed according to his own pattern and potentialities.

As a result of these studies, educational objectives and procedures were greatly revised. The emphasis in education shifted to the development of the individual child.

The schools of today strive for the maximum growth of each individual and for a "tolerant understanding" of others in a world society. Educational systems plan carefully calculated group experiences, in order that each child will grow according to his own pattern of development and at the same time will learn to live and work happily with others in a democracy. Curricula provide for the development of skills and for the teaching of facts and subject matter which are essential to every child's happiness, but the methods of teaching have greatly changed. "Unified learning" and meaningful experiences are gradually replacing the teaching of isolated subject matter. Children are guided in their learning so that they understand the reason behind facts and knowledge. Modern education emphasizes creative self-expression, and at the same time it provides for social growth and coöperation.

REQUIREMENTS FOR A CREATIVE DRAMATICS PROGRAM

The schools of our country are in a unique position to reach all of the children of all of the people. Creative dramatics, when offered through the schools can go to every child, regardless of his dramatic or scholastic ability, for this program has been planned for the development of every child. Dr. Arnold Gesell firmly believes that dramatic play should be included in the public schools from the primary grades on up.[2] Creative dramatics is an inexpensive program which does not require an extra fee for materials. In this creative activity, scenery and costumes are largely imaginary. Ordinary chairs, when carefully arranged by the children who are creating the play, may represent a magnificent golden throne, the deck of a pirate ship, the concealed opening in a treasure cave, or whatever setting the story may require. Imaginations are constantly stimulated, and many a classroom becomes a far more beautiful "Secret Garden" in the minds of the children who are participating than even the finest of artists might devise.

The three basic requirements for an effective creative dramatics program consist of a group of children, a space large enough for the children to move about freely, and a leader who understands the philosophy and technique of creative dramatics as stimuli for the development of a well-integrated child.

---

[2] Dr. Gesell, in the opening address at the American Educational Theatre Association, New York, 1949.

Schools can readily provide the first two requirements. A group of children may range in number from three or four to as many as thirty or thirty-five; however, twenty children have been found to be an ideal number. In a group of this size, every child has an opportunity to participate several times during a forty-five-minute period.

The space for playing does not necessarily mean a stage or a gymnasium. Many teachers who are making use of creative dramatics find the space in the classrooms to be entirely satisfactory, particularly in rooms where tables and chairs may be shifted about freely.

The leader or teacher is vitally important to a program of this kind, since she is the one who motivates the children's thinking and leads them into the delight of many and varied creative experiences. An educator observing a group of children participating in this activity wisely stated that the teacher must be the greatest creator of all, for she must create the faith within each individual in the group until he feels confident and eager to think and do for himself. Once a teacher understands the basic principles of creative dramatics and recognizes its values in an educational program, she will want to master its techniques and methods, for she will find many uses for it throughout the school day.

CREATIVE DRAMATICS IN THE SCHOOLS OF TODAY

Let us consider the basic foci in the schools and see how sound the philosophy and technique of creative dramatics are in carrying out the purposes of child education.

Programs Based on Knowledge of Child.   When children are highly motivated, their interest is strong, and learning flourishes in an atmosphere where attention is active, concentrated, and intent. Motivation is the first consideration of a leader as she guides a group of children into creative dramatics experiences.

Because drama has a universal appeal for all children, dramatic activity provides a strong and natural motivation for learning. The

challenge of "making up a play" or of "putting on a show" appeals
to almost every child, and each one regards it as play rather than
work. "When are we going to have more fun?" was the question
asked by a timid eighth-grade girl after the activity of creative
dramatics was first introduced by her classroom teacher. This girl,
who had been passive in her interest in other classwork, suddenly
found herself enjoying and contributing to this new activity which
had a freshness and an aliveness about it.

"To delight is to instruct." This belief of the great poet, Horace,
is as sound today as it was nineteen hundred years ago. Delightful
experiencing is fundamental in all creative arts. Creative drama
provides a variety of situations, allowing each child to delight in
many experiences which it would be impossible for him to enjoy in
reality.

Creative dramatics is based on Kilpatrick's theory that *we learn
what we live*. We learn to the extent that we live an experience.
When a child reads a story he may identify himself with a character
and live the experience to a degree. Likewise, when he hears a
story read to him he may live the experience to an even greater
extent. However, when a child participates in the activity of bringing the story alive, he gets "inside" the story, so to speak, and as he
does so he "becomes" the characters in the play. *As he creates he
lives the story*. If the story is funny, he becomes funny. If it is
beautiful, he experiences its beauty. If it is jolly, he delights in
being jolly. If the story is strong in adventure, he too goes adven-
turing. A twelve-year-old boy describing playmaking to a newcomer in his class explained simply, "You don't act the part. You
are the part."

John Dewey's accepted belief that we learn by doing is fundamental in the process of creative dramatics. Children learn to appreciate literature by experiencing it, by understanding, enjoying,
and thrilling to soul-stirring moments which they live as they bring
vital material to life. Active participation characterizes every creative dramatics experience. Children enter into a lively group dis-

cussion to formulate a plan for their story. With the plan carefully in mind, they work together to play a scene from the story. In the dynamic discussion that follows each playing, children learn to evaluate their work with a purpose.

Social Growth and Understanding Through School Programs. The group activity of creative dramatics would appear to have been designed particularly for the purpose of helping children to work and play together and for developing a feeling of security in a social situation. "The finest thing about creating a play," a leader tells a group of children, "is that we can make it as exciting or as beautiful or as interesting as we want it to be. It is up to every one of us. Our play will be thirty times as fine if everyone in the group shares his ideas and helps with our plan." It provides a constant challenge for every child to enter into the discussion, to participate in the playing, and to respect the ideas of others. Group coöperation is essential to the process of making a play.

Make-believe has an almost magical effect in bringing harmony and enthusiasm to a group of children, for it immediately invites merriment and delight. Since the leader endeavors to keep the activity in the realm of art, children strive for excellence in the creation of their play. They gradually develop a freedom in expressing their ideas and in considering the ideas of others. They recognize quickly that by working together and sharing ideas they are able to create a far stronger play than they had ever imagined they were capable of doing. The pure joy that they experience as a result of coöperative creative effort spurs them on with an even greater spirit of teamwork as they create more plays and as they approach other group projects or problems which arise.

Creative dramatics provides unusual experiences in human relations, which in turn lead to a gradual development of understanding. Tolerant and friendly attitudes toward one another are constantly encouraged, as a group enters into a lively discussion for the sake of a play. Dramatic activity of this kind may bring an understanding of another person's point of view, or it may bring an understanding of a character from the story itself. "What kind of a person is Cinderella's stepmother? How do you think she feels inside? Why is she cruel to Cinderella?" Questions similar to these stimulate thinking at the beginning of each new play and help a child to analyze and to understand the reasons behind character actions and reactions. Since drama has to do with many kinds of people in multiple emotional situations and conflicts, the experience of being many different kinds of characters gradually develops within a child a better understanding of himself and of others.

When a class of six- and seven-year-old children had finished listening to the story of "Little Black Sambo," a little boy, the only Negro child in the group, jumped to his feet and shook his hand vigorously.

"What is it, Julius?" the leader asked.

"I think I should be Sambo," Julius said eagerly.

"Why do you think you should be Sambo?"

"Because I'm black," Julius said proudly.

"That's a fine idea, Julius, but it isn't one's skin that matters. It's how you feel inside that really counts."

"I can feel just like Sambo," Julius said with confidence and a big smile.

The children voted unanimously for Julius to play this important part in their story. As he played he *was* Sambo, and the other children responded to his enthusiasm as they played the story with high feeling. Through the use of this and other folk tales, these children grew in tolerance and understanding.

When children act out stories which are concerned with people living in other lands, such as China, Norway, Switzerland, and Mexico, they project themselves into the lives of these far-away people. As a child becomes a Chinese farmer earning his living by toiling in a rice field, he begins to understand many of the customs of the Chinese people. As he lives through the experience of an elephant boy in India or of a goatherd tending goats in the mountains of Switzerland, he gradually gains a better understanding of how and why people live as they do in different environments.

Development of the Whole Child and the Individual Child. When a leader first meets a group of children who have come together for creative playing, she discovers personality traits almost immediately. Children who are engaged in genuine fun are off guard and concerned wholly with the jollity of the moment. As the children plan and play together, a leader recognizes a shy child or one with leadership qualities, one who is secure or insecure, one who shows aggressive tendencies. She finds a well-adjusted child, one who is liked or disliked, accepted or rejected, one who needs only the slightest stimulation to set his creative power into action. She sees a timid sensitive child who always prefers to be in the audience. Individual problems, individual drives, individual desires are brought out into the open as the group enters into dynamic play activity.

A group of third-grade children who were being introduced to creative dramatics wanted to play "The Three Billy Goats Gruff." After the leader had told the story, she started a lively group discussion by asking, "Why do you think the troll felt mean and grumbly? Why wouldn't he let the goats go across the bridge?" One girl answered immediately, "The troll wants to tease the billy goats. He likes to scare everybody. Sometimes I like to tease just like that." Another child said, "He's mean and he's selfish. He isn't teasing. He's really bad!" Several children expressed opinions, many of which corresponded to the first suggestions. Among the children was a small boy named Herbert whose eyes were noticeably crossed. He had not been accepted by the group, and he was often belligerent in his attitude and actions toward the other children. The teacher felt that this story might prove particularly helpful to Herbert, and she gradually led him into the discussion by asking in a friendly manner, "Maybe you have an idea about the troll, Herbert. Why do you think he didn't want the goats to go over the bridge?"

"He's lonesome," Herbert said at once. "None of the other trolls like him. They leave him out of everything. He found this bridge and it's his. I think he's mean 'cause everybody's mean to him."

After further discussion, the class decided to use Herbert's idea, and they chose Herbert to be the troll for the first time. He played the character with strong feeling, and when the scene was over, the children cheered and praised "such a good mean troll."

When a child is given opportunities day after day to release inner tensions in a satisfying manner such as this, and when he gains the approval of others, he gradually develops a feeling of harmony within himself as he becomes "all of one piece" emotionally, mentally, physically, and socially.

Creativity, the native delicate power within each individual is constantly nurtured by experiences which stimulate one's imagination. Individual creative power may be likened to a hidden spring. It may require only the slightest tapping to uncover it, or, again, it may take many months of skillful digging to cause the spring to bubble forth with a stream of clear thinking. Each child must exercise his own creativity and bring it into action for himself; however, constant exposure to and participation in dramatic literature helps a child to discover his unique and priceless power. Hughes Mearns, in referring to the creativity within each individual, states that "the new education becomes simply wise guidance of enormously important native powers."[3]

When a child, bursting with enthusiasm, spontaneously calls out, "I have a wonderful idea," a leader knows that the child's creativity is being generated, and she encourages him to express his idea and share it with others. Many such experiences stimulate and encourage a child to do something for himself. Creative skills which are essential for self-entertainment are developed and nurtured in the activity of playmaking. These skills equip a child with the necessary tools for making wholesome use of his leisure time.

---

[3] Hughes Mearns, *Creative Youth*, Doubleday, Doran and Co., 1925.

The world of ideas and beauty is opened to boys and girls when they live through sensitive and beautiful dramatic experiences. In the minds of many, creative dramatics, more than any other experience, helps a child to satisfy his aesthetic and spiritual desires, for in this activity a child learns about beauty by living beauty. He learns to enjoy poetry by feeling poetry. A leader, understanding the value of having a child reach for experiences which lead him onward and upward in his thinking, provides episodes from literature and experiences from life which broaden horizons and open gateways to beauty.

Real Problems of Living Met in School. The procedure which is followed in the group activity of creating a play is readily carried over into the real problems of living as children learn to work together in a group. They learn to organize, to arrive at conclusions based upon the collaborative thinking of all the members and to solve problems in a democratic way. A group which has experienced the planning, the playing, and the evaluating of many creative plays will be in a position to meet problems which arise in school and in community living. Individual members will know how to approach a problem intelligently, to discuss it from various angles, and to formulate a plan of action for working it out in a satisfactory manner. Whether the problem be one of planning a school party, arranging an excursion to a factory, or providing entertainment for a community program, the students will know how to coöperate for a common purpose.

Many classroom teachers have found the activity of creative dramatics exceedingly helpful in teaching children how to make an introduction, how to answer the door, how to use the telephone, how to make an announcement, how to give directions, and how to meet many social courtesies which arise in everyday living.

When an "open house" was being planned in an elementary school, children from kindergarten through the sixth grade approached this situation in much the same way that they approached a new story which they were going to dramatize. They discussed the reason for "open house" and concluded that their parents were to be their guests. In one second-grade class the discussion became so lively that Helen, a seven-year-old, called out, "I'd like to bring my mother and daddy right now!" Helen was encouraged to choose a mother and a father right then and there, and this family hurried into the hall while the rest of the room waited in eager anticipation. When the teacher invited them to come in, Helen proudly introduced her mother and father. After the parents and the teacher had a short visit, Helen showed her mother and father the most interesting units in the room, including the farm set, the book tree, the aquarium, and her work-book. After Helen's experience every child wanted to play "open house." For several days the group played this new game until every child enjoyed making introductions. These second graders looked forward to this special occasion, for they were prepared to meet it both socially and emotionally. On the evening of the "open house" all of the children in the room brought their parents, and in a few instances a child brought his grandparents as well.

An eighth-grade class which was planning a school tea for the faculty and parents prepared for this occasion in a similar way. In one of their group meetings the entire class worked on introductions. Many of the students took the roles of their parents, others took the roles of faculty members, and they acted out various introductions in a creative, spontaneous manner, giving each student the experience of participating and of observing. Other meetings were spent in dramatizing the presentation and acknowledgment of awards, in working out the procedure of a receiving line, and in experiencing the etiquette of serving and being served.

Chapter VII

CREATIVE DRAMATICS IN THE SCHOOL PROGRAM

> Could you tell me how to grow,
> Or is it unconveyed, like melody or witchcraft?
> —EMILY DICKINSON

With the understanding that creative dramatics is fundamental in education, let us see how this activity carries over into the school program. Since one of the major problems of teaching is that of interesting children in their work, we shall consider creative dramatics not as an isolated subject, but as a motivating force which vitalizes learning in many different ways.

CREATIVE DRAMATICS AND GROWTH IN LANGUAGE ARTS

By the time a child is ready for school he has a good many words at his command. The school recognizes language as an art, and it strives through a carefully planned program of reading, listening, speaking, and writing to equip a child with language skills that will enable him to speak freely and naturally and with honor to this age-old art. Speaking is one of the most important considerations of every individual, for a person is immediately judged by his language. "As a man speaketh so is he." Since speaking is continuous throughout life, the school endeavors to help each child discover his native powers of expression, in order that he will be able to communicate with others and in turn to receive communications from others.

In the friendly atmosphere of playmaking, children learn to express themselves in a realistic environment which closely reflects reality. Children learn to talk freely, to enter into group discussion, to think on their feet, to "keep the play going," and to evaluate their efforts. Because of the strong appeal of drama, a child's interest is always high in a playmaking class. Children enter into dramatic activity with a "glad-to-be-here" attitude which immediately establishes a relaxed and sociable feeling. Children who are usually indifferent in their attitude toward working in the usual routine manner generally respond with active attention to playmaking activities, and they become eager to join in actual playing. In a spirited creative dramatics class, children tend to achieve increased emotional and social stability. Creative drama, therefore, can and does make a valuable contribution to the language arts program, for until a child is emotionally and socially secure, he will not be able to express himself with ease.

Vocabularies are increased as children enlarge their experiences. Dramatic participation in many experiences provides a rich substitute for experiencing in reality. Since it is not possible for every child to go beyond the physical boundaries of his environment, nor would it be possible for a child to experience a good many things first-hand even if it were, creative drama offers rich experiences in converting and in reconstructing reality.

A leader indirectly stimulates an interest in new words. "Who can think of an adjective that describes the character of Ebenezer Scrooge?" she asks, after telling Dickens' *Christmas Carol* to a group of seventh-graders. Real thinking is required in order to recall that Scrooge was a "squeezing, wrenching, grasping, scraping, clutching, covetous old sinner." "Covetous," the leader may repeat as a child recalls this adjective. "Covetous is an interesting word. Let's say it together. Who knows what covetous means?"

Younger children become interested in words as a leader suggests, "Let's find words that will paint the elf in our story." After the children have thought of such words as "tiny, merry, gay, happy, brown, green, and quick," the leader may say, "Now let's think of action words, words that tell us how the elf moves about." Children delight in searching for words such as "dance, spring, jump, fly, lilt, run, and skip."

Good voice and diction are identified with creative drama. Again the leader guides rather than directs the children into good word usage. "Why was the town crier such a fine character in our play?" she questions, as she leads the group into an evaluation of their play. By further questioning she helps the children to see that the clear, distinct chanting of the crier helped to make his character interesting. By participating in many such experiences children discover that their voices can become powerful instruments for expressing exactly what they wish to say. Children will delight in being fairy godmothers, giants, genies, brownies, witches, and other imaginary characters which require careful use of their voices, for they soon recognize that their voices are among their most important assets. In the friendly activity of playmaking, a child readily accepts the challenge of speaking clearly and loudly enough to be heard.

Good speech habits are developed from good listening habits. "Ain't," "git," "jist," "huh," and other careless forms of speaking are indirectly improved in the activity of creative dramatics. Children become interested in improving their language as they begin to see how important it is to have the right words to express what they want to say. By using a positive approach, a leader stimulates an interest in close observation. She praises rather than criticizes, and she draws favorable comments from the children in the group. "Wasn't the Queen a stately person? Did you notice how carefully she said *just* three wishes?"

A leader emphasizes good speech habits rather than calling

attention to incorrect forms. If children fear that they are to be criticized, they will be self-conscious and hesitant about volunteering for character parts. They will cease to be free and creative in their thinking if they are too conscious of speech. Realizing that she exerts a strong influence on the children, a leader always uses fine and acceptable language herself. She never violates a rule of rhetoric unless she feels that it accomplishes a purpose.

Training in listening is a strong factor in every creative dramatics experience, for the activity gives each child an opportunity to be both a participant and a spectator. The entire experience requires active attention on the part of every child. In order to plan a scene, children must be receptive and alert when the material is being presented. In the process of developing a play a part of the group is chosen to be the audience, which places this group of children in the role of observers. The audience is given the responsibility of watching the story from the standpoint of improving it. To encourage good listening, a leader occasionally chooses the audience before she chooses the cast. "Who would like to be in the audience this time?" she asks. "Good listeners are good helpers, because they are watching for good ideas and for ways of making our story stronger."

Educators and librarians have recognized creative dramatics as a splendid medium for introducing children to good literature. When children experience enjoyable moments in dramatic art, they grow in their appreciation of good reading materials. When a child has been exposed to the very best in literature over a period of time, he is able to discriminate for himself, and, when given a choice, he will always choose the better thing. This does not hold true, however, unless the child has been introduced to the good as well as to the poor in reading material. As a child dramatizes stories he identifies himself with the characters, and in so doing his reading takes on new meaning. Once a child becomes acquainted with the finest English of the past and with the finest English of the present, he is no longer content with mediocrity. When his appetite for good literature becomes sharpened, he wants more and more of this nourishing diet. Creative dramatics is powerful in making this transformation. Catharsis is at work, and whenever a child experiences high moments in creative drama, his appreciation for literature is strengthened.

Primary teachers find that reading content is improved when children identify themselves with the characters in the story. Interest in reading, both silent and oral, develops as a result of playing stories. Reading for information is motivated in the process of story dramatization, for children read with the definite purpose of finding new material for improving their play. Comprehension in reading is strengthened when children are given opportunities to play parts of the stories which they have read. A child grows in his ability to comprehend the funniest part, the saddest part, the most exciting part of a story, when he is allowed to choose a scene for creative playing.

Written expression comes as a result of having something to say, something to write about, something exciting or interesting enough to tell to others. Experiences which have been strong enough emotionally to stir a child's thinking generally result in finer written expression than the mere assignment to write a theme about anything the child wishes. Dramatic experiences which penetrate deeply have a strong and lasting effect on a child's thinking.

CREATIVE DRAMATICS AND GROWTH IN SOCIAL STUDIES

An alert teacher recognizes limitless opportunities for using creative dramatics in the field of social studies. As a group activity, dramatic participation develops the capacity to work together, to think together, and to get along together. It encourages each child to reflect and to interpret, and, by the interchange of ideas with other children, to get a more complete understanding of the material presented than is perhaps possible by any other method of teaching.

In addition to offering first-hand experiences in good social living, this activity can vitalize the subject matter of geography, of history, and of social developments throughout the country and the world. It is useful with younger groups of children in dramatizing units of study on the home, the farm, the community, and the field of transportation.

Dramatic episodes from the history of our country, including periods of discovery, exploration, and expansion, afford rich opportunities for real learning when the teacher allows the children to create scenes or a play from a specific social movement. Early historical developments, including the voyage of Columbus, the landing of the Pilgrims, the settling of Jamestown, the beginning of our government, George Washington's experiences at Valley Forge, and other impressive happenings which contributed to the growth of our country, provide vital material for creative playing.

The Civil War period will be long remembered by boys and girls when they relive humble experiences from the life of Abraham Lincoln. Reconstructing experiences from the life of Clara Barton and dramatizing touching episodes from *Uncle Tom's Cabin* will be effective in teaching children both historical facts and conflicting attitudes of Civil War days.

A group project in which children become early settlers pushing westward to the California gold fields in the days of '49 motivates vital reading. When a class decides to create a play from this experience, many questions are immediately aroused. How did the settlers learn of the gold in California? What is a wagon train? How many covered wagons generally traveled together? Was the trail blazed? How did the wagons cross large streams and rivers? What provisions did each family carry? How did the settlers dress? Was there real danger from the Indians? Why did the Indians feel bitter toward the white man? What kind of weapons did the settlers use? How did the settlers arrange their camp at night? What did they do for entertainment?

To answer these questions each child reads avidly, searching for information that will contribute to the play. He learns the folk songs of this period with a refreshed interest, for in order to be a red-blooded scout riding ahead of the wagon train he, too, must know the songs when he joins in the merry-making around the wagon camp at night. Square dancing and folk games have real significance for a child when he sees how they functioned in life, and he is eager to learn exactly how the dancing is done.

What child wouldn't be entranced by a series of striking dramatizations which brings to life the progress of the westward movement? How much more meaningful social studies can be when children work intensively in groups to prepare historical scenes to share with others than when they simply read and report in a routine manner! A seventh-grade class of thirty-nine students developed an interesting project based on westward expansion. The class was divided into eight groups, and a leader was chosen for each group. Rivalry and competition among the children spurred each group on to intensive effort. Many of the groups worked on their scenes in after-school hours. One group painted a large mural on wrapping paper to suggest a mountain setting for their scene. On the day when the groups combined their efforts, each child witnessed impressive scenes showing the development of Alexander Graham Bell's telephone, the driving of the last spike on the Southern Pacific Railroad, the arrival of the first white woman in the Oregon territory, the defending of the Alamo, the discovery of gold by Sutter, the bravery of Custer's last stand, the inauguration of the Pony Express, and the camping of covered wagons at sunset.

Expeditions into various parts of the world have been dramatized by groups with a zest that contributed to good learning. A fifth-grade class which had been studying South America in a geography class developed an original dramatization in which two explorers returned from the Andes and brought back moving pictures to share with American friends. The children became the characters in the pictures, and they pantomimed interesting South American customs and sang South American songs.

Imaginary flights to remote places never fail to stimulate interest among the most apathetic group of children. When they become passengers aboard a large transport plane and hear a loud voice speaking from a make-believe public address system calling, "Flight 106 leaving for Guadalajara, Acapulco, Mexico City!" children respond to the tingling excitement of adventure and become interested in learning about the new country to which they are traveling.

When a good foundation has been established for creative thinking, older groups of children may be ready to develop an original play based on such interesting concepts as democracy, peace, war, beauty, happiness, and America. Biographies of historical figures furnish an abundance of dramatic material which promotes good learning.

CREATIVE DRAMATICS IN ARITHMETIC

A variety of close-to-life situations, such as playing store, operating a transit system, establishing a post office, and other experiences which allow for a practical application of arithmetic skills, may be dramatized effectively in the classroom. When dramatics is used for the specific purpose of helping children to understand the number system, the dramatization is always kept close to reality.

When children play store they are encouraged to set up a "real" store, and "real" money is used in the business of buying and selling; or if the customers are permitted to buy on credit, the clerks will work out detailed sales slips. Experiences in recognizing money values, in making change, and in applying fundamental number skills are readily provided by dramatic participation.

In many classrooms bank day has become an experience which the children anticipate with strong interest, for through dramatization banking has taken on vital meaning. Each week different children are chosen to be cashiers and tellers, and they assume the responsibility of checking each deposit carefully as they work in the school bank, which is arranged in a realistic setting. The experience of making a loan, of computing interest, and of transacting business in many different ways can be dramatized in a realistic way which will give children a good understanding of how-to-do-it.

A teacher will correlate arithmetic with dramatics only when she feels that the children gain by dramatic participation. She will not use dramatics as a vehicle for teaching fundamental skills but rather as a meaningful experience for the application of such skills. Motivating the interest and effort of the children and keeping the experience alive with a wake-up-and-go attitude are the responsibilities of the teacher whenever she uses dramatics in an arithmetic situation.

CREATIVE DRAMATICS IN NATURE STUDY AND SCIENCE

Creative dramatics is more than playing a story or creating a play. It can and should be a stimulating experience which arouses thinking on the part of each child who participates. Creative dramatics can open new horizons to the world of nature and awaken a new awareness to the world in which we live. Whenever children dramatize nature stories or nature poems, the teacher approaches the material from what the children know about it, and she gradually leads them into a discussion which arouses a new interest in something which may have grown to be commonplace or ordinary to them.

For a child to be ready to create a play from Robert Louis Stevenson's poem, "The Wind," his imagination must first be kindled with such questions as these: "Where does the wind come from? How does the wind feel when it blows so hard? What kind of a song does the wind sing? What does it sing about? How do the trees feel as they sway in the wind? Do you think the birds enjoy being blown about by the wind? What causes the kites to be tossed so high? How do the fleecy white clouds feel as they float and drift in a blue sky? Where does the wind go when the blowing stops?"

Since children must first envision and imagine an experience before they can create it, guide questions serve not only to stimulate creative thinking but to cause the child to wonder about the experience in reality.

On a wintry day when a fifth-grade class created a play from a poem about a snowstorm, the children watched the falling snow with new interest. As one of the boys looked out of the window, he called out eagerly, "Look how large the flakes are! You know this is the first time in my life that I've ever really watched a snow-flake."

In the natural environment there is an abundance of material which comes with each season of the year, with changes in the weather, and with fascinating experiences in the animal world which offer a rich variety of dramatic experiences. "The Little Plant," by Kate L. Brown, and Edith Nesbit's "Baby Seed Song," are excellent nature poems for young children to play in the spring of the year. A teacher who appreciates the beauty and wonder of the outdoor world will recognize opportunities each day for making vital material live as she guides children into dynamic dramatizations, and as she uses the dramatization to motivate further investigation into the how and why of things in the world around us.

CREATIVE DRAMATICS IN SAFETY EDUCATION

Dramatics has been widely used in safety education and has proved to be exceptionally useful in preventions of accidents. "An ounce of prevention is worth a pound of cure" illustrates what can be accomplished when dramatic participation becomes so meaningful to the participants that the emotional and psychological transfer affects their thinking.

Traffic safety has been dramatized effectively in classrooms when children have been encouraged to create improvised scenes, such as crossing a street against a traffic light, attempting to cross a busy highway without using a crosswalk, hurrying into the midst of traffic to retrieve a pet kitten, and riding bicycles on sidewalks carelessly, weaving in and out among busy pedestrians. Scenes in which violators are arrested by police officers and dramatic scenes which take place in hospital rooms are emotionally strong and therefore can be useful in teaching children to be cautious.

Home safety may be emphasized in a similar way when children create such dramatic accidents as those that might result from playing with matches or experimenting with chemical compounds and with electricity. Scenes in which toys or dangerous objects are scattered in doorways and scenes in which medicine is left carelessly about are effective in causing children to use care in preventing similar accidents in reality.

CREATIVE DRAMATICS IN THE RELATED ARTS

Music. Singing games, such as "Here We Go Round the Mulberry Bush" and "Did You Ever See a Lassie," contribute a pleasant motivation for leading young children into the genuine fun of pantomime. Story-telling songs and songs which emphasize strong character feeling are used often for dramatization, for they combine action and music in a charming way. "A Frog Went Courtin'," "The Farmer in the Dell," and "The Lovely Princess" have proved to be favorites for children of all ages to play. Rather than playing "The Farmer in the Dell" in the accustomed manner, children are encouraged to be a farmer, a farmer's wife, a child, a nurse, and each of the characters in the song.

Sea chanteys, American folk ballads, and cowboy songs provide a wealth of dramatic material for playing. Occasionally children enjoy dramatizing a song entirely in pantomime while a part of the group sings. Mountain ballads, Negro spirituals, songs of the lumber camps, songs of the railroad builders, and other folk tunes enrich a child's experience when they are rewoven into their original fabric in a creative play.

An appreciation of music is developed when children listen to recordings in order to find appropriate selections to heighten the mood of a particular play. A group of third-graders had listened to several recordings for the purpose of finding suitable background for their Hallowe'en story. After listening to "Dance Macabre," one little girl exclaimed, "We must use this! It's so full of secrets and surprises!"

From time to time children express a desire to create a play from a musical selection. Among the favorites which children's groups have worked on with great satisfaction are "Home on the Range," "Hansel and Gretel," "The Dance of the Blessed Spirit," "Copelia Ballet," "The Nutcracker Suite," "Dance Macabre," "The Sorcerer's Apprentice," "Til Eulenspiegel," and "Peter and the Wolf."

Whenever a play requires an original song or a melody, children are encouraged to create the music. A child with musical ability may respond to this desire and work with zest to compose appropriate words and music for the sake of a play.

Arts and Crafts. Creative expression in all the arts is of considerable value to the individual. One child may find that he can best express himself through the medium of dramatics, another child may prefer to express his innermost feelings through writing, still another may find a great release in painting, another in dancing, another in singing. A leader often finds that the activity of creative dramatics stimulates a child's creativity to such a degree that it carries over into other creative activities. If a child is a king, a prince, or a beggar in a play, these people become a part of his experience, and when he reads or sings or paints, these characters are very real to him.

Many leaders unify a learning experience for children by guiding their groups into creative writing or creative painting experiences at the conclusion of each creative play. A leader may suggest, "Now that we've had such a fine time playing 'Jack and the Beanstalk,' I wonder if we can show how we feel about this story in another way? What part of the story do you like best? What part do you think you will always remember? When you close your eyes, what picture keeps coming back to you? Try it and see. Let's paint 'Jack and the Beanstalk' pictures—each one of you paint whatever you like best in your very own way."

Presenting a play for another class may motivate the construction of certain properties or of simplified scenery to suggest a setting for a play. Many children put forth their best creative effort when they are given opportunities to work with their hands.

CREATIVE DRAMATICS AND AUDIO-VISUAL METHODS

Audio-visual methods of teaching and creative dramatics procedures are in complete accord in their major purpose, for each is primarily concerned with helping children to learn effectively. Audio-visual methods recognize the value of creative dramatics in a learning program. Edgar Dale states that "Restrictions of time and place make it impossible for any of us to experience directly much of what we need to know if we are to be educated . . . Dramatic participation can help us get as close as possible to certain realities that we cannot reach at first-hand."[1] Mr. Dale regards dramatic participation as the third band on the "Cone of Experience," since it is a reconstructed experience which closely reflects reality.

Creative dramatics leaders recognize the value of sensory aids, such as recordings, radio, exhibits, films, and pictures, as strong motivating material for leading children into dramatic experiences. An audio-visual program is concerned with providing rich experiences for children, in order that they will be able to make sound and logical generalizations through the use of verbal symbols. One of the primary objectives in a creative dramatics program is to develop a freedom of expression within each individual so that he will learn to think and to speak for himself.

CREATIVE DRAMATICS FOR HANDICAPPED CHILDREN

Pioneer work has been done in providing creative dramatics for handicapped children. The results have shown remarkable success,

---

[1] Edgar Dale, *Audio-Visual Methods in Teaching*, The Dryden Press, 1946.

particularly in promoting good life experiences. Boys and girls in schools for spastics have responded enthusiastically to opportunities to participate in dramatic play activities. In many situations the children have traveled to interesting places entirely in their imaginations. In a school where creative dramatics was being introduced, the handicapped children imagined themselves to be walking in the forest at daybreak. As they sat in their chairs, some of the children identified themselves with trees, others with flowers, others with forest animals. The leader became the sun who awakened each one and helped to bring the forest to life in a manner which was enchanting to the children.

In another group, where the children had enjoyed dramatic play throughout an entire school year, the leader told the story of "The Nutcracker Suite." After they had heard the story, they listened with great interest to Tchaikowsky's "Dance of the Sugar Plum Fairy," "Chinese Dance," and "Waltz of the Flowers." After a short discussion of the story, the children became sugar plum fairies. As they listened to the music, a few of the children danced freely about the room, others danced with their arms, some with their fingers, and all with their hearts. As they played, they projected themselves into a world of beauty and fantasy. The experience proved to be refreshing and stimulating, and the children asked to be sugar plum fairies over and over again.

Creative dramatics has opened a new world to many blind children who were living in a world of darkness. Through word pictures, touch sensations, and smells, the children have enlarged their concepts of the world around them. They have found great joy in interpreting new impressions and in pantomiming their ideas of such delightful things as bluebirds, violets, and butterflies. Through creative dramatics the blind child is given a chance to get outside himself. When his imagination is carefully guided, a blind child is able to hear and see fairies just as vividly as any other child.

Creative dramatics gives blind children a chance for normal play.

It provides a friendly situation in which they can apply the skills that they have previously learned. They gain practice in direction and in handling themselves physically. They learn to guide themselves through the action of a story by sound and by touch. And, above all, they have a good time working and playing together for a real purpose.

Deaf children can live normal lives in spite of their handicaps, once they are helped to become a part of the hearing world. Creative dramatics has been used effectively in giving them confidence and a sufficiently secure feeling to participate in community living. Oftentimes parents of deaf children become frustrated and disturbed over a child's handicap when they lack an understanding of what can be done to help the child. It is not uncommon in a situation of this kind for a child to sense his parent's feelings to such a degree that he becomes extremely insecure and oversensitive.

Such was the case with six-year-old Tommy, who had been deaf since birth. Tommy was usually kept out of sight when anyone came to his home; or, if he happened to appear when guests were present, his parents became embarrassed as they hurried him away and offered an explanation of his disability. Tommy was fully aware of side glances, and he sensed a humiliation which added to his fears. A friend of the family who was aware of the outstanding progress that had been made in teaching deaf children in one of the public schools asked if she might take Tommy to visit one of the classes. On the day that Tommy went to the school he saw a room full of friendly boys and girls. They were watching the teacher tell a visual story as she placed colored cut-out figures on a felt board. Tommy watched the teacher point to a picture of an elephant, and then saw her make a wonderful trunk with her arms. As the teacher lumbered around the room like a heavy, jungle elephant, the boys and girls who were watching became eager and delighted. The teacher motioned for them to follow her, and each one became an elephant and tramped around the room in his own way. Tommy watched closely as the teacher and the children pantomimed many different kinds of animals. The children could readily associate the visual with pantomime, and in a short time they formed an animal parade with ponies, dogs, camels, elephants and monkeys following the teacher, who led them merrily around the room. As they paraded about, each child had a chance to think and to feel independently.

When Tommy went home he became each of the animals that he had seen the children pantomiming. He looked for pictures of animals in magazines, and whenever he found an animal that was familiar to him, he delighted in pantomiming it. When his father came home that evening Tommy put on a circus for his parents, and, for the first time in his young life, he had a real incentive for communication—the actual aim of which is to encourage deaf children to try to speak. As Tommy continued to go to school, he gradually became a participating member of the group and a well-adjusted child at home.

CLASSROOM TEACHER OR SPECIAL TEACHER FOR CREATIVE DRAMATICS

Is it more desirable to have creative dramatics taught by a classroom teacher or by a special dramatics teacher? If the school program is arranged on a departmentalized system, creative dramatics will be scheduled as an elective or as a part of each child's weekly program. In this system a special dramatics teacher works with many different groups of children each day. She may work with each class for a thirty or forty-five minute period twice each week, or, if it can be arranged, she may work with them oftener. Many schools regard creative dramatics as one of the fine arts, and instruction is scheduled in much the same way as it is in music and art departments. A creative dramatics specialist is skillful in her guidance of each individual, because she uses this activity as an art and succeeds in guiding children to creative heights.

On the other hand, a classroom teacher who works closely with her pupils from day to day has a good understanding of the needs, the problems, and the differences of each individual. A classroom teacher is in an ideal position to use this activity whenever a strong motivation presents itself and to correlate it with various units of work. In a self-contained classroom a teacher is in a position to combine the time that is scheduled for language arts, let us say, with the time that is set aside for social studies, and thereby she is able to arrange a longer period for developing a creative play. A classroom teacher who works closely with her students will be able to provide specific reading and resource material to enrich each learning experience.

In an ideal situation, children benefit by experiencing creative activity daily under the guidance of a classroom teacher and by working with a creative dramatics supervisor once each week.

Chapter VIII

CREATIVE DRAMATICS IN THE HOME

A great man is he who has not lost the heart of a child.
—MENCIUS

Home is a child's first world. It is his place of beginning, for a little child, not unlike a young seedling, secures his roots wherever he is born and begins to grow. A child's family is the cultural base of his universe, and the influence of home determines to a great degree what kind of an individual a young infant will be. He may be allowed to grow in harmony with himself, or he may be hampered as he struggles to become himself. In addition to providing food and shelter and love for a child, a family must consider each child as an individual and must respect the child's inner self. In this one consideration many parents have failed. They have neglected or perhaps have not known how to nourish a child's inner feeling which we may think of as his creative spirit, his imagination, his bubbling spring of native power, or his soul, which is the very essence of his individuality. If a child is to be a confident, secure, creative person, parents must begin early to encourage and guide this delicate yet vital power. Unless the creative spark which lies deep in every child is fanned to a flame which fires his whole being, life will not be the soaring, challenging experience which each young individual dreams it to be. A child must have an opportunity to develop his native ability, to be strong in that which is his own.

MOTHER AS A LEADER

In recent years more and more mothers have applied the principles of creative dramatics with children at home and have found the experiences of great benefit in helping a child to find himself. As we go into the home we shall speak of mother as the leader, but this does not mean that father or grandparents, aunts or uncles, or older brothers and sisters cannot stimulate a child's thinking in a similar way.

A busy mother does not set aside a special time for this activity; rather she makes it a part of whatever the child is doing. Creative thinking can begin with the child's day and carry through to the "Now I lay me." As a leader, a mother uses the magic of suggestion. Her attitude is one of positive thinking. Her role is one of recognizing the interest of the child and of stirring his imagination until he becomes the creative thinker. A positive suggestion by mother is many times nothing more than a single thought or an idea used at the right moment to set a child's mood for an activity which follows. It may seem easier to say "no, no, no" in an attempt to make the child stop whatever he is doing, but it is hardly fair to insist that he stop his activity without being able to substitute another one.

MAKE-BELIEVE FOR THE PRE-SCHOOL CHILD

Play is all in all for the very young child. His play is his work, and through his play he grows and learns. We have but to watch a little girl playing house to see how much she discovers about living as she bakes make-believe cakes, washes dishes, tidies up a house, feeds her dollies, and entertains with make-believe tea parties. A wise mother will not interfere with a child's play, yet she will not overlook its importance. She will be a good audience for her child's playing even though she continues with her own work, and now and then she will offer a friendly suggestion or praise the child's efforts. She may knock at a make-believe door where her little girl is playing, and with a twinkle in her eye she may exclaim, "Mrs. Smith, I just brought some fresh rhubarb in from the garden. I would be delighted to have you and Mary Jane come over at twelve o'clock and have lunch with me today." An invitation such as this will not only prepare the little girl for lunch time, but it may send her imagination soaring as she dresses herself and Mary Jane, her favorite dolly, for a lovely luncheon with mother.

Since the creative instinct is so natural in all children, a mother will find that it works its way out in many kinds of make-believe. It may be necessary from time to time for a mother to play with her child for a few minutes and to offer a suggestion or two in order to get the child started on a new flight of fancy. As mother joins three-year-old Skippy in his playing with blocks, she remembers how much Skippy enjoyed visiting on grandfather's farm. "Come on, farmer Skip, let's build a barn big enough for all your bossy cows and for all your horses that are in this big pasture!" This idea may be enough to turn Skippy's dreaming into vital action, and he may become a farmer for a good part of the day. He may remain in character while he is eating his noonday meal and again when he is ready for his afternoon nap. He will enjoy resting on his bed when it suddenly becomes a soft clover field or a comfortable stack of hay.

Whenever a child is playing in character, a mother will encourage him in his make-believe fancies. She will enrich his thinking by reading to him from an illustrated "Mother Goose" and from other children's books, and if possible she will play recordings of fine music which have a strong appeal for children. A mother will be pleased to see how these experiences stimulate a child's thinking and carry over into his dramatic playing.

CREATIVE THINKING IN EVERYDAY LIVING

One of the most practical values of creative dramatics is in the routine of everyday living, for through its use routine tasks may become pleasant and meaningful. Let us see how a mother may use creative dramatics throughout the day. Up to the child's eighth year, mother has little trouble in awakening him in the morning. Generally, it is the other way around. Mother wishes fervently that Billy and Susan would stay in bed an hour or even a half hour longer at the start of day. In this situation she might tell them the story of "Rip Van Winkle" or "Sleeping Beauty," encouraging them or perhaps challenging them to be Rip or Beauty throughout the night and into the morning.

Or a mother might tip-toe into a child's room after he is asleep and pin a picture on the wall. She will have told him earlier that there would be a surprise program on the "television" screen waiting for him in the morning. When children are encouraged they can readily imagine a story around a picture, and when they learn to enjoy such flights of the imagination, the rest of the family is able to sleep a little longer.

Some children respond to the enchantment of being a prince or a princess and enjoy the luxury of playing in bed an hour before breakfast. With a suggestion from mother or father the night before, a child, as soon as he is awake the next morning, will quietly gather up his toys, hop back into bed and imagine his toys to be pages and servants grouped around his bed awaiting his orders. Should he inquire after the health of the queen, one of his make-believe pages may whisper softly, "Oh, your honor, the queen isn't awake yet, and we have to be quiet."

After the early-bird age a child sleeps later, and parents may then find it quite a problem to arouse a child each morning. If a mother has to call nine-year-old Johnny several times each morning, she may try creative magic and see how it helps in getting him up. Since she knows that Johnny's strongest interest at this particular time is in cowboys, she may either assume the character of a cowboy herself or say or do something that will awaken in Johnny a responsive chord so that he will begin to think and to feel like a cowboy himself; then he will want to hurry out of bed. Mother may stride into his room calling, "Hi Pardner! It's time to be up and off to the range!"

She may give him a friendly jostle or pull on his pajama sleeve and call cheerfully, "Come on, cowboy! You'd better roll out of the covers and have breakfast with the rest of us cowhands."

If Johnny's mother does not feel confident in creating a character, she may jangle his spurs together or beat on a skillet with a pancake turner and call loudly, "Wake up, cowboy! Breakfast's ready! Can't you smell the bacon sizzling over the campfire? You'll have to eat in a hurry if you're going to get the shorthorns up to the hills by noon."

Creative dramatics suggestions such as these will no doubt be enough to awaken Johnny; then his mother may find that singing or whistling a cowboy tune as she finishes preparing breakfast may further motivate Johnny's thinking and start him off with a good feeling for the entire day. What's wrong with a mother wearing a bright plaid shirt and fastening a cartridge belt around her waist as she sets about making biscuits, not for the family's breakfast but for all the "farmhands" or "big game hunters"?

If a mother knows that her child is for the time being fascinated with ships and sailing, she may sound an alarm or ring a bell outside his room and enter with a snappy salute. "Four bells, Captain Jones. We're sailing into New York harbor."

This may immediately arouse the ten-year-old captain, or he may need further dramatic persuasion. "Do you wish your breakfast served in the cabin sir?" or "What are your orders, captain?"

Sounding reveille with a make-believe bugle and awakening a would-be soldier with "Good morning, general," many times works magic in getting a child up and dressed and washed and ready for "chow" in record time. Many a child has an irritating habit of dawdling—dawdling while dressing and dawdling in getting to the breakfast table. How could a five-star general who reviews troops and issues directives dawdle over dressing or brushing teeth or tying shoe laces? When a child starts the day with a spirit of fun and in the mood of make-believe, he has a stronger incentive to keep moving than merely that of buttoning buttons and lacing laces.

"Last call for breakfast! Breakfast is served in the diner," may be a pleasant awakening to children who have enjoyed overnight train trips. A mother entering her daughter's rooms in the character of a Pullman porter with a white towel over one arm, may greet the child, "Good morning, madam. It is seven o'clock, Thursday morning, and we're forty minutes out of Baltimore. Do you wish to have me call you later, madam?" In a surprisingly few minutes "madam" will be ready for breakfast and hurry into the diner. Mother may then become the dining car porter who hands the child a make-believe menu and asks, "May I have your order, please?"

The grapefruit may become a vine-ripened cantaloupe from Florida, and the strips of bacon may suddenly turn into fresh mountain trout from the streams of northern Maine.

A little child, especially a little girl, may enjoy waking up to the sound of a crying Mary Jane, a dolly, who is in great need of her young mother to prepare breakfast or a six o'clock feeding. A little boy may feel important when his day is started as the caretaker of a hungry little puppy or of a meowing kitty that is waiting to be fed.

Personalities from real life or storybook heroes and heroines become idealized characters for some children. A mother may find that she has only to call "Cinderella" or "Sleeping Beauty" or "Tom Sawyer," and her child awakens into a pleasant make-believe world of reality.

Many a little child enjoys being "Black Sambo" and will hurry out of bed to eat pancakes with Black Mumbo and Black Jumbo. And many a little child enjoys being Baby Bear and will hurry out of bed to eat his porridge with Mother Bear and Father Bear.

A creative suggestion makes a great difference in the entire feeling of the child who must be called to help with the morning chores. "Come on, farmer Bill, the horses need feeding," or "Wake up, milkman! It's time to drive the bossies into the barn!" make waking up out of a sound sleep much more pleasant than a harsh alarm or a sharp command.

The creative suggestion is a miraculous time-saver for parents. As a first reaction, many mothers may perhaps say, "My, that sounds like it takes a lot of time." The beautiful thing is that it saves infinite amounts of time, for it serves as a springboard for getting a child's imagination started. A mother cannot remain aloof, however, and expect the magic to work by itself. She must enter into the spirit and give thought and attention to the suggestions she makes. Once a child starts thinking for himself, he is not only able to enjoy moments of solitude, but he becomes engaged in self-initiated activities that free his parents from the constant need to provide entertainment or amusement for him. When a child's day begins in a creative way, the impetus can last for hours while he plays out his role as general, cowboy, or whatever he wishes to be.

The positive suggestion is not only a time-saver but a nerve-saver as well, when parents wish to improve a child's manners and habits. The child who slumps might be greeted each morning with a friendly salute followed by a brisk, "Good morning, Major!" The Major, of course, could not return a salute properly unless he, too, was straight with his shoulders thrown back. The heavyfooted child could be welcomed with a cheery "Hello, Miss Fairy Foot," after she had shuffled clumsily down the stairs. A laugh, a gentle humorous suggestion and an imaginative approach keep the child in good humor while the parent gets the idea across. Nagging and picking on a child merely make him rebellious or resentful, and when a child is in this mood very little, if anything, can be accomplished.

Tasks and chores can be a pleasant part of a child's day when they are motivated by parents who use their imaginations to guide the child's attitude toward them. Johnny, who is playing cowboy in the back yard, may be disturbed if mother interrupts his play with an abrupt order, "Johnny, stop whatever you're doing and run to the store for a loaf of bread. We need it for lunch."

A mother who is aware of her child's cowboy interests may walk out into the yard, admire the shorthorns and give Johnny a friendly pat, "My you're working hard. You're the best cowboy in the state of Texas. It looks as if you'll be through here in time to ride down to the village store and get some supplies before noon."

Instead of a task, this becomes a friendly cowboy jaunt, and Johnny welcomes the chance to carry home not only a loaf of bread, but a heavy knapsack full of groceries as well.

Suggesting that the young captain cruise down to the supply dock and get a loaf of bread can send him happily on this errand, and he will probably ask to bring a cargo of supplies.

"How would you like to be Louie, the vegetable man, and go shopping in the market?" is a question that invites creative fun for girls as well as boys. When the child returns with the groceries, a mother may add to the enjoyment by buying and bargaining with Louie as he shows her the vegetables. "What fine looking carrots you have, Louie! How much are they?"

Louie, catching the fun of bargaining, holds the carrots proudly and says, "One dollar a bunch!"

"My, my," says mother, handing Louie an imaginary dollar, "everything is expensive these days, but we do need carrots!"

A big basket and a bright red hood may send a little girl merrily on her way to a nearby store in character of Little Red Riding Hood. Again, going to the jungle bazaar to get milk and butter and eggs may be pleasant for the child who awakened as Sambo and had pancakes for breakfast.

Daily tasks, like mowing the lawn, sweeping the sidewalks, and raking the yard, can be enjoyable when children make use of creative thinking. A few words from mother or father may work like magic in turning a lawn mower into a large mowing machine or into a high-powered combine moving across the wheat fields of Montana. Johnny maneuvering the lawn mower may suddenly become the owner of a large ranch, or he may become a hired man or a chief engineer operating a new machine, or if he prefers he may be a team of work-horses pulling the machine around the alfalfa field. He may want to be a gardener who takes great pride in keeping his own yard as neat and clean as the city park.

Many a child will thoroughly enjoy weeding and caring for a garden when he becomes a farmer working on his eighty-acre farm.

Washing dishes, sweeping the floor, making beds, and dusting need not be dull and uninteresting tasks. If mother will find a small white apron and perhaps a headdress for her daughter Ann and suggest that Ann be Rosie the cleaning lady or Bridget the maid, she will see how easily work can turn into play. Giving a word of praise to Bridget when any task has been nicely done is important for an appreciative mother to remember. "Sure, and the kitchen's pretty as a picture, Bridget. I couldn't have cleaned it better myself."

And if mother surveying the kitchen notices crumbs on the floor and says, "Look Bridget; sure and the leprechauns are playin' tricks on you," Bridget will very likely get the broom and with a smile will start sweeping up the crumbs.

On days when mother is sick, creative dramatics may be especially helpful. It is surprising what a small white towel fastened over a little girl's head and a suggestion that she be a hospital nurse can do for both the child and mother on a day when mother has to be in bed. The nurse may proudly take the responsibility of the entire household. She will attend to her mother's requests with professional importance. She will find joy in surprising her patient with breakfast and luncheon trays, in arranging flowers in the room, and in answering the telephone and saying efficiently, "I'm sorry, Mrs. Smith is ill today. Who is this calling please? Do you wish to leave a message?"

When a child's thinking becomes creative at the beginning of the day, a mother finds that it often carries through into routine activities. Taking a bath becomes something more than a daily scrubbing to the young captain who has a fleet of ships and an aircraft carrier floating in the harbor beside him. "Rub-a-dub-dub, three men in a tub" keeps a little child soaking for a long time as he delights in being the butcher and the baker and the candlestick-maker.

A little girl of eight years had such a good time playing with two toy boats in her bath that she made up the following rhyme after she was out of the tub:

> I saw a little tug boat
> Out upon the sound.
> It was pulling a great big steamer
> Around and around.
> The great big steamer seemed to say,
>   "I want to go to Elliott Bay
>   But I don't want the people to see
>   A little tug boat pulling me."

A child looks forward to helping with the evening meal when mother encourages his creative ideas. A girl likes to set the table and make it attractive with surprises and flower arrangements. She enjoys being a waitress, setting the table properly, and serving the meal to the family to show that she knows exactly how every-thing should be done. A boy may like to be a waiter or a steward or a chef.

A teen-aged girl may hurry home from school two or three evenings each week to prepare the family dinner if the family encourages and appreciates her efforts. A word or two of praise serves to stimulate her imagination and to develop her ingenuity.

There should be time in every child's day for solitude—for quiet thinking and for dreaming. Poetry, literature, and past experiences many times motivate delightful flights of the imagination. A. A. Milne's poem, "Halfway Down," has encouraged many a young child to have all sorts of interesting thoughts while playing alone—

Halfway down the stairs
Is a Stair
Where I sit.
There isn't any
Other Stair
Quite like
It.
I'm not at the bottom,
I'm not at the top;
So this is the Stair
Where
I always
Stop.

.   .   .   .   .

Halfway up the stairs
Isn't up,
And isn't down.
It isn't in the nursery,
It isn't in the town.
And all sorts of funny thoughts
Run round my head:
"It isn't really
Anywhere!
It's somewhere else
Instead!"[1]

Going to bed is another everyday happening that can be made pleasant and relaxing by the use of creative dramatics. Stories may be told and read to children at bedtime. Or, mother or father may become an audience, an attentive listener, encouraging the child to tell about his daily experiences. "Tell me about today," or "Was this a good day or a mixed-up day?" may be enough to kindle the child's thinking. As he tells about the fun he has had or about the trouble he has had with the boy next door, these experiences live again for him. Every child needs to have someone to listen to him. He needs to have time to talk. He needs to share his dreams and

---

[1] Reprinted from *When We Were Very Young*, by A. A. Milne, published and copyrighted 1924 by E. P. Dutton & Co., Inc., New York.

his troubles with an understanding mother or father or grownup friend.

After the child has told his stories and released his innermost feelings, a wise parent enriches the child's thinking with new ideas and impressions. He remembers the child's interests. He may tell first-hand experiences or stories from literature that are particularly meaningful to the child at this time. He may share poetry that he likes, or he may set the child to wondering about distant lands or about the greatness of the universe. Together they may travel on imaginary journeys to South Africa, or to the far-away moon or to a bright star that they can see from the bedroom window. Five or ten minutes spent in this way at the end of the day open new worlds of thinking to a growing child, and it builds a closer relationship between the child and his parent.

WORK CAN BE FUN

If the dramatic instinct is encouraged within the child day after day, he will not only learn to perform the most tedious tasks but will develop a spirit of responsibility toward their continued performance. Some parents may begin to wonder if we are doing the right thing for the child in making work seem like play, for as he grows older he will find it necessary to perform real work. If we remember that our attitude toward everything we do depends entirely on the spirit with which we set about to do it, we will see the value in helping a child to develop a friendly spirit toward something that needs to be done. We must remember, too, that a steady diet of mere amusement becomes exceedingly tiresome, whereas the work which one cares for may be refreshing and stimulating. It would seem important from this standpoint to help children develop a spirit of attack toward work such as will bring it into a realm of interest. If we can help children carry their imaginations into their work as well as into their play, we will go far in building attitudes which will serve children well throughout life.

PREPARING FOR NEW EXPERIENCES

Through the medium of creative play a mother can prepare a child for new experiences which are a vital part of his growing-up days. Together they create the new situation and make it as realistic as possible. They act it out again and again until the child feels confident and secure when he encounters the situation in reality.

A young child can be prepared for a first trip to the dentist, for going to kindergarten on the very first day, for staying overnight with Aunt Cecelia, for answering the telephone when mother is busy, for going to Bobby's birthday party without mother, and for other experiences which the mother realizes are new and may involve insecurity.

Going to the store by herself is a great responsibility for five-year-old Nancy who has always gone before with mother or father or friends. A wise mother will help Nancy by playing store with her several times before she permits the child to go alone. Playing store will be pleasant, and it will be played like a game with mother being careful to see that Nancy is learning exactly what to do. On a day when mother and Nancy return from the store, mother may put the groceries on the table and say, "Wouldn't it be fun to play store? I'll be Mr. Boggs, and you come to buy groceries from me."

However, mother may prefer to play store on a morning just before she and Nancy go shopping, in order that Nancy will be more observant when they do go. Mother may find that a direct question will motivate a desire for playing. She may arouse a strong interest by asking, "Wouldn't you like to go to the store alone sometime and buy a surprise for us?" Or, it is more likely that the motivation may come from Nancy herself when she asks to go to the store to buy an ice cream cone or some candy.

Mother will probably say, "Let's play store, and you come to buy an ice cream cone from Mr. Boggs. Our kitchen will be Mr. Boggs' store."

Mother may open the cupboard doors to suggest the grocery shelves, and she may ask Nancy to help push the kitchen table into the center of the room so that they may use it for the counter. Mother will explain to Nancy that the kitchen door is the door to the store. She will remind her that it is not necessary to knock on the door of the store before entering. To make the situation meaningful, Nancy may wear her hat and coat and carry her purse, just as she will when she goes to Mr. Boggs' store.

Mother as Mr. Boggs may be arranging the grocery shelves as Nancy enters. "Good morning, Nancy," Mr. Boggs will say. "What would you like to buy today?"

Nancy may think that playing store is funny and she may laugh, or she may say, "I don't know."

Mr. Boggs, very much in character, will say, "Did you want a loaf of bread? Maybe your mother wants a pound of butter or some cookies?"

After several suggestions from Mr. Boggs, Nancy will undoubtedly remember. "I want an ice cream cone, please."

Mr. Boggs in pantomime will pick up a make-believe cone and ice cream dipper. "Do you want strawberry or vanilla, Nancy?"

"Strawberry," Nancy will probably answer.

Mr. Boggs will hand her the cone when it is ready. "There you are, Nancy. That will be five pennies."

Nancy may give Mr. Boggs the money, or she may hesitate. Mr. Boggs may ask, "Do you have a nickel, Nancy?"

If Nancy is hesitant about giving him the money, he may ask, "May I see if you have five pennies in your purse, please?"

Nancy may hand him the purse, or she may decide to give him the money herself.

"Thank you, Nancy," he will say. "Come back again someday."

During the first playing, mother will find out whether or not Nancy is ready to go to the store alone, and she will learn in what ways she can help her. If Nancy is eager to play store again, mother will offer a positive suggestion. "Mr. Boggs is a busy storekeeper. Be sure you know what you are going to buy when you go to the store."

The second time they play, Nancy will be much more confident, and mother can see how helpful creative playing can be. After they have played two or three times, mother will introduce new situations which might prove to be problems to Nancy.

What will Nancy do if the door to the store is difficult to open? Rather than have Nancy come crying all the way home because she couldn't get in, mother will prepare her for this possibility as they create this scene together.

If other customers in the store get in line ahead of Nancy while she is waiting to pay for her groceries, what will she do? Mother being many different customers hurrying to the counter bewilders Nancy. When mother sees that Nancy does not know what to do to meet this situation, she will break character, and she and Nancy will discuss the problem. When they arrive at a solution which is satisfactory to Nancy, they will play it again. This time when mother is a busy lady going in front of Nancy with her groceries, Nancy will say, "Excuse me, please. I have been waiting to pay Mr. Boggs for a long time. I think I should pay him now."

Mother, in character, says, "Excuse me, little girl. I didn't notice you. You *are* ahead of me."

After playing this situation several times, Nancy is prepared to meet it in reality when it occurs. When a mother uses this medium, she helps her child with situations which are difficult problems as she faces them alone.

A little girl, nine years old, had been so well prepared for a tonsillectomy by the use of creative playing that she could hardly wait for the day when it was time for her operation. When she arrived at the hospital, the room and the bed and the nurses were familiar to her. She had been the doctor wearing a white jacket so many times when she had played at home that she was not afraid when the real doctor came into her room. She was familiar with the stethoscope and with the careful examination that the doctor made of her nose and throat. Having her temperature taken and being wheeled into surgery where she was given an anesthetic were experiences that she had acted out so often with mother that she anticipated rather than feared them. At home they had created a scene in which she would have difficulty in speaking after the operation, and when the little girl experienced this feeling in reality she had no anxiety or fear about her discomfort.

Situations acted out together by the child and his parent enable the child to solve problems logically, to develop independence, and to express his feelings with ease and confidence. An older child can be prepared to meet such experiences as traveling alone on a plane or a train or a bus, being a guest at a luncheon and accepting an award, acknowledging an introduction, escorting a guest to a formal party for the first time, or going to the office to discuss a problem with the school principal.

MEETING EMOTIONAL SITUATIONS

Every child in his growing-up years experiences strong emotional situations which become high or low moments in his living. A mother can help a child to meet emotional problems in much the same way as she prepares him to meet new situations; however, she must be alert to recognize the right time for offering her help. This is particularly important for a mother to remember when her child reaches the sensitive adolescent years.

A fourteen-year-old boy who has to give a report may suddenly exclaim at the breakfast table, "I hate school. I've never liked to give speeches anyway!"

If the child's mother understands this emotional outburst, she will try to get him to talk about the report. After they have discussed the situation, they may act it out once or twice or until the child feels emotionally secure about giving the report.

A mother who knows that her seventeen-year-old daughter has been nominated for high school president will watch for an opportunity whereby she may be of real help to her. The girl may be so emotionally disturbed on the evening before the election that she will say, "I'm going to bed early tonight. I can't do anything until the election is over."

The mother will recognize this as the time when her daughter is ready to release the many fears that have been tormenting her. They will discuss the election thoroughly and will consider several possible outcomes. When the mother feels that her daughter is ready, they will first create a scene in which the daughter was victorious. The living room will become the assembly hall with the chairs and stage arranged as realistically as possible. Mother will be the retiring president who announces the outcome of the election and introduces the newly elected president. The girl will stand and give a short speech, for she will have discussed with mother what is important for her to say. Together they will act out this scene until the girl's thinking becomes flexible, and she speaks with assurance. When the mother feels that her daughter is prepared for this particular situation, they will create and play a scene in which the girl has been defeated in the election. In a comparatively short time, probably no longer than fifteen minutes, the mother will have helped to prepare the girl to meet one of the most meaningful days in her life.

One family acted out a dramatic situation while they were driving home from a basketball game. When the parents learned that their son Dick was not going to the formal junior dance because he was afraid to invite a girl to go with him, the mother realized that she could help Dick with his problem. The mother and father talked about the significance of the occasion, and the father recalled a similar dance he had enjoyed when he was in high school. After a few minutes, Dick explained that he would like to invite Mary Brown but that he didn't want to call her on the telephone for fear that her father or mother might answer his call. As they rode along in the car, the family discussed the situation in detail.

The father entered into the spirit of the playing, and he readily became Mr. Brown, who was the first person to answer Dick's call. When Dick had talked to Mr. Brown several times, they acted out a scene in which Mrs. Brown answered the phone. At first mother was Mrs. Brown, and later she became Mary. Dick acted out the telephone scene with Mary three times. When he called her the first time, Mary accepted his invitation graciously. The second time Mary declined, for she had already been invited to go to the same dance, and the third time she thanked Dick and invited him to come to her home for dinner on the evening of the dance. By the time they had reached home Dick was ready to meet his problem, and he immediately went to the telephone and made his call.

CREATIVE PLAY AT HOME

Creative playing at home can be the most fun of all, for it is spirited, lively, spontaneous play. A wise mother will endeavor to turn her child's idle play toward creative pathways. This she may do by suggesting ideas to the child, by encouraging his own original ideas, and by providing him with objects or material that will quicken his own thinking. A child must have freedom in his play if he is to develop his creative power. A parent will block rather than free a child's thinking if he attempts to direct the child's play too closely.

One young mother who was late to a meeting explained her tardiness by telling the others that she had been detained in a department store elevator. Her young son, David, indoors on a drizzly day, had become fascinated with her suggestion that he be an elevator man. He had commandeered the use of a wardrobe with a sliding door, and he eventually succeeded in getting his mother as a passenger. The mother, huddled under the clothes in the closet, named the floor where she wanted to get out, but she had an independent and solicitous elevator man. He said that they were remodeling the fifth floor, so he didn't stop there. The fourth floor was having a sale, and it was too crowded for him to open the door. He explained that there was nothing but furniture on the third floor, so he went on to second. Since there were no toys on the second floor, he went straight down to the main floor, but so many people were waiting to get on the elevator that David's mother didn't have a chance to get off until he finally let her off in the basement. After his mother had gone, David spent the rest of the morning operating the elevator for imaginary shoppers. He delighted in answering questions and in volunteering information as he opened and closed the sliding door for imaginary customers.

Another young lad found great satisfaction in being a garage man parking imaginary cars. Rickie's mother, who was entertaining at tea, wanted to keep him happily occupied during the afternoon, and when the guests started arriving she said quite casually, "Whom will we get to park all the cars this afternoon?" This suggestion was enough for Rickie's fast-growing imagination. Every time a car drove up in front of his house, he pretended to drive it into the driveway and to park it in perfect order, using great care not to scratch or bump the fenders.

When a child complains, "What can I play? There's nothing to do around here," a parent will realize the importance of firing the child's imagination until he rouses himself into action. An attic trunk that contains discarded clothes or costumes may be just the thing to help a young lad become a noble king or a brave knight or a bold pirate or an outlaw. It may help a young girl become a beautiful queen or a lovely princess or a wicked old witch or an old beggar woman.

An old blanket thrown over the clothesline and fastened down on either side may become a tepee or a long house for an eight- or nine-year-old boy who quickly becomes Chief Running Wolf. He may spend most of the summer playing under the Indian tent, eating and sleeping in the character of an Indian chief whenever he is permitted to do so. His friends and playmates may be young warriors or Indian maidens or squaws coming daily to a council meeting or a pow-wow or a harvest festival.

A flag on a stick may mark the spot where secret treasure is buried for a young boy whose thinking has been sharpened until he becomes a pirate or a robber or a plunderer or a mutineer. A crown of leaves and flowers may set a little girl to dancing like a princess or a dryad or a fairy queen.

When a child asks if he may play store and sell lemonade on the street corner, a wise mother will not only encourage this idea but will be helpful with suggestions and will take time to enjoy buying a refreshing drink from the young storekeeper.

Having a pet show, planning a circus, building a hide-out, making a throne, having a doll's birthday party, climbing to a lookout tower in an apple tree are a few of the many ideas which may spring up in a child's mind when he starts thinking creatively. These ideas should be encouraged by a mother who strives to develop the natural creative impulse within the child and who wants to provide a wholesome release for a child's energy and strong inner feelings. By daily experiences a child gradually learns to think for himself. He may soon learn to meet disappointment with a substitute plan. If a downpour of rain puts an end to a family picnic, he may be able to plan a different kind of picnic around the living room fireplace or a scavenger hunt throughout the entire household for the family to enjoy.

As she encourages dramatic playing, a mother will find that she, too, becomes more creative in her thinking. Once she starts exercising her imagination, she will discover many ways for using creative dramatics at home. She will find it comparatively easy and will make use of it often, once she sees creative magic working its way into the hearts and minds of children.

Chapter IX

CREATIVE DRAMATICS IN COMMUNITY PROGRAMS

Man cannot live by bread alone.

If creative dramatics did nothing more in a community than keep alive the tales of its "old timers" for each new generation of boys and girls, it would well justify its unique place in community living. Every community, large or small, has its quota of old pioneers who dearly love an audience for the true tales they can tell of earlier days when America was young. Many of these stories have been handed down from pioneers before them, while others are personal memories of long, full lives. What experience could be more thrilling for an American youngster than to listen to an "old timer" spin exciting yarns of experiences that actually happened when "we came to the Oregon territory in a prairie schooner," and then for the youngster to join with his neighbors and friends in reliving these eventful incidents! Creative dramatics has brought many such experiences to boys and girls in small communities, and thus has increased their awareness of the colorful past.

But creative dramatics has gone even further in enriching community life for growing children; it has proved itself a strong factor in influencing a child's social, moral, and spiritual development. It can strengthen the very fabric of children's lives by bringing them to an appreciation of religion as they reconstruct Bible stories during an active Sunday School hour. It can help children to appreciate their great heritage in art and beauty, and it can introduce boys and girls to literature in a way that leads them thoroughly to enjoy reading good books in community libraries.

While boys and girls laugh and play together, as they share ideas and participate in creative activity, they experience the very fundamentals of democratic living. They form strong friendships, and they become good neighbors. When children are guided into understanding their heritage, they learn to appreciate and honor their American traditions. Since a large percentage of our country's population is rural, creative dramatics is an effective way of bringing the beauty and culture of the world to the doorsteps of children living in small country towns and industrial settlements.

Habits and attitudes which a child forms in his early years have a strong and lasting effect on the way in which he lives and grows to adulthood. What a child does with his after-school time, his Saturdays, and his Sundays, should be a matter of concern to parents and community leaders, for a child's daily living and person-to-person relationships go far in guiding him into being the kind of individual he becomes. The habit of going to Sunday School, of going to the library, of going to a museum, and of participating in other desirable community activities will become second nature to the child who finds these experiences satisfying and friendly. Creative dramatics can make community living vital for young people in both large cities and small towns by encouraging boys and girls to become active participants in experiences which are interesting to them. Creative dramatics is a magical means of enlarging a child's interests, of developing his curiosity in many directions, and of encouraging his finest creative expression.

CREATIVE DRAMATICS IN RELIGIOUS EDUCATION

On earth peace, good will toward men.

Drama has its beginnings in religious worship. Greek drama originated in the religious dances that interpreted the worship of Dionysus, the god of fertility, and the rebirth of the seasons.

In a similar manner, the drama of the Middle Ages developed from the liturgy of the medieval church. In order that the masses of uneducated worshipers might better understand the meaning of the Scriptures, the priests acted out simple little scenes. The priests became Biblical characters reliving happenings which were recorded in the Scriptures. Thus the people of the day, as they reverently watched scenes unfolding before their eyes, were impressed with the significance of the story of the birth of Christ, of the dialogue between the angel and the three Marys at the tomb on Easter morning, of the Epiphany, and of other Biblical episodes which were brought before them in simple, dramatic form. The mystery plays which developed at this time gradually introduced characters which were not in the scriptures to heighten the dramatic action and to clarify the dialogue, until at length the whole story of the life of Christ was enacted in one complete cycle. As these plays became more elaborate, and as the crowds of people who came to the churches to see them grew in numbers, the plays were finally staged out of doors in the church yards. At last, however, the clergy ceased to be the actors, and the plays were taken over by members of the guilds, who presented them in the towns.

The profound influence of Christianity during the Middle Ages in building a faith which unified and civilized its people is of great significance today. It emphasizes the role that religion can play in forming patterns of understanding, peace, and brotherly kindness in human lives. Like the drama of medieval days, creative dramatics can be a potent force in a child's religious education. Whereas the religious drama of earlier years was presented by the clergy for the

benefit of worshipers, old and young alike, creative dramatics in
the Sunday School encourages the children themselves to become
the Biblical characters, reliving Bible stories not for an audience,
but solely for the enjoyment and the values which they gain from
the experience.

Influencing Religious Growth.   When Bible stories, which are the
finest examples of basic truths, are brought to life by boys and
girls who reconstruct them in a dramatic way, the experience indirectly guides their living. When children work intently to create
dramatic scenes from material found in the Scriptures and base
their dramatizations on many different Biblical stories—parables,
legends, histories, biographies, sermons, songs, letters, and fables—
it is understandable that their religious concepts will be enlarged
and the Bible will take on new meaning for them. Once a Biblical
characterization is adequately created by children it becomes a living power, and a child participating in the experience is better able
to grasp the spiritual thought behind the concrete exemplification.

Active participation in dramatizing many Bible stories gives a
child an opportunity to explore the emotional content of many
different characters and to understand the character's position in a
situation which closely parallels reality. When a child acts out the
story of the "Good Samaritan" and identifies himself with the kindness and goodness of this worthy character, he vicariously experiences charity and generosity. It is equally important, however,
for him to experience the feelings of the villainous robber who set
upon the victim, to become the man who went down from Jerusalem
to Jericho and fell among thieves, and to identify himself with
characters such as Pharaoh, Goliath, and Judas. By experiencing a
variety of emotional characterizations, a child will learn to distin-
guish between destructive and constructive emotions, and he will
find this experience of value in personal application.

Creative dramatics contributes to a gradual deepening of spiritual consciousness within a child when he is given opportunities to
act out scenes that emphasize the manifestations of a supreme

power. Young children delight in dramatic play centering around the wonder of nature. At the slightest suggestion they become small seeds growing into plants and blossoming into many different kinds of flowers. They readily become the sun, the wind, the rain, and the stars, and each one imagines and interprets these powers in his own way. An older child makes wonderful use of his imagination as he re-enacts scenes which are characterized by "signs and wonders and mighty works." The vision of Moses revealed by the burning bush, the Israelites being guided by a pillar of a cloud and a pillar of fire, the deliverance of the people of Israel as the waters of the sea divide and make a pathway before them, the sending of quails and manna, the handwriting on the wall, and the experiences of Daniel in the lion's den are among the many dramatic and vivid happenings which children have created with thorough satisfaction.

Encouraging Sunday School Attendance.   Belonging to a Sunday School is an experience that should be a part of every child's life. Many children attend Sunday School regularly and willingly, other children attend occasionally and perhaps reluctantly. A goodly number attend at Christmas time and on Easter Sunday, but there are many teen-aged boys and girls in communities today who have yet to attend Sunday services. It has been estimated that the average attendance of the child who does go to Sunday School is for a period of four years. When one considers that a child could start when he is four or five years of age and continue until he is ready for college, or for approximately fourteen years, it becomes a real challenge to make Sunday School programs dynamic enough to encourage children of all ages to attend over a longer span of years. If a boy or girl should attend Sunday School for a period of twelve or fourteen years, he would spend well over five hundred hours in religious training.

Creative dramatics has proved to be effective in bringing boys and girls of all ages to Sunday School of their own accord, since it offers a dynamic program capable of satisfying the child's constant desire for self-expression and of providing an active participation which inevitably makes children feel that the service belongs to them. In many Sunday Schools where creative dramatics has been introduced, the attendance has not only increased, but the regularity with which children attend has been noticeably improved. The very fact that religious education is concentrated into one hour on Sunday morning emphasizes the importance of using a force as effective as creative dramatics to make religion meaningful for children. Significant developments can result from a one-hour period each week when the experiences are planned so that they reach within the child and affect his thinking and feeling.

Sunday School Teacher as Leader.   When a Sunday School teacher introduces creative dramatics, she will go a step further in her regular preparation as she plans how she will guide her class into dramatizing the story or lesson material which she intends to use. If a teacher plans to use the dramatic story wherein Pharaoh's daughter finds the baby Moses hidden in a small basket along the river bank, at the time when King Pharaoh had commanded that all Israelite boy babies be thrown into the River Nile, she will first make certain that she can present the story vividly. She will then consider the characterizations of Miriam, Miriam's mother, the princess, and her attendants, in order that she may lead the class into purposeful pantomime and characterizations. She will reflect on several possible scenes of action which will enable her to ask stimulating questions to guide a class into informal playing within a one-hour period. A teacher will realize that beginning dramatizations will be somewhat crude, but, as the children grow in their ability to characterize, and as she gains confidence in leadership, dramatizations will gradually become more powerful and satisfying. After several experiences, the children and the teacher will see opportunities for expanding short incidents into dramatic scenes, and the children will gradually feel free to elaborate on the dialogue.

A Sunday School teacher may use carefully planned and graded lessons, or she may use the Bible as her guide. In either event, she will strive for variety in the way in which she motivates an interest in each new lesson. If she tells a story one Sunday, she may read directly from the Scriptures on the following Sunday. Occasionally, she may have the children read the lesson, or she may use pictures which clearly tell a story. If colored slides or moving pictures are available, they may be used to arouse a strong interest. A letter from a missionary, a hymn, architecture or woodcarving within the church, an act of kindness, and other resourceful material will be used frequently to lead children into specific Biblical happenings or related experiences.

After a story has been presented, the teacher will guide the children into dramatizing it in the same way that a leader works with children in other creative dramatic situations.

Kindergarten and Primary Departments.   Teachers in the nursery school, in the kindergarten, and in primary departments will lead little children into dramatic play activity based directly on the lessons for the day. Since the imaginative play of young children is closely related to reality and is concerned with familiar and definite things, a teacher will help them to grasp an understanding of Creation by encouraging them to be animals, birds, trees, flowers, and other growing things in a variety of situations.

The significance of Old Testament teachings will probably have the greatest meaning for young children when they are guided into dramatic play centering around family life, such as showing through pantomime the many different ways in which they help mother, father, sisters, brothers, and neighbors. Make-believe based on sharing, thinking of others, remembering kindnesses, making decisions, following "laws," such as necessary rules and routines, will be useful in helping a young child to understand Christian ways of living. The fellowship of neighborliness may be dramatized by encouraging children to live together as good neighbors in a make-believe town or along a friendly street that may be quickly arranged by the use of chairs and benches. Children will be guided into acting out housekeeping activities and ways of neighborly living within the community either as one large group or as individual families.

Among the many activities that young children enjoy pretending will be that of going to church on a Sunday morning, during which they will be guided into conducting services in their own way.

Incidents and episodes from the childhood of Jesus will provide understandable situations for primary groups to play. Identifying themselves with shepherds, fishermen, herdsmen, and tillers of the soil will be pleasant experiences for little folks and will give them something of an idea of life in Biblical times.

Many of the songs, stories, and verse that are supplied with the lesson material will furnish excellent opportunities for group play and pantomime. Being soldiers, marching for peace, while they sing "Onward Christian Soldiers" will be worthwhile for kindergarten and primary groups. Playing the story of Noah and the ark has a strong appeal for children of all ages. When older children identify themselves with the characters of Noah and the members of his family, they experience great concern over the significance of the coming flood, and they work industriously to carry out explicit orders which have been given to Noah. Young children enjoy the pantomime of building the ark and feeling the excitement which comes when the rain begins to fall. They find pleasure in being the many different animals, entering the ark in twos. Seven- and eight-year-olds like to be Noah and his sons watching the rain for forty days. When make-believe becomes "real" for them, they express themselves freely in dialogue as they talk together for forty days about why God has sent the flood. They enjoy the dramatic action which comes with the abating of the waters, with the sending forth of a dove, and with the appearance of a great rainbow in the clouds.

Junior and Senior Departments.   The hundreds of stories in the Bible which contribute to the one great story of God afford rich experiences for older boys and girls to reconstruct creatively. Since a Sunday School teacher who is working with older children is concerned with giving them an over-all knowledge of what the Bible is and what it means to them, she will guide them into dramatizations wherein they become kings and prophets, humble followers, good and evil people, wise and mighty rulers, conquerors, traitors and disciples. Stories from the lives of Joseph and his brothers, stirring incidents which occurred during the conquest of the Promised Land, including the story of the two spies, crossing the River Jordan, Joshua directing the siege against Jericho, and incidents from the lives of Achan, Gideon, Samson, Ruth, Samuel, David, and Solomon have been enjoyed by boys and girls in both junior and senior departments.

New Testament teachings have significance for boys and girls when they are guided into becoming apostles traveling throughout the Roman Empire spreading Christianity in countless different ways.

Real life situations will be used for dramatizations from time to time to help children see what they may do to participate in good ways of living. By acting out short scenes from actual happenings, a situation comes alive with such force that children feel a responsibility toward the situation and an urgent need to do something to improve it. An alert teacher will recognize material of this kind in current reading, in local happenings, in newspaper or magazine articles which describe the plight of people in other countries, in letters from families living in Displaced Persons' Camps, in newsreels which picture suffering, in radio reports from flood, tornado, fire, or other disaster areas, in first-hand accounts from missionaries, and from conversations or other incidents that not only lend themselves to dramatization but indirectly teach good neighborliness and brotherhood.

When Sunday School lessons are planned around a certain theme, such as The Life of Christ, The Bible, or The Church, the teacher will lead her students into dramatizations which are closely related to the major emphasis of study. If, for instance, a class is considering the development of the Church, they would benefit from dramatizing solemn and telling scenes from medieval days when the construction of cathedrals was first begun. Exploring and recreating the history of music in the Church would enhance the children's appreciation of the beauty that is so integral a part of religious education.

Reliving the story of the first Christmas, which is beautifully told in the second chapter of St. Luke, is an experience in which every child should participate, for the interest which children have in seeing a play presented by others is not half so great as that which comes with being a part of a play. The stirring drama of Easter morning will be another impressive event for children to recreate. There is literally no end to the possibilities for informal dramatizations within the church school, once a teacher increases her awareness of such opportunities. Wordsworth, in his "Ode on the Intimations of Immortality," recognized the broad creative world of childhood when he said:

> See at his feet some little plan or chart,
> Some fragment of his dream of human life,
> Shaped by himself with newly learned art;
> A wedding or a festival
> A mourning or a funeral.

In Sunday Schools, Synagogues, and Bible Camps where creative dramatics has been introduced, children have responded with sincere enthusiasm to the opportunity to act out religious material. When dramatic play which has been enjoyed by children throughout the ages is introduced into religious worship and children are repeatedly guided into good ways of living, they gradually learn to identify themselves with religion in reality. When they experience the serenity and deep satisfaction that comes from doing for others, they slowly but surely build toward peace.

CREATIVE DRAMATICS IN MUSEUMS

A thing of beauty is a joy forever.

—JOHN KEATS

"They are imitations, lies, falsehoods. They have no souls—they only pretend," said the stately Dresden mirror.

"Oh dear," said August anxiously. "If Hirschvogel would only talk." The museum visitor had pulled open the auditorium door, expecting to find another gallery. Instead she found herself in the land of make-believe, in a quaint curiosity shop where pieces of bric-a-brac were all in motion. The story she witnessed was "The Nürnberg Stove," which a group of nine-year-olds were bringing to life.

A facsimile of a picturesque Nürnberg House that had stood in a children's case at the museum had been the inspiration for the story. The children had seen a moving-picture acquainting them with the beauty of Nürnberg's countryside and showing local people at work in many different ways. In the museum they had seen the work of many great artists. Every Saturday morning for several weeks, while the boys and girls played this story, they felt that they were in Nürnberg, and they learned with August that "fleeting mortal lives pass so soon.—Only we endure, we the things that the human brain creates. So in us our masters being dead, yet may speak and live."

Building Appreciation for Art and Beauty.   Impressive dramatic experiences such as this are of real value in opening up a new world of art and beauty for children. When boys and girls dramatize material based on works of art, they are brought into an appreciation of their cultural heritage in a way which is both understandable and inspirational to them. In a small community where there is no museum of art, it is quite possible that paintings by American artists or fine reproductions of great masterpieces will be found in a church, a school auditorium, or a community hall. Some of the finest paintings are of the Nativity and other religious subjects, and good reproductions of old paintings may be used effectively in leading children to an interest in art. Stained glass windows, Gothic arches, tapestries, woodcarving, hand-wrought articles, or other creative handiwork may be found in a community when a leader is desirous of correlating creative dramatics with art.

Quite frequently when children are taken through an art museum in a city there is a guide, a teacher, or a parent with them who reads the information which accompanies each painting. They hear the title and the name of the artist, or they listen to an explanation which is read concerning a piece of statuary or other art objects. When a child sees a museum in this way, the experience is generally not stimulating enough to impress him with the significance nor the beauty of the art which is exhibited there. How much more meaningful all art becomes for a child who, on the other hand, is guided through a dramatic experience in which he becomes Michelangelo living in Florence in the fifteenth century, patiently learning the art of sculpturing, chiseling a great statue of David and Goliath, and later working deftly with his brush, painting the ceiling of the Sistine Chapel.

By identifying himself with Michelangelo, Leonardo da Vinci, Raphael, Botticelli, and other great artists and craftsmen in spirited, dramatic situations, a child gains an insight into mankind's universal desire for lofty expression, and he begins better to understand his own creative impulses. The empathic response which a child experiences as he becomes an artist, expressing his innermost thoughts and feelings on imaginary canvas, frequently transfers into reality, and a child will then freely express his own feeling of beauty through painting, sketching, clay modeling, woodcarving, writing, dancing, or in other creative ways. When a child repeatedly identifies himself with experiences closely related to art, his appreciation for beauty is strengthened, and he seeks out museums, galleries, paintings, and works of art for himself.

A group of young girls who had been in creative dramatics classes planned to visit a Degas exhibit. They were extremely tired from walking when they arrived at the museum, but as they viewed Degas' great paintings they caught a glorious feeling of buoyancy from the dancers in the pictures. The children's clumsy little saddle shoes became ballet slippers, and for several minutes the girls themselves were beautiful dancers skipping about and dancing lightly, completely oblivious of their surroundings or their earlier feelings of tiredness.

Another group of boys and girls thoroughly enjoyed an exhibit of the works of the French impressionists. As they watched the pictures, they felt the warmth of sunshine. Each one experienced an exhilarating feeling of being inside the paintings, surrounded by glowing light as he basked in this unusual beauty.

Interpreting Customs and Cultures of Other Peoples.   Rare collections of art may be the motivation for leading children into dramatizations which will help them to understand many of the customs and cultures of people from other lands. In the Seattle Art Museum, an extensive collection of oriental art has been the center for dramatizations of many old Chinese legends, for observing traditional customs of the Chinese New Year, and for acting out other Chinese and Japanese stories, including "The Wonderful Pear Tree," "The First Chinese Flute," "The Mountain of Jade," "The Dancing Tea Kettle," and "The Tongue-Cut Sparrow." As the children played these stories, they experienced many different ways of living which were traditional with the people of China and Japan. Habits of bowing, removing one's shoes before entering a dwelling, sitting on the floor, eating with chopsticks, and drinking from cups without handles proved of real interest to the children as they wove these and other customs into their plays. By working entirely creatively—that is, without costumes, properties, or scenery—the children's imaginations were constantly exercised. In one of the stories, a group of Chinese children parading with lanterns stopped to show them to an old Chinese grandfather. In describing his imaginary creation, an eight-year-old said, "It is a big blue eye with lightning coming out of it." A girl of the same age described her lantern as "a butterfly of different colors with music in its wings." And a younger child said, "Mine is a brown flower with golden petals drooping from it."

Proudly gracing the entrance of the Seattle Art Museum are several large marble figures that were found at a tomb near Peking some years ago. These beautiful figures hold a singular appeal for almost every child who sees them. In one of the creative dramatics classes that was meeting at the Museum, a group of eight- and nine-year-old children decided to create an original play based on the information that they gathered concerning the animal figures. The children planned their play to begin shortly after the death of Prince Kao Sui, a Ming Prince of the early fifteenth century. Several of the children became Chinese sculptors carving significant animal figures to guard the approach to the Prince's tomb. The "spirit road" which they arranged stretched in a long avenue away from the tomb. On either side they placed large camels which were to provide transportation for the Prince in his new life. The sculptors made large rams for the "spirit road" so that the Prince would be well fed and clothed. They carved two Chinese dogs to bring pleasure, and they placed two noble lions near the tomb to signify the royal estate of Prince Kao Sui. When the sculptors had finished carving the animals, they made strong warriors. Each warrior was equipped with golden bows and arrows studded with pearls and rubies. In their dramatization, the children planned the second act to take place several hundred years later, when a young Chinese Prince was visiting the tomb of his ancestor. While the young Prince was in prayer before the tomb, he dreamed that the "spirit road" came to life and paraded in a great procession before Prince Kao Sui. The rams brought great trays of Chinese delicacies, the dogs entertained with dancing and with tricks, and the warriors demonstrated their great powers of protection. When the festivities were over, the old Prince commanded the two camels to hasten to the end of the "spirit road" and to bring the young Prince to join him. At this moment, the young Prince awakened and hurried away from the tomb, relieved to find that he had only been dreaming. Through their playing, these children had enlarged their concepts of Chinese history and art in a way they would long remember.

Vitalizing History and Tradition.   As one travels across the country and stops in towns, villages, and cities along the way, he is immediately impressed with landmarks he sees—totem poles, hitching posts, old forts, log cabins, statues of historical figures, bronze plaques, and monuments of many different kinds that have been preserved or erected in honor of pioneers whose vision, courage, ideas, and ideals have led them on to great achievement. Together with these monuments, one finds colorful exhibits in national, state, and local museums that also serve as records of American progress. The exhibits may include objects which have been handed down from the days of the early American Indians, articles preserved from the Revolutionary and Civil War periods, relics which mirror pioneer traditions and exploration movements, and evidences of discoveries and inventions that have played an important part in the growth of our country. Many of these treasures have vivid and triumphant stories behind them. Through the imagination and resourcefulness of a leader in making use of such museum pieces, creative dramatics can be one of the most magnetic mediums for bringing children into an appreciation of their human past.

Each community is different from every other community. Each community has something distinctive to offer culturally. The written or traditional history of a town or city offers excellent material for dramatization. When children relive history through creative dramatics and dramatize events that led to the founding and naming of the town in which they live, they develop a community consciousness, a loyalty and a pride that strongly influence their lives.

Every American town is close to the legends of the Indians who once occupied the entire country. Many of the legends that have been handed down from generation to generation are strong in dramatic action. This vigorous material holds a fresh interest for children when it is relived out of doors around a make-believe tepee or a campfire. History and human tradition live for a child who, after seeing an Indian tomahawk, an arrowhead, a wampum belt, or other Indian relics, is guided into becoming a redskin living on the lawless frontier, taking part in ceremonial war dances, observing religious rituals, and adapting himself to the white man's mode of living.

A deerskin suit, deeply fringed and beaded, or a pair of deerskin moccasins, might very well lead a group of children into becoming pioneers along with Daniel Boone, pushing their way through the trackless wilderness to found the settlement of Boonesborough in the wilds of Kentucky.

When a child becomes one of his country's ancestors, encountering hardships and joys with a true pioneer spirit, he experiences a warm companionship with courageous men and women, and he develops an awareness of the grandeur of human achievement. When history and creative dramatics are combined into eventful experiences, they inspire youthful participants with a strong urge to travel forward into new pathways and frontiers of knowledge.

Politics and current events are better understood by children when they participate in elections, make campaign speeches, witness a presidential election, and take part in a vigorous town meeting on issues of peculiar importance one hundred years ago.

The famous collections of dresses worn by the wives of our country's presidents that are on display at the Smithsonian Institution would serve as excellent motivation for leading a group of junior high school girls into eventful historical dramatizations. A series of signal episodes that took place at the White House from colonial days up to the present time could be re-created, wherein the girls would find great satisfaction in identifying themselves with the presidents' wives and imagining themselves to be wearing many of the same costumes they had seen.

Younger children would be intrigued with Charles Lindbergh's small plane, "The Spirit of St. Louis," also on display at the Smithsonian Institution. With the guidance of an imaginative leader, each child could experience the heroic flight across the Atlantic, and he could arrive victoriously at Paris amidst great cheering from a crowd that had been waiting anxiously.

An old flintlock gun, a newspaper carrying the headlines of Abraham Lincoln's election, a spinning wheel, pioneer farming implements, a homesteader's cooking utensils, picks, shovels, and goldpans that were used by early day prospectors, and countless other treasures that have been salvaged from the past, will serve as priceless material for bringing today's children into vivid dramatic experiences that develop a consciousness of our country's rich heritage in its men and women of vision.

Leader in a Museum Program.   If it is convenient for a children's class to meet in an auditorium or study room within a museum, this experience will go far in helping each child to develop the habit of visiting a museum for himself. If such facilities are not available, the class may meet elsewhere within the community, and a leader will arrange to take the children to the museum several times during the period in which they are working on a specific dramatization. It is quite possible that an American painting, such as one of Charlie Russell's Indian or Cowboy subjects, may be loaned to a leader for several weeks when a creative dramatics class is developing an original play based on a picture of this kind.

Many museums are making splendid items available to schools and study groups in large and small communities. Framed and mounted reproductions from many of the old masters are being loaned for a small fee; copies of rare fabrics, films, colored slides, and other authentic materials are being sent to communities upon request; and reproductions of some of the finest religious paintings can be had for very little money. To place some of these works of art along corridors, in churches, and in school rooms to help children develop an appreciation for beauty would go far in improving the quality of their living.

To take advantage of the wealth of museum materials that are available, the demand must come from the community. If one person not only has the imagination to see the need but does something about it, an entire community life can be enriched. University extension courses and adult education classes have been influential in bringing creative dramatics to many children. Parents, Camp Fire and Scout leaders, Sunday School teachers, librarians, and classroom teachers have become enthusiastic creative dramatics leaders once they have learned how to proceed in working with children. Volunteer leaders should be encouraged to pursue cultural programs for children. They should realize from the beginning that they will encounter difficulties and will no doubt be rebuffed often, but they should remember, at the same time, that with persistent effort on their part worthy ideas will grow, for it is always the tall trees that catch the breeze.

CREATIVE DRAMATICS IN LIBRARIES

As for me, I'll take a book.

One of the most gratifying rewards which comes from working with young people is the realization that when they are provided with quality of any kind they soon learn to prefer it over poor or second-rate "stuff" which comes their way. An appetite for good reading and an appreciation of quality in literature can be developed by providing a child with literature experiences that are dynamic enough to satisfy his emotional needs.

Librarians have found creative dramatics of great value both in bringing children to the library and in stimulating their reading. Creative playing provides an active library program for active boys and girls. Instead of sitting quietly and reading when they come to the library, lively children are given a chance to work off their energies as they play stories with zest and enthusiasm. When boys and girls thoroughly enjoy acting out a story, almost every child wants to read the same story in order that he may become better acquainted with storybook persons whom he has learned to know.

A group of children who were content with cheap and sensational reading were invited to the library to watch other boys and girls act out vigorous historical legends. In a comparatively short time, most of the children who had been watching asked for books containing the legends in order that they might read for themselves the same tales that they had watched the other children playing. A few of the boys who had been reluctant to visit the classes asked if they might join in the playing, after they had discovered from three or four meetings that creative dramatics wasn't just a "sissy club," as they had thought.

Reading takes on new meaning for children when they act out worthy stories together. Not only does the story live, but the storybook characters become living people as well. When children create characters, they exercise their imaginations to such a degree that they soon learn to identify themselves strongly with the characters they find in books. As well as reading about *Little Women*, children become Beth and Jo and Laurie, and their many experiences become the children's experiences. They find a warm and understanding friend in *Uncle Remus*, and they learn to enjoy *Mary Poppins* in the same way that Jane and Michael do. They learn to know the *Prince and the Pauper*, for the Prince and the Paupers' heartfelt emotions and desires are akin to those of child readers who have learned to read with their hearts and their minds. When reading becomes meaningful, children are able to travel far beyond the physical barriers of the little town or village where they live. If their surroundings seem drab or commonplace, they can go on glorious adventures and project themselves into a world of beauty through their reading. With books they may find themselves traveling to the ends of the earth, visiting far-away places that hold a special lure for them. History and geography have far greater meaning for children whose creative imaginations have been kindled. They read the pages of history books as they would read an exciting story, and names in a geography become romantic places of adventure. Through active participation in creative dramatics, a child's imagination is exercised to the degree that his reading becomes vital. It is then no longer necessary for him to act out each new story, for he vicariously identifies himself with the characters he meets in his reading. A child who has learned to read in this way will find himself free to fly on a magic carpet over the streets of Bagdad with Sinbad the Sailor, without leaving his own front porch. He will thoroughly enjoy moments of solitude in which he conjures up dreams growing out of all his past experiences. It is during such moments that he nurtures his creative powers.

Building Appreciations for Literature.   Creative dramatics stimulates an interest in literature far beyond the stories used immediately for playing. When boys and girls play a story that has a strong appeal for them, they inquire whether the author has written other stories or books. Children who play "Ali Baba and the Forty Thieves" are generally eager to read "Aladdin" and other fascinating tales of Scheherazade. Children who have a good time being Tom Sawyer whitewashing the fence are not content until they have secured the book and read all of Tom's adventures and perhaps those of Huckleberry Finn. A vigorous playing of "The Elephant's Child" is sure to create an immediate liking for Kipling's rare humor, and a child will not be satisfied until he has read many of the *Just So Stories.* When boys and girls in a junior high school class were creating scenes from "A Midsummer Night's Dream," many of the class members went to the public library to get copies of *Shakespeare's Works.* One of the boys told the librarian about the enjoyable time they were having being artisans preparing a play for the Duke. "From what I knew of Shakespeare," he went on to say, "I always thought of him as a stuffy old man, but I see now how mistaken I was."

Books on handcraft, costuming, music, books on other countries, and historical information hold a strong interest for a child when he finds a real purpose in reading them. In a Saturday morning dramatics class that met for two hours at a public library, the children found great delight in creating scenes from several of Dell McCormick's *Paul Bunyan's Tales.* To make their plays exciting and colorful, the children decided to make Indian drums for sound effects. In the children's room they found books on Indian crafts and books describing primitive musical instruments, which they studied with unusual interest. Coleman's *Drum Book* was widely used by this group, and several children searched carefully through many books for Indian symbols so that their drums would be authentic both in design and color. As their plays grew, their imaginations grew, and they decided to make hand puppets to show the comparative sizes of Bunyan's different characters. The interest in puppetry opened a new field of reading for many children in the group. They were eager to find books on puppets and marionettes. A nine-year-old boy became so interested in the information he found that he built a stage and made puppets for many different stories. Many of the girls asked for books on costuming, and they created interesting and unusual clothes for the puppets. One of the boys learned to use a sewing machine, and he and his friends spent many evenings designing and sewing puppet clothes. One of the boy's fathers helped his son and several neighborhood children to build a Paul Bunyan bunkhouse from discarded cartons. These children created their own plays during the week as they played together in the backyard, and they had many unusual ideas to offer each Saturday morning when they went to the creative dramatics class.

Leader in Library Progam.   A children's librarian, with her rich background in children's literature and her understanding and love for children, should find the experience of leading children into creative dramatics both pleasant and easy. She will be able to acquaint children with many of the finest story book characters who are sitting quietly on the library shelves hidden away behind their bindings. Likewise, she will be in a position to guide children's reading, and she will find that by enthusiastically referring to fictional characters as real people she will invite a strong interest in reading. Instead of saying, "Here is a book that I think you will like," how much more inviting the book becomes when a leader suggests, "How would you like to go to a place where there are peppermint tree trunks and lollypop flowers? There's a young fellow named Pinocchio who is just waiting for someone like you to go with him." Or, "One of my best friends is a girl about as big as you who lives up in the Swiss Alps. Her name is Heidi, and I would like for you to know her tco."

If a Story Hour is being conducted for children at the library, creative dramatics may readily be introduced as the next step beyond listening to a story. After a story such as "The Princess

Who Never Laughed" has been told, a librarian may guide the children into pantomiming only a small part of the story which is strong in dramatic action. In this story each one in the class may become a villager, parading along behind the boy who is carrying an imaginary golden goose. Each character will be encouraged to feel that he is stuck fast to the one ahead and that he is anxiously trying to free himself. Or, a librarian may prefer to have the children work on group characterizations for several meetings. If she should tell the story of "Rumpelstiltskin," she would probably continue by guiding the children into a variety of emotional situations, such as having each one be Rumpelstiltskin as he spins straw into gold, as he dances joyously when he feels that he is to claim the baby for his own, and as he leaves the castle angrily after the queen has guessed his name. On the other hand, if creative dramatics is being introduced as an entirely new program at a library, the librarian or a volunteer leader from the community will proceed in a way very similar to that of the teacher who introduces creative dramatics at school.

One young leader, who organized a creative dramatics class for eighteen boys and girls who lived in a rural area, began the class by showing the children how much fun it was to pantomime and to be characters from Mother Goose. In a comparatively short time the children were creating plays from their favorite stories, and they became so interested in reading that the leader requested good children's books from families living in the vicinity. Many of the older people found children's classics on their bookshelves or in their attics, and they happily contributed books to the creative dramatics class. This leader was also influential in getting a bookmobile to come out to the country once each week, bringing books for both children and adults. The children found great interest in selecting books from the bookmobile and in reading for the specific purpose of finding good stories to bring to life in the Saturday morning classes.

In a similar way, parents and volunteer leaders may establish creative dramatics classes for the children in their neighborhoods and communities, for when children learn thoroughly to enjoy reading good books, they experience a freedom of the mind that gives them a broad outward look and enables them to live more abundantly. Yet not all stories lend themselves to creative dramatics —some are better read than played. The appendix of this book includes many that are especially fine for playing by children at different age levels. Most libraries in even the smallest communities will have a useful number of children's classics.

CREATIVE DRAMATICS IN SOCIAL WORK

Live, let live, help live.
—Ralph Waldo Emerson

There is an area in which a creative dramatics leader and a practitioner of social work, particularly in the group work field, are on common ground. The similarity is the common aim of helping a person, adult or child, to use, conserve, rebuild, or release his or her own strength. Both are fundamentally supportive of the living experience, and both aim toward self-directional, more creative, more comfortable, and therefore happier social functioning. The difference lies in the deeper diagnosis and treatment by the group psychotherapist.

The techniques are similar in that both recognize the needs of children for gratifying experiences, and they both tend to promote the gratification of such needs by a variety of means available to an individual or to a group.

In trying to help the more normal child who is troubled or has personality or emotional problems, the creative dramatics leader works with the child in a group situation, endeavoring to gain his confidence and helping him to gain confidence in himself. When a child participates with others in enjoyable creative play experiences, he may reveal many of the inner tensions that are troubling him. A good creative dramatics leader will encourage this process by indirection. If a child reflects an environmental problem, the leader may recommend to the child's parents an agency that will be able to give them whatever aid they need. If the problem appears to be largely with the child, the leader will diagnose carefully, and, if she understands the point of referral, she can confer with the parents and recommend whatever assistance she feels is best for the individual.

Many children are hiding troubles of many kinds, some serious and some trivial. As a creative dramatics leader wins a child's confidence, many of these problems will gradually be revealed to her. They may be reflected in the child's attitudes toward the leader and toward other children. They may show up in the way he develops a characterization or in his interpretation of the meaning of a story. Again, a child may reveal his inner self through discussions or reactions to situations that he considers funny, sad, good, or bad. Whereas a leader of creative dramatics in most cases aids the child in releasing his tensions, the social worker takes the case a step further in seeing that something remedial is done about it.

In just such a way a creative dramatics leader helped to solve many of twelve-year-old Mike's disturbing problems. The leader was preparing to tell a story to a class of eight- and nine-year-olds on a Saturday morning, when the door to the auditorium suddenly opened. A twelve-year-old boy stood on the threshold in a defiant manner. As he remained in the doorway, the leader detected a hostile attitude. "Won't you come in and join us?" she asked cheerfully, as she went over to the boy. "We are just ready to hear a story."

"Nope—I don't like stories," Mike answered sharply as he looked toward the leader. She then noticed that one of his eyes was crossed.

"Well, it's such a nice day, I'm sure you'd rather play football," she said, hoping to make the boy feel comfortable.

"There isn't anybody to play football with," Mike said crossly.

"Then you might as well come in and hear the story," the leader said as she turned back to the group. She added, "We'd like to have you, if there isn't anything you'd rather do."

Mike came in. He sat in the front row. He folded his arms belligerently and listened as the leader told "The Golden Arrow." She had planned to tell "Cinderella," but, being faced with a new situation, she immediately switched to the Robin Hood tale. She told the story with all the zest she could muster. As the boy listened, he relaxed. He laughed and responded along with the others. When the story was over, everyone clapped except the older boy. When the leader asked if he liked the story, he was ready with an abrupt answer. "Not very well," he snapped.

He had quickly assumed his hostile pose and had pulled away from the others. The chip was back on his shoulder.

"Would you like to hear another story?" the leader said to the group. Everyone was eager except Mike. "Suit yourself," he said, in an utterly bored tone, when the leader put the question directly to him.

Because this leader had also had social work training, she immediately sensed an insecurity and recognized that the boy had disturbing problems. When the Story Hour was over, she asked Mike if he would like to stay and help tidy up the room. Mike stayed, but he said very little. The following Saturday, however, he was waiting at the auditorium door. It took several weeks before the leader got acquainted with the boy. He then told her that other children laughed at him and teased him about his eyes. She learned, too, that he liked stories as well as any other boy of his age. He even told her he would like to be Robin Hood and join a group of his own age, if she thought the other boys would not laugh at him.

The leader made two recommendations to Mike's parents—medical attention and creative dramatics. The children's aid program to whom Mike's parents were referred was influential in seeing that the boy's eye was gradually straightened through corrective therapy and the use of glasses. Meanwhile, he participated in creative dramatics experiences. He enjoyed the companionship of boys and girls of his age and became a more pleasant person to live with.

Creative dramatics generally provides a release for a child's problems, rather than a cure. The tensions and conflicts that have been built up inside a child are given a chance to come out, but the cause will still remain. The creative dramatics leader herself is not in a position to tackle the basis of the trouble. Quite by chance, a first-grade teacher discovered an unsolvable problem in a six-year-old child during a creative dramatics situation. When she was telling the story, "Ask Mr. Bear," she noticed that Billy, a shy little boy, seemed uneasy about something. When the story was finished and the children started talking about the presents they would like to give their mothers, Billy listened to all the others and then said abruptly, "When I am sixteen I can do anything I want to do."

"And what are you going to do?" the leader asked.

"I'm going back to my mother. She lives far away from here. My brother's going with me, too!"

"Good for you, Billy! That will be nice for you and your brother and for your mother, too," the leader said cheerfully. The teacher had known that Billy was living in a broken home, but she had not realized the degree to which the circumstances had affected the child. As the children played the story, the leader was aware of Billy's eagerness to identify himself with the characters, particularly with the mother and the little boy. Although the teacher could do nothing to remove the cause of Billy's trouble, she provided many creative situations that were related to family life. When children have missed love and sympathy in their homes, they often find comfort and compensation in living through satisfying family experiences in dramatic play. Miracles in a child's behavior can be accomplished when he finds satisfactory release for suppressed troubles.

COMMUNITY LEADERS

Community programs do not evolve without the coöperation of its people. A community should not be indifferent to its cultural advance. Through creative dramatics, all phases of community life can be made more interesting. It is a technique that has no age limit. It is inexpensive, practical, tried and proved. The leaders of today are building our children's tomorrow. Through creative dramatics, they can explore the very depths and heights of living. Many homes have fine libraries that could be shared. An interested parent could make the stories live for many neighborhood children as well as her own. The volunteer who works for the pure love of children is not to be overlooked. Very often a lay person can work as effectively as a professional. Margaret Hickey has said, "You will make mistakes, but you will learn more from your mistakes than from your successes. Above all, you must be convinced that the job you are doing needs to be done, and that you are doing it to the best of your ability. Then pray hard for spiritual wisdom, which is the most important qualification for leadership.

"There will be times when you ask yourselves why you ever took this on, and you will want to remember what Jane Addams so often said: 'Who, if not you? When, if not now?' "[1]

---

[1] Margaret Hickey, "We Are Appraised," *Junior League Magazine*, June, 1950, p. 15.

Chapter X

CREATIVE DRAMATICS IN RECREATION

> Build in me, hills, the granite of your heart.
>
> —LEW SARETT

"When a town forgets how to play and its people fail to participate in creative recreation, it is likely to become dull and uninteresting."[1] When a town finds time for creative activities and its people
learn to laugh and play together, it is likely to become wide-awake
and enterprising. An up-and-coming community that wisely tunes
itself to the tempo of youth and provides worthy recreational programs benefits by a society that is worthwhile and wholesome.

Communities can be fun. A community can grow with its children. It can respect the needs and desires of youth by offering
recreational programs that utilize the energies of active boys and
girls. Creative recreation programs can go far in enlivening and
strengthening a community that is struggling for a way of life.

Childpower should not be overlooked. Healthy children are
human dynamos. When their energies are tapped and harnessed to

---

[1] Baker Brownell, Joseph Kinsey Howard, and Paul Meadows, *Life in
Montana: as Seen in Lonepine, a Small Community,* The Montana Study,
University Press, Missoula, 1945.

satisfying, constructive projects, they have neither time nor inclination to be destructive. When children are enthusiastically engaged in creative activities that draw on their deepest resources of power, they thrill to the joy of accomplishment, success, and recognition. Growing children who learn to play together in the routine of everyday living learn also how to work together. Through their play they learn to season their lives with genuine laughter. They learn to face the real situations of life squarely. When a child finds his "home town" stimulating, not alone from entertainment, but also from creative group experiences, he develops a strong community loyalty. He builds a feeling of responsibility toward the town in which he lives.

A community should not be lulled into inactivity because of the absence of cultural institutions or recreational facilities. Community leaders should survey the possibilities at hand and find ways to make creative recreation a vital part of the lives of growing children. Recreational programs will probably be organized under a park department in a large city. In a smaller community or town, they may be planned by community groups or by volunteer leaders. Once a program has been organized and set up, the children may meet on a large vacant lot, in an idle ball park, on the school grounds, in an open field, in a community hall, or on a space of prairie land near the edge of town.

PHILOSOPHY OF RECREATION

Recreation may be thought of as any form of experience or activity in which an individual joins from choice because of the enjoyment it brings him. A close examination of the word itself reveals re-creation, the act of creating anew. Many recreation leaders have looked upon the word and have seen but one channel through which people may be re-created; that is, the physical. Some have recommended dancing as the ideal means, while others have concentrated on hobby training. The average librarian naturally thinks of books as the finest form of recreation, while a person who has worked with children's theatres readily chooses formal dramatics as an ideal medium for children's recreation.

But recreation is not limited. It is good use of leisure time. Good use of leisure time, again, implies a complete use. It is important that it embrace all phases of a child's being—the mental, the emotional, the social, the physical, and the spiritual. It is important, too, that recreation be a positive doing, for it is a change of occupation for the body and the mind. It is a change that the individual wants to make. When a child becomes active in something that he wants to do, he does it cheerfully, joyfully, wholeheartedly, and with power.

Recreation leaders have a responsibility which they hold in common with parents and teachers everywhere—a job to keep alive, to release, and to channel human energies. Since children attend centers of recreation purely voluntarily, they should all be included as a part of the fun. Recreation leaders should strive to make each child a participant instead of a spectator, a doer instead of a watcher. There are some children who are never so gloriously alive as when swinging a bat, throwing a ball, or performing feats of physical skill. There are other boys and girls who prefer more artistic undertakings, such as painting, sketching, or clay modeling, and others who thoroughly enjoy stamp collecting, while some find real zest and satisfaction in playing checkers and other board and table games.

Since creative dramatics is an activity that is aimed toward the development of the whole child, it has been found to be an ideal medium for recreation. Creative dramatics helps dissolve tensions and lessen frustrations. "Be what you want to be! Feel the way you want to feel!" a leader encourages again and again. When she discovers suppressed ideas and desires, she opens the way for creative expression. If a child has always wanted to be a ballet dancer, the leader guides the entire group into delightful creative experiences in ballet dancing. If a child has secretly hoped that one day he might conduct a symphony orchestra, a leader helps the child to satisfy this desire. She makes it easy for him to become a great conductor in a dramatic situation that closely parallels reality. Perhaps the child finds himself to be Sir Thomas Beecham, while his friends will be members of the London Philharmonic. Through the joy of make-believe they will find themselves in London, playing Franz Schubert's beautiful "Unfinished Symphony." Or, again, they may become members of the Philadelphia Orchestra finding thorough enjoyment as they play gay Strauss melodies, particularly "On the Beautiful Blue Danube." Creative dramatics is a magic carpet sort of play, and children of all ages respond to the spell of make-believe. The possibilities of creative dramatics in recreation programs are limited only by the skill and understanding of the leader.

Creative dramatics is a flexible program that is wonderfully adaptable to the playground which, because of location or circumstances, has a more transient attendance. Informal playmaking, with youngsters playing first one role and then another, creating fresh dialogue and action with each playing, does not collapse because of the absence of a few members. It includes equally well the newcomer and the seasoned trouper who has learned to create characters readily. A creative dramatics program can be organized over a long-term period, or it can readily lend itself to a satisfying experience that takes place in a twenty- or thirty-minute period.

CREATIVE DRAMATICS ON THE PLAYGROUND

"The farmer in the dell, the farmer in the dell!" So sang a group of forty boys and girls who ranged in age from six to twelve years. It was a Saturday morning, and the children were skipping around in a big circle on the schoolyard lawn.

"What kind of a farmer is Toby?" the leader called out as the children came to a stop. Everyone watched Toby, who was busy shocking make-believe grain in the center of the circle.

"Oh! He's feeding chickens! He's a chicken farmer!" shouted one of the six-year-olds.

"No, he's not," piped up nine-year-old Mary. "He has a wheat farm. I can tell, because he stands tall and straight like wheat."

Several of the others were sure that Toby was a wheat farmer. Toby was pleased when they guessed that he was shocking grain.

"What kind of wife would a wheat farmer want?" asked the leader. Already the game was beginning to take on meaning. Several of the boys as well as the girls had ideas about this. "I wonder who will feel the most like a farmer's wife?" the leader continued. "I'm sure the one who really thinks and feels like a wheat farmer's wife will be chosen."

Everyone became wheat farmers' wives. Some of the girls pretended to be working on quilts; some made bread; some fed chickens. One of the boys mixed biscuits, another made cookies, and one put on a freshly starched apron. Toby chose the wife who had been pulling turnips, for he said she looked as though she could cook for the threshers and keep the house neat and clean.

Next, they considered an important problem: what would a wheat farmer and his wife need on their ranch? The group immediately started singing, "The wife takes a cat," and at once, without even a suggestion from the leader, the children became many different kinds of cats. They lost themselves completely in the spirit and fun of the game.

And so the song went on. The farmer took two dogs; the wife took a team of horses; together they chose four pigs, six cows, a dozen chickens, and at last a child. And what fun all forty of the children had! They had played more than a game. They had sung more than a song. They had had a jolly, creative experience, and they were ready and eager for more of this kind of play.

Bringing games to life is one of the many ways that creative dramatics can be used in children's recreation. "London Bridge Is Falling Down" could result in a Saturday morning holiday to visit all of London. "Oats, Peas, Beans, and Barley Grow" could take the children to a large farm or perhaps to a cattle ranch. "A-hunting We Will Go" could set the mood for an exciting fox hunt, while

"Row, Row, Row Your Boat" could be the beginning of interesting trips down big or little rivers in this country or in far-away lands. Singing games provide excellent motivation for getting the children started toward creating their own plays. "The Muffin Man," "Go Round and Round the Village," "Yankee Doodle," and "Home on the Range," have been used with notable success in outdoor playing.

On the playground a child has the whole outdoor world as a background to use in his creative interpretations. He is free to use more space and to pretend more vigorously, perhaps, than when he is playing in his school room, in a museum, or in a library. Out of doors in the open air children can, in their minds, fly farther and faster than airplanes. When they feel like taking off and soaring high into the blue, they find great satisfaction in being airplanes running the full length of the playground and circling back again.

Creative dramatics is democratic. When it becomes a part of the recreational program, children from every part of town and from every type of home learn to coöperate as they play together. Each child is given a fair opportunity to join in. Each one is given responsibility for his part in the total effort of creating a play that is successful, and when it is a child's turn to be a member of an audience, he becomes just as interested and critical an audience as he can be. Every child has ideas, and in this kind of creative recreation every child's ideas are respected. With sufficient time, a good leader can draw out even the shyest child.

Creative dramatics can be just as exciting and satisfying an outlet for pent-up rebellious attitudes as a baseball game. Boys as well as girls find that informal dramatics can be as vigorous and as real as they want to make it. If young boys wish to play red-blooded games like pirates or explorers, they can do more than act like these characters. They can *be* bold pirates and brave explorers.

In several instances, creative dramatics has proved to be the answer to rebellious children looking for excitement. One group of nine-, ten-, and eleven-year-old boys had satisfied their need for adventure and gained a certain recognition among some of their contemporaries by indulging in a "Mysterious Mission" at frequent intervals. The mission was assigned to different boys on different days, and it set forth specific orders for the boys to set fire to the grass on a hillside between their playground and a railway track. The youngsters were so cleverly sly about their pranks that often they would set fire to the hillside, disappear momentarily in their hideouts, only to reappear on the scene as "good samaritans" to aid the firemen in putting out the rapidly spreading flames.

The playground supervisor, as a last resort, asked the creative dramatics leader if there was any way in which she might help the boys, as the next fire episode would result in the boys visiting the local detention home. When the resourceful leader went in search of the boys, she found them romping through the wooded area between the park and the railroad tracks, playing a game of cops and robbers.

Joining their game, she seized upon a quiet moment in their play as they sat around a make-believe campfire to tell them some of the red-blooded and spirited adventures of Robin Hood. In no time at all, the area became Sherwood Forest, and the oldest boy in the group became the bold outlaw, while the others became his trusty followers.

For the next few days, the adventures of Robin Hood were meaty material for the boys' outdoor playing. They became so engrossed in their active dramatizations that they forgot about their mischievous pranks, and they began reading more stories of the English "outlaws." They fashioned elaborate bows and arrows, quivers, and crude costumes. Long underwear was brought from home to be dyed Lincoln green during the craft hour. Pennants were made for the shooting tournament at London, where Robin Hood matched his skill against Clifton of Buckinghamshire and Gilbert of the White Hand.

So proud was the group of their informal dramatization that they shared it with the other playground children at a Friday night family-fun program. "You're good!" was the enthusiastic response of the members of the informal audience. Here was recognition much more satisfying than starting fires on the railroad right-of-ways, recognition that put an end to the fire episodes and motivated a continued interest in dramatic adventures and anticipations.

Such elaborate properties as the boys fashioned for themselves are not at all necessary or even desirable for creative dramatics. A constant use of costumes or properties tends to limit the imagination when children are playing creatively; however, in this case costumes and properties served a real purpose. Once the boys had kindled their imaginations sufficiently, they thoroughly enjoyed playing other stories without the use of such helps. Physical properties are not necessary to the child whose imagination is at work. A creative child is able to imagine a far more magnificent king's crown when he is encouraged to wear an imaginary one, than he is when a yellow paper crown is placed upon his head.

PROCEEDING WITH LARGE GROUPS OF CHILDREN

Since twenty is considered an ideal number for a creative dramatics group, what does a leader do when fifty children arrive at a playground, each one eagerly waiting for the fun of playmaking? She may divide the children into two groups and arrange for each group to meet at a different hour, or she may work with the entire group at one time. Children from five through eight years of age will be organized into one group, while children who are nine years old and older will play together in another group. While the leader works with the younger children, the older children may enjoy watching them play, or, if facilities are available on a playground, they may spend their time in unsupervised activities.

If circumstances within a community make it necessary for a leader to work with a large number of children during a single hour, she will plan to use material that may be readily expanded or contracted. A recreation leader will always be prepared with a central theme, pantomimes, or stories that are flexible enough to be used with anywhere from five to fifty children.

Since every child loves a circus, a leader might very well use a circus as a central theme. After an enthusiastic build-up for the "greatest show on earth," she would invite the entire group to use the large open space and to be elephants, lions, clowns, and tight-rope walkers. Once the youngsters were inside the magic and using their imaginations, she would organize the fifty children into eight or ten smaller groups. Each group would be encouraged to create an act for the circus. If there were a wide range of ages among the group, the leader could include a few of the younger children in each of the groups, or she could work with eight or ten of the youngest children herself.

While each of the older groups was working independently, the leader could guide the little children into being trained dogs, galloping ponies, dancing monkeys, or whatever they wished to be. If any of the older groups needed help in planning an act, a leader could suggest a few ideas to set the children's imaginations working. Girls like to imagine themselves as pretty statues on turntables, aerial artists swinging high in the air, beautiful ladies wearing sparkly, fluffy costumes and riding around circus rings on milk-white ponies. Some girls find special delight in being fat ladies, or, again, in being midgets. Boys like to be talking seals, dancing bears, trained lions, and other circus animals. Almost every boy enjoys being a clown, particularly when he has an appreciative audience for his pranks and antics. Some boys like to feel that they are riding bicycles on narrow ledges high above the heads of spectators. All children enjoy making make-believe music, and every circus needs a brass band.

After five or ten minutes of individual group planning, or when-ever the leader felt that it was time for the circus to start, she would bring all of the children together into one large circle. The leader or one of the older children would be the ringmaster who would begin the ceremonies and get the circus started in a jolly holiday spirit. The ringmaster would see that the circus continued to move along with high interest. When the children were not performing in the circus ring, they would perhaps enjoy being spectators who would cheer for the various circus acts. When the acts were over, the ringmaster could lead all of the performers around the make-believe tent in a grand parade. A circus parade would serve as a satisfying finale to a gay circus day.

Carnivals, county fairs, and rodeos have been enjoyed by children when they were created in a similar manner. A rodeo has proved to be a favorite theme for outdoor playing. Children find genuine pleasure in identifying themselves with Indians, cowboys, horses, bucking bronchos, and steers. When a large group of children is organized into six or seven smaller groups, a rodeo may include a series of colorful and fast-moving events. An Indian ceremonial dance, a cowboy running race, a cowgirl relay event, trick riding and roping, a pony express, bucking, bulldogging, and stage-coach races never cease to thrill active boys and girls.

Make-believe trips provide excellent material for children to play in an outdoor setting. A group of thirty-five youngsters who lived in a small community on the West Coast thoroughly enjoyed an imaginary visit to the New England states. One Saturday morning they walked to an evergreen forest not far from the town where they lived. They pretended that they were on a sugar-gathering expedition in the midst of a large maple grove in Vermont. Each child gave serious thought to selecting a fine sugar-maple. He then pretended to cut the bark, tap in the plug, and hang a tin pail on the tree. Some of the children started fires in the large stoves in the imaginary sugar sheds. They made ready the huge copper kettles, in order that they could boil the maple syrup while they were still in the forest. While the syrup boiled, samples were taken from time to time, to see if the syrup would granulate. At the end of their busy morning, the children walked back to town and enjoyed munching on make-believe maple sugar bars.

Legends and ways of life from other lands offer stimulating material for creative play. Children may like to feel that they are gathering tea leaves on the hillsides of Cochin-China, and they may like to travel through the jungles of the Amazon tapping rubber trees. They may also become interested in being Arabs traveling in a caravan across a desert, pitching their tents, tethering their camels, and eating meat which they have broiled on their swords.

Being traders from Hindustan might have a strong appeal for some youngsters. They could travel in caravans across the Himalayas on their way to Tibet and experience the danger of climbing rugged mountain peaks. They could set up their tents against a wild blizzard or a sudden snowstorm.

Some children like to pretend that they are scientists on an animal-hunting expedition in the Belgian Congo. Before the scientists are guided into the dense jungles by their native guides, other children become jungle animals and hide among the trees and behind bushes in the playing area. As the guides hack their way through the thick undergrowth with huge machettes, they lead the scientists into dangerous wilderness. The scientists see large snakes, cobras, pumas, elephants, alligators, and whatever jungle animals the children decide to be. They see colorful birds and vultures and listen to their constant screeching. To add to the interest of the expedition, the scientists often capture a leopard, a jaguar, a wildcat, a lion, or an animal that has been requested by a museum. The scientists find great sport in capturing the hunted animal alive and taking it back to camp.

Pantomimes for Large Groups. Children of all ages enjoy charades. When a leader is working in a situation where the attendance is irregular, she will find pantomimes of exceptional value for creative recreation. Although the activity is likely to be less informal than it would be if the children were creating a play, a leader will always work for character feeling. Pantomimes are of little creative value when children are doing surface work rather than thinking and feeling.

When a group is large, the children will be organized into several smaller groups, and each group will plan a pantomime for the others to guess. Mother Goose rhymes, short scenes from favorite stories, famous characters from history, sports, occupations, or holidays may suggest interesting pantomimes to children. In working out a pantomime that depicts a holiday, each group will be encouraged to create a situation that will make others feel that it is New Year's Day, Valentine's Day, St. Patrick's Day, or any other red-letter day during our calendar year. If the children are eager to use dialogue to accompany their scenes, they may do so, unless a leader feels the necessity of having them strengthen their feeling of character. In this event, she will suggest that each group play a scene in pantomime for the first time, and for the second playing dialogue may be added to the same scene.

Some groups have become fascinated with pantomimes based on single words, such as acting out the names of flowers, trees, animals, birds, fish, and insects. Younger children create pantomimes of this kind according to concepts, that is, each child within a group becomes a flower according to his idea of a flower. Older children have enjoyed playing single word pantomimes according to the syllables within the word. When a group of boys was pantomiming the word "dandelions," the boys first became hungry lions. They roared loudly and paced back and forth in an imaginary cage. After a zoo keeper brought their food, they became extremely graceful lions. Each one strutted around the cage calmly and beautifully. Since the children who were watching were aware that the pantomimes were based on flowers, they found little difficulty in guessing.

A mixed group of junior high school students enjoyed pantomiming scenes from pictures on postage stamps. Many of the students were avid stamp-collectors, and the idea for the pantomimes originated with them.

Occasionally, a leader may invite children to create short scenes from specific objects. She may place an object or two in a paper bag and ask the chairman of each group to select a bag. The objects will serve to arouse the children's imaginations, and each group will create a scene based on specific objects. Objects may include such articles as a wallet, a policeman's badge, a bandana handkerchief, a pair of dark glasses, a newspaper, a map, a compass, or a sealed telegram.

Stories for Outdoor Playing. Forest and animal stories are ideal for outdoor playing. There are trees to hide behind, rocks to clamber over, and hills that many times serve as hideouts or provide a perfect background for a certain story. When a leader is working with a large group, she will choose a verse or a story in which the characters may be readily multiplied, in order that many children may participate in the playing.

When boys and girls are playing out of doors, they generally feel completely relaxed, and they like to tumble and romp and stretch their arms and legs freely. Little children have enjoyed being spiders crawling across the grass to see for themselves what Miss Muffet is eating. Again, they have enjoyed being villagers galloping on imaginary horses, riding great distances around the playground to arrive at Banbury Cross. There they have gathered on either side of a village street and have waited eagerly to see their beautiful Queen, a fine, fine lady riding upon a fine horse, with "rings on her fingers and bells on her toes," and a courtly procession riding along behind her.

Young children have found the playground to be the finest kind of barnyard road when they have played Marjorie La Fleur's "Little Duckling Tries His Voice." When Little Duckling starts on his journey, he finds little Kitty Cat living with a whole family of friendly kittens. He sees that Puppy Dog lives with many younger puppies and older dogs too, and he finds that Yellow Bird lives in a deep forest with beautiful bluebirds, blackbirds, sparrows, canaries, and robins. When he meets Big Cow, he sees a herd of cattle grazing in the meadow, and he listens to each one making a loud, mooing sound. When Little Duckling's mother comes looking for him, he is happy to see all of his brothers and sisters waddling after her. But even greater than this, Little Duckling is happy to hear the pretty sound of his mother's "Quack, Quack," and he decides that he will talk that way, too. In examining this delightful story, a leader will see that it may be played with as few as six children or by many, many more when it is expanded in the above manner.

Other stories that have been used in a similar way when children were using a large playing area include "The Three Bears," "Ask Mr. Bear," "The Three Billy Goats Gruff," "The Little Rabbit Who Wanted Red Wings," "The Timid Foolish Rabbit," "The Boy and His Goats," "The Animals That Found a Home," and "Little Mouse Sees the World."

One of the most delightful stories for outdoor playing is "The Three Wishes." One group of children created a fantastic forest scene before they brought the woodcutter into the story. They pretended that the forest creatures—birds, rabbits, deer, squirrels, and fairies, pixies, elves, and dryads—were invited to a birthday party for the Fairy Queen. As the Fairy Queen sat on her toadstool throne, each of the creatures presented her with a beautiful birthday present. Some brought butter from the buttercups, while others brought honey from the honey bees. One tiny fairy brought a lacy shawl that had been spun by silver spiders. Two young elves brought a ring that was set all around with dewdrops. After the queen had thanked everyone for her presents, the creatures entertained her with dancing and singing and forest reveling. While they were in the midst of their merrymaking, the old woodcutter tramped into the forest. The fairies hurried away, and the story then proceeded in much the same way that it has been written.

Uncle Remus tales, Just-So Stories, Paul Bunyan legends, and Robin Hood tales have provided excellent material for large groups of older children to dramatize. Children who have had a strong desire to be pirates have enjoyed working on scenes from *Treasure Island*. Other groups have delighted in playing "Old Pipes and the Dryad" in an outdoor setting. A group of junior high school students who had become interested in archery on the playground found real satisfaction in working out dramatic interpretations of "The Shooting Match at Nottingham" and "William Tell."

Munro Leaf's *Ferdinand* was used to introduce creative dramatics to a large group of youngsters in a summer park program. The children became so enthusiastic about playing the story that they worked on it eagerly for eight meetings. The younger boys thought it great fun to be frisky young bulls, running and jumping and butting their heads together. The little girls liked to identify themselves with Ferdinand, and they, too, found a peculiar delight in sitting quietly and smelling flowers. The older boys and some of the girls liked to be the important-looking Spaniards who came from Madrid to choose the fiercest bull they could find for the famous bull fights. A keen rivalry developed among the older boys, as each one created the rollicking scene wherein Ferdinand was stung by a bumblebee.

Attending a bull fight in Spain held a romantic appeal for the older girls. On the days when they were planning the great bull fight, the girls came to the playground with bouquets of flowers. Each one wore flowers in her hair and felt that she was gaily dressed for the occasion. The parade into the bull ring was glorious and exciting. Many of the boys found genuine pleasure in being the famous Maniletti. It was difficult for the children to decide whether they wanted to be *banderilleros* or *picadores* or the great and graceful *matador,* but once a cast was chosen, the parade was always a gay spectacle.

Each new cast tried to make the experience in the bull ring more exciting than the time before. One cast was not content to have the people leave without seeing a real bull fight. After Ferdinand was led away, a fierce bull (one of the boys) came roaring into the ring and put on an excellent show with the *matador*. Another cast entertained the spectators with Spanish songs and folk dancing.

CREATIVE DRAMATICS IN SCOUT PROGRAMS

Learning by doing is a byword in the Scout program. Using creative dramatics in many situations can make Scout learning more fun and more complete. Scout and Cub leaders can bring regular meetings to life through dramatic situations. They can help boys dramatize specific outdoor learnings. The ritual will be customarily the same at all times, but the meaning of the ritual can be re-created in order that the boys may better understand the meaning of scouting.

Indian lore is very much a part of the Scout tradition, and along with it is the emphasis on being able to take care of oneself in the woods safely and sanely. Ideal material for reinforcing these teachings can be found in the lives of old scouts, tribesmen, pioneers, and backwoodsmen. When boys relive vivid incidents in dramatic situations, they learn lessons in ways that they will always remember.

Creative dramatics has been used effectively in many Scout camps. Leaders have found that when Scouts are assigned to certain Indian villages, they enjoy becoming real Indians. As young braves, some of the boys hunt for food for the tribe, others gather firewood, while others who are hunting in the forest send smoke signal messages back to the braves at camp.

Nights around the campfire have become known as creative dramatics time in several camps. Troops work with real challenge to create five-minute scenes, either to entertain or to inform others. This form of creative recreation is gradually replacing the more common stunts and acts that require little thinking on the part of the participants or spectators. In helping the boys to create spontaneous scenes, leaders encourage them to live their surroundings. Some Scouts have developed scenes around such possible happenings as being lost, being bitten by a rattlesnake, starting a fire on a morning after an unexpected storm, and giving first aid to a Scout who has been injured in a fall down a mountain ledge. How much better to bring home lessons on safety and caution in this way than by actually living the circumstances!

Preparing for bird badges has become more interesting to some Scouts when, along with their study of the habits and habitats of specific birds, the boys have become these birds. Many boys have had a good time in identifying themselves with different kinds of snakes when they have been working for snake badges.

When a Scout camp is located near a lake, a stream, or an ocean, an ordinary canoe race can be more exciting when it becomes a race between Indian villages or a crew race at Poughkeepsie. Swimming races take on new meaning when Scouts feel that they are participating in the Olympic games. One boy may be proficient at the Australian crawl, while another is a back-stroke expert. How thrilling the day becomes when each entrant from a different country is out to beat a world record!

Camping days become enriched when the Scouts identify themselves with American pioneers and travel through thickets and wilderness in imaginary Conestoga wagons on their way to new homesteads or to rich gold fields. Being a member of the Lewis and Clark expedition and being guided through dangerous mountainous country by Sacajawea is an experience every Scout will remember.

Creative dramatics is of value in Girl Scout programs as well. Leaders have guided the girls into dramatizing much of the suggested material that is found in their handbooks. They have created dramatic scenes from their Scout songs and have developed interesting scenes from the life of Juliette Low, founder of the Girl Scouts in the United States. At one summer camp, a group of Girl Scouts acted out a series of scenes which told the story of Juliette Low's grandmother. When the grandmother was a little girl, she was kidnapped by an Indian tribe, and she lived happily with them for four years until she was finally returned to her mother.

Citizenship training is of utmost importance in Boy and Girl Scout programs. Both at summer camp and throughout the year, Scout leaders should encourage the discussion of current events. When children are guided into playing many of these events, they gain a broader understanding of the world around them.

CREATIVE DRAMATICS FOR CAMP FIRE GIRLS

Like Scouts, the Camp Fire Girls can live their outdoor experiences all the year around, whether they are meeting in somebody's living room or spending a summer at camp. They can relive last year's camping experiences and live next year's outdoor program ahead of time. They can learn by anticipating and living through meaningful, dramatic experiences.

The emphasis on Indian lore opens the way for vivid material in their playmaking, for the Camp Fire program is as explicit and well-planned as the Scouting programs. Honor beads and badges have greater significance for Camp Fire girls when they dramatize events related to specific ranks. For instance, if a Camp Fire girl has chosen *E ha wee* for her Indian name and she is working for a Trail Seeker's Rank, the experience becomes pleasurable if she becomes a laughing Indian maid going on a hike for berries or with another real purpose, rather than simply hiking in order to earn a rank. Newly organized groups have found real enjoyment in dramatizing the Indian name which they have chosen for their group. Each member has enjoyed pantomiming her Indian name, in order that the other girls will recognize her as an Indian maid of outstanding character.

Some Camp Fire Girls have dramatized their trips to summer camp by imagining themselves to be Indians or pioneers scouting for new hunting or fishing grounds. They have set up camp in pioneer or Indian fashion. Morning swims have been included as part of an Indian ritual. Cooking breakfast over a campfire has taken on new meaning when the girls have imagined themselves to be early-day pioneers preparing to cross the Platte River as soon as the morning meal was over.

When summer camp was organized around a specific theme, the girls have created short skits for evening programs that emphasized the summer theme. When the girls gathered around a campfire for song fests, they enjoyed being southern folk singing plantation songs. They became ranchers in the far West singing cowboy ballads, and they felt that they were pioneers camped for the night as they joined in the songs of the Forty-niners.

CREATIVE DRAMATICS IN SUMMER CAMPS

"We're going to camp! We're going to camp!" What a joyous and familiar saying this has become among American children today! There was a time when only the children of the very poor or the well-to-do attended summer camps. Today camping is available to almost every child from every part of the United States. The camp life experience has been found to be of such value that many schools, both public and private, are setting aside time for camp. Camping has been found to foster good teacher-pupil relationships, since the teachers and the pupils relax and play together in a way quite different from the formal atmosphere of the schoolroom.

Creative dramatics has gone to camp, too! Many counsellors have used creative dramatics the minute children have arrived at their destinations, to help them forget any fears they may have had about being homesick or lonely. Children have been greeted as members of an Indian tribe and have been guided into becoming young braves or Indian maidens gathering for a great council meeting or for a summer hunting season. They have unpacked their belongings and set up camp in character of young Indians. They have chosen Indian names and have taken great pride in living up to their names. Each child has been made to feel that he was an important member of the tribe, and through this experience he has felt secure in his new environment. Ordinary hikes have become journeys into the hills to gather roots or berries. Campfires at night have become council meetings. Ceremonial dances and authentic Indian games have been learned with real purpose, and young campers have returned to civilization several weeks later with many new skills and accomplishments.

Other counsellors have helped children adjust to their new surroundings by orienting them for camp many months in advance. They have sent literature to children inviting them to spend the summer being ranchers, vagabonds, scientists, beachcombers, gypsies, pirates, or voyagers. They have written letters to prospective campers informing the would-be rancher or gypsy about the necessary clothing and equipment for the summer. When summer arrives and a child is met at a station, many miles away from his home, he is greeted with a friendly, "Hi Pardner! We've been looking for a good ranch-hand like you!" or "Hello there, Gypsy. You're just the one we've been waiting for! How about joining us on the gypsy trail for a big bonfire tonight?" When a child has said goodbye to his parents somewhat reluctantly, a creative suggestion works its magic at once in putting him at ease and starting his summer in a comfortable way.

Dallas Lore Sharp's stories, "Things to Hear This Spring," and "Things to See This Summer," have been used by many counsellors to help children develop an awareness and an appreciation of the outdoor world. After boys and girls have watched squirrels or chipmunks scurry in and out among trees and undergrowth, they find real joy in becoming these forest creatures. When camps are located near lakes or streams, children enjoy the fun of dramatic play during their swimming hours. Some children like to play that they are seals, walking on the beach and swimming and splashing in the water. Others find an exhilaration in gliding through the water as they pretend to be different kinds of fish. Being frogs has brought many hours of jolly fun to young campers. When children are guided into understanding their new surroundings, they experience a oneness with the outdoor world. They listen to night sounds, rustling sounds, and the sounds of water with new and curious interest. They become as much a part of the forest as the trees and the wind.

In a natural outdoor setting, history can live for children through creative dramatics. In their boating hours, children could re-enact the discovery of America. They could dramatize the courageous voyage and landing of Christopher Columbus. They could experience the hope in the hearts of all the men when they saw some weeds and land birds after many long weeks on a limitless sea. They could experience the disappointment of the crew when, several days later, there was still no land to be seen. They could plead with Columbus to turn back and could start a mutiny aboard the vessel. They could feel the courage of Christopher Columbus, who quieted their fears and said, "Sail on, Sail on."

They could fire an imaginary cannon shot from the Pinta and feel that they were sighting a new land early on the morning of October 12, 1492. Some of the children could be Indians who greeted the voyagers from Spain. They could relive the awe and astonishment that the natives experienced in seeing white men for the first time. They could experience the curiosity that the Indians felt toward Christopher Columbus as he landed, wearing his velvet Admiral's robes.

Independence Day offers further rich material for playing at summer camps. Celebrating the Fourth of July was such a glorious experience for boys and girls at Trail's End Camp that each young camper finished the day by sitting down and writing home about it. Betsy, an enthusiastic ten-year-old, had this to say:

Dear Mother,

All the campers at Trail's End Camp went to the shore for the 4th of July Pageant. There were three people who told the story of why we celebrate the 4th of July, and then different tribes acted out the different ways we gained our freedom.

One skit was about the pilgrims landing on Plymouth Rock. The boys took a row boat and rowed from one side of the dock to the other where there was a big rock, and boys dressed like Indians came out to meet them. They made friends and smoked a peace pipe.

Another one was a town meeting to make plans against the British. Two boys walked up and down the dock with a lantern and bell, yelling, "Town meeting tonight." The meeting was held, and they talked against the British and the tea tax. Then we had the Boston Tea Party and it showed how the boat guards were tied up and gagged. The Indians threw the tea into the water and then when they finished, they drank the water that had the tea in it.

The oldest girls did Paul Revere's Ride. A girl rode in on a horse and there was no mistake—she was Paul Revere. She said, "The signal is—one if by land and two if by sea." They came by land. One fire was built across the lake. Paul Revere warned the sleeping people in the Lodge—"The British are coming!"

The next skit was the Battle of Concord Bridge. The British soldiers and the Minute Men guarding the bridge had a fight. One from each side fell in the water but the Minute Men won.

I sure like the 4th of July.

Love,
BETSY

Betsy's mother was quick to admit that the Fourth of July in the past had meant picnics, fireworks, and parades, with little emphasis being placed on the significance of the day. Not only did Betsy and other campers at Trail's End have the fun of playing and making the Fourth of July come alive, but they understood the feelings of the people involved. The counsellors had told the stories, and the children had played them many times before the holiday.

The landing on Plymouth Rock was preceded by a meeting aboard the Mayflower before the Pilgrims landed. The children in a little rowboat identified themselves with the Pilgrims on the Mayflower. They discussed plans for their new community, and they elected John Carver for their governor. The boys rowed carefully near the shore, and they made their first landing on Cape Cod. Some of the men scouted the shoreline, and they found an Indian storehouse full of corn. Since the storehouse appeared to be deserted, the men took the corn. When the Indians returned and found their corn missing, they were angered. They shot arrows at the Pilgrims and tried to frighten them away. Although nobody was killed, the Indians and the white men had an exciting battle. After the Indians had gone, the Pilgrims planned their community house and a storehouse. They set to work at once, for winter was upon them.

Camp experiences as vivid as these carry over into the children's homes when the campers return. Children are eager to share all that they have learned with friends and family. Parents are likely to be introduced to new chapters in history when they learn, for instance, that the men in the Boston Tea Party drank the water that the tea had been dumped in, and that just one man fell from each side in the battle of Concord Bridge. More important, however, parents will discover that their children's fast-growing imaginations have been guided through rich camp experiences in group living, learning, and sharing.

Chapter XI

THE LEADER

> As a man thinketh in his heart so is he.

Vacation was approaching. The schoolmaster, always severe, grew severer and more exacting than ever, for he wanted the school to make a good showing on "Examination Day." His rod and his ferule were seldom idle now—at least among the smaller pupils. Only the biggest boys, and young ladies of eighteen and twenty escaped lashing.[1]

Mark Twain's vignette of Mr. Dobbins, a schoolmaster of Tom Sawyer's day, leads us to see that the way of the classroom teacher has changed considerably within the last century. In reminiscing about one's own childhood days at school, certain teachers stand out clearly not perhaps because of their severity, but probably because of desirable qualities which children instinctively recognize and respect.

Why is it that some teachers are long remembered, while others are soon forgotten? What qualities in an individual's personality contribute to good teaching? What kind of person does it take to make a good teacher? When these questions were considered by

---

[1] Mark Twain, *The Adventures of Tom Sawyer*, Whitman Publishing Co., 1931.

various members of a class of college students, each one of whom was beginning his training for elementary teaching, the answers that were given pictured an ideal teacher in such realistic terms as these:

"A good teacher should have a well-rounded personality and should be strong in character worth."
"A teacher should know how to teach—learning should be fun!"
"A teacher should be thorough in the way she teaches."
"She should be enthusiastic about her work."
"A teacher should be friendly."
"A good teacher should always be neat and well groomed."
"She should try to understand every child and should respect each one for what he is—she should not show favoritism."
"A teacher should be community- and world-minded."
"She should have a professional attitude toward her responsibility as a teacher."
"She should recognize good work and give credit and praise."
"She should be firm, but always just."
"A teacher should have a pleasant speaking voice."
"A good teacher will laugh with children."

These desirable qualities set forth by prospective teachers are outstanding among the attributes one looks for in choosing a young man or a young woman to work with children in the specialized teaching of creative dramatics. Although many more women than men have entered this field in the past, an ever increasing number of young men are combining creative dramatics with study in the related fields of education, recreation, social work, and psychology. In considering the requirements of an ideal creative dramatics leader, it should be understood that the same basic qualities that are desirable in women leaders apply also to men who are entering this profession.

In setting up a measuring stick for a good creative dramatics leader, one begins by asking what a child needs most from a leader in order to be creative. First of all, he needs security within a group. A leader should help him to feel happy, relaxed, and at ease. He needs freedom, yet he requires a certain amount of firm guidance in which specific goals are made clear to him. He needs to be understood for what he is. He needs to be recognized as an individual with ideas and differences of his own. He needs opportunities for asserting his independence. A leader who directs a child's every move, restricts him by thinking for him, instead of stimulating him to grow by challenging his thinking and widening his horizons. A child needs a worthy example in a courteous, warm-hearted and creative adult. A child's imagination needs to be fired, and his thinking and feelings need to be steered tactfully into natural, truthful, and complete expression. He needs encouragement and specific praise for worthy attainments, however great or small. He needs someone who can bring out in him what he likes best about himself. A leader who judiciously celebrates a child's success gives him a powerful urge to go on creatively, striving and succeeding.

VITALITY AND PERSONALITY

Vitality is essential. One of the first and always immediately noticeable qualities which one observes as he watches a good leader at work is the amount of vitality that a leader uses as she skillfully guides children through a meaningful creative experience. It takes real vitality to fire children's enthusiasm to the place where they become as excited about discovering America as Columbus was, and where they fight the Battle of Bunker Hill with a patriotic spirit second only to that of the British and the Americans in the days of the Revolution.

Although good health contributes much to a leader's dynamic energy, her personality is an important factor in determining the quality of her aliveness, for a leader's personality immediately reflects the kind of person she is—her ideals, her conduct, her standards, her appreciations. An ideal leader will be recognized by outstanding traits of sincerity, spontaneity, friendliness, tolerance, optimism, humbleness, and patience. She will not allow her personality to dominate or overshadow to the degree that the children imitate her, but rather she will exert a strong influence for bringing out the best in each individual.

Sidney Pressey and Francis Robinson have observed that "An alert vigorous teacher can vivify almost any subject; a routine colorless teacher will make it lifeless."[2] A strong spirit of enthusiasm must dominate every creative dramatics class, and it is up to an energetic leader to create a friendly, zestful working environment if she is to encourage each child to participate cheerfully.

When a leader has confidence in herself, she works freely and easily with children. When she has faith and conviction in the values of creative dramatics, her enthusiasm and inspiration penetrate deeply into her work, and she becomes sincerely interested in each child who comes under her guidance. Faith in creative dramatics, faith in children, and faith in herself go far in reinforcing a leader's natural vitality and thus contributing to her dynamic leadership.

A leader's personality makes an immediate impression on those with whom she works. After a newly organized class in creative dramatics had met for several times, Bill, a shy nine-year-old, told his mother that he liked creative dramatics because "Miss Brown was so pretty." Bill's younger brother, who had also worked with Miss Brown, commented, "Boy, she's neat!" Actually, Miss Brown was quite a plain looking person, but she had an inner spirit of beauty and a radiant personality to which the children had responded, and she had been wholesomely attractive in her appearance as well.

A leader's appearance is vitally important, for outwardly she expresses her inward feelings. What a person wears becomes a part of her personality, and her manner of dress provides an immediate index to her character. This does not mean that a leader needs to dress expensively, but she must use good taste in her choice of clothes and must observe cleanliness and neatness with utmost care.

---

[2] Sidney L. Pressey and Francis P. Robinson, *Psychology and the New Education*, Harper & Brothers, 1944.

"A good teacher should always be neat and well groomed." Children respect and appreciate careful grooming, and they respond to variety and color in a person's appearance. A small cluster of flowers, a sprig of holly, or a colorful scarf may readily brighten an otherwise dull costume and will cost little in time, effort, or expense. A leader whose appearance is always crisp and clean will have a stimulating and refreshing effect on others, and what she wears may serve to enrich a child's living in more than one way. This was exemplified during the past war when a leader who was working with a group of housing-project children in an after-school program went to meet them one afternoon with a small sprig of apple blossoms tucked in her hair. At the very next meeting, many of the little girls were proudly wearing different kinds of flowers in their hair.

VISION AND IMAGINATION

"A teacher should know how to teach—learning should be fun!" It takes only a few minutes of watching a leader working with children to tell whether she is an imaginative person. A leader who can think of new and refreshing ways to approach old and familiar stories is one who will be distinguished by her richness of imagination.

Many a beginning leader is surprised to find that once she begins to exercise her imagination, she awakens latent powers within herself, and consequently she becomes much more flexible in her ability to suggest and to suggest rightly. She also grows in her readiness to receive the children's suggestions and in her ability to utilize and synthesize these suggestions, thus giving the children a strong feeling of success. A creative leader will not be content with ordinary effort on the part of a child but will work patiently for the good that she knows is there. As a leader taps the reservoir of creative power within each child, she constantly develops a child's imagination to the forgetting of self and gradually leads him to the visualization and expression of the character outside himself.

A leader who has the power of clear visualization will be characterized by thoroughness in her work. She will be able to help children see a wealth of possibilities for enriching and enlarging a single idea. She will never try to hurry a child, realizing from her own experience that creative thinking cannot be forced. Likewise, she will readily appreciate the simplicity with which a child expresses himself. She will be quick to accept differences in interpretation and to recognize creative thinking when she sees it. An imaginative person will be able to detect creativity which reveals itself in a natural, simple, childlike way, regardless of how crude or how exquisite it may be.

With a good understanding of the what and why of creative dramatics, a resourceful leader will be able to apply her knowledge and imagination readily. How happy a group of children will be whose leader, when the first snowflakes fall, stops a reading lesson or whatever activity may be going on and invites each one to become a snowflake as she calls:

> Lightly falling, lightly falling,
> Snowflakes dancing 'round!
> Gently whirling, gently twirling,
> Fluttering to the ground.

One can imagine the delight children gain from a leader who joins with them and becomes a whirling snowflake, or from a teacher who provides the pleasant refreshment of imaginary ice-cream cones after an intent study of arithmetic or spelling.

He was a wise philosopher who said, "Most of us miss the gold under our feet." If a leader is characterized by abundant living, she will recognize countless opportunities for creative playing, and she will in turn awaken an awareness on the part of each child as she constantly opens new horizons of thought. Current events, geography, history, literature, nature, and everyday occurrences can be richly enlivened by a leader who has learned to exercise her creative power. A creative adult, regardless of age, will always be youthful in spirit, for an aliveness always accompanies creativity and serves to keep its creator eternally young.

COMMON SENSE

James Stephens, in *The Crock of Gold*, emphasizes the need for common sense in creative living when he says, "A man has said that Commonsense and a woman has said Happiness are the greatest things in the world. . . . Commonsense is Thought and Happiness is Emotion, and until they embrace in Love the will of Immensity cannot be fruitful."[3]

Just as it takes a considerable amount of good common sense in living, likewise it takes good common sense in teaching creative dramatics, for a leader indirectly gives children a philosophy by which to live. Creative imagination will be valuable to a child only when it is combined with the soundness of common sense application. Imagination which is stirred up and then left uncontrolled or disregarded may become a dangerous, frivolous, or even disastrous force. If a leader kindles a child's imagination without instilling careful judgment, she is very likely to do him more harm than good. On the other hand, if these two qualities are blended in a leader's personality, she will be in a position to help a child develop stability and seriousness of thought at the same time that he develops his creative power. A leader will find her good judgment challenged often as she strives to guide children's thinking toward ethical standards of living, particularly when they are creating an original play, for with children's natural interest in excitement, they may be inclined toward thrilling situations based on illogical or unsound motives.

Creative work is likely to go off on terrible tangents of mediocrity unless a leader keeps a proper perspective on the high goals which may be reached and approaches her responsibility with humility and challenge. An ideal leader will remind herself often of the

---

[3] James Stephens, *The Crock of Gold*, The Macmillan Company, 1936.

specific objectives in a creative dramatics program and will strive toward maximum accomplishment of these desirable aims.

Creative dramatics has its high moments and its low moments, its ups and downs. There will be days when even the most confident leader will wonder what it is that she is doing or not doing that results in group confusion or lack of interest. In encountering a situation such as this, a leader will attempt to determine the causes by evaluating fairly: Was she sufficiently prepared? Was the story or material right for this specific group of children? Has the class worked too long on the same story? Was the planning balanced with sufficient active playing? Was there enough fun in the class? Was specific praise given when merited? Was the motivation strong enough to arouse imagination? Was too much expected from the children?

Optimism on the part of a leader is essential, for whenever a lag or a recession sets in, she will not only recognize it, but she will put forth a special effort to recapture her enthusiasm. A leader will guard against becoming tense and worried over a puzzling situation but will be justified in believing that with sincere effort on her part the long trend will be upward. She will allow the children's best efforts in previous experiences to spur her on to stronger guidance and also to overshadow the poor efforts of the moment at hand. A leader will not expect moments of rare creativity often, but she will use the utmost patience in motivating, guiding, praising, and working with each individual within a group to try to reach his creative depths. She will set her goals high, and when magic moments do occur she will realize that they are constantly worth striving for.

A leader will use care in not overtaxing a child. She will never insist that he play a character part until he is ready, for one failure can quickly undo the results of weeks of careful building.

POINT OF VIEW

Why does a person choose to work with children in the first place? If an adult can answer this question fairly and say in all honesty that she has a genuine love for children and enjoys being with them, she is likely to have a tolerant understanding of children, and this is one of the most essential requirements for a creative dramatics leader.

To be able to help a child find himself, a leader must have a sincerity of purpose and really care about working with him. She will be kind to a child without overwhelming him with attention. She will be able to control and guide him without resorting to severity. A very special kind of friendship exists between a sincere leader and a child. This friendship is more than an acquaintance-ship. It is a friendly attitude which reveals itself in a leader's point of view, and it is accompanied by a dignity, a warmth, a respect, and an understanding which quickly establishes complete rapport among a group of children. In other words, when a leader's point of view is rightly placed, she will get along with children happily, for they will respect and admire her, and she will understand them. She will never be too busy to listen to a child's problems or to his joys. If a child has something to tell, it is important that he be allowed to tell it, but it is even more important that someone listen. A leader will have a lenient heart and will be sympathetic with a child's needs and desires.

If a leader can remember herself as a child, how she thought and felt in many different situations, she will better understand a child's point of view and will be sympathetic and receptive on matters that are close to his heart. Every child has ideas and feelings that must be respected, and a good leader will know how to tunnel patiently to the innermost depths and uncover the real child in order that he may talk about the things that are deepest within him and thereby be more at peace with himself. Thus through encouragement, indirection, and understanding a leader will be able to help a shy child blossom, a "show-off" grow in his respect for others, and children with emotional and physical problems make more wholesome adjustments toward the people with whom they live.

When a young leader told the tale, "The Stone in the Road," to a group of restless teen-age boys who met in an evening class in a city park, she very wisely told only the brief plot of the story. After explaining that a duke living in the medieval days had placed a bag of gold under a stone in the middle of the road to see if any of the complaining villagers might remove the stone and thus be rewarded for unselfishness, this leader asked the boys if they could conceive of such a thing happening today. An interesting discussion then arose, centering in a civic problem which was of great concern within the city at that time. Since the problem had to do with the expense involved in paving city streets, the boys decided that in their play the mayor of the town would place a substantial reward under a stone along one of the streets in question. Considerable time was spent in deciding just what the reward would be, each boy trying hard to out-think the others. When a fifteen-year-old lad finally suggested that a key to a new Cadillac be placed under the stone, the other boys responded wholeheartedly to his unique plan, and they set to work in earnest to create a play which had real meaning for them. This young leader, who was inexperienced in specialized teaching, made up for the lack by her unusual ability to place an experience on a child's level of understanding.

An ideal leader will always be sensitive to a child's feelings. She will be open-minded to new points of view and flexible enough to change her original plan when it is to the advantage of a group that she do so. No one can tell a leader what she should do in a given situation, but each leader will feel her way along, keeping the child's viewpoint in mind at all times.

An experienced leader, working with a group of eight- and nine-year-olds in a class that met one hour each week on a Saturday morning, observed in a gratifying manner the importance of recognizing a child's viewpoint. The children were working on "The Nativity," and were planning to share it with their parents on a Saturday before Christmas. Since they were a beginning class and had only this last meeting in which to work together before the parents came, the leader was anxious to have them strengthen their characterizations, and she felt that every minute of the class hour was vitally needed. When the children hurried into the auditorium, the leader noticed that a new girl had come with Rosella. As soon as everyone was seated, the leader inquired about the new little girl, and Rosella stood up proudly to introduce her friend. "This is Judy Smith," she said. "She just moved next door to us, and she came to visit today."

"We're glad you're here, Judy," the leader said sincerely. "Maybe you would like to be in our class, too."

Judy, who was standing beside Rosella, moved back shyly and sat down without answering. The leader understood. She knew how it felt to know only one person and to have many others watching you.

"We have two Judys now," she said pleasantly. "Isn't it fun to have two people with the same name? We have a Judy Smith and a Judy Nelson."

The leader looked around the circle. "Where are you, Judy Nelson?" she asked, taking everyone's eyes away from the new little girl.

Judy Nelson laughed as everyone looked and pointed to her. "I'm right here, Miss Dawson," Judy Nelson said cheerfully. Then she added, "May we do our Christmas story for—for Judy?"

"Yes, yes!" the others called eagerly, and several hands went into the air. "May I be Mary?" "May I be Joseph?" "I'd like to be a donkey."

The leader could see that the children were confident about giving their play for the new little girl. She could sense the spiritual significance of Christmas in the children's eagerness to share. She recognized the importance of their readiness, and she understood exactly how they felt. After a friendly approval of Judy's plan, she chose the characters and the stage managers for the first scene. In a few minutes, the front of the room became a busy street in Bethlehem where four innkeepers and their families lived. There was an old innkeeper whose inn was crowded, a young, haughty innkeeper who was cross because his sleep was interrupted so often, a meek innkeeper who depended on his wife to attend to the business, and a kind innkeeper who humbly offered the manger as a place to rest for the night. As the children played the scene, they became weary travelers. Some were old, some were young, some leaned heavily on imaginary crooks and canes. When Mary and Joseph and the donkey came to the inn where the kind innkeeper lived, Joseph knocked on the doorway and waited anxiously.

"Why do you come so late? What do you want at this hour?" the old innkeeper asked, as he stroked his chin and rested on an imaginary staff.

"Do you—do you have any vacant apartments?" Joseph asked hopefully, as he searched for words to explain his need.

When the scene ended with Mary and Joseph going off to the stable, Judy Smith and the other children who had been watching clapped their hands appreciatively. The children praised the fine characters and offered specific suggestions for making the play seem more like Bethlehem in the early days before there were apartments. Because Judy was visiting, the children wanted to show her the manger scene before working to improve the scene at the inn. The leader recognized the value of allowing them to continue with their plan, and she chose different children for the characters from the children who had played in the first scene. In this scene, everyone played except the new Judy and the leader.

One of the boys had made a small wooden manger, and when the scene opened, Mary knelt reverently beside it. Three oxen, several lambs, the donkey, and many angels were watching peacefully. Joseph stood near Mary, and he greeted one of the Wise Men kindly. "Where did you come from, sir?" he asked.

"From the East," the Wise Man said confidently.

"How did you come?" Joseph questioned.

"By camel," he answered.

"Did you have a nice trip?" Joseph inquired kindly.

"A fine trip, thank you," the Wise Man said, and then he turned to Mary and knelt down before her. He placed a small imaginary gift beside the manger. "This golden chest is for the Christ Child," he said quietly.

"Thank you very much," Mary said with real gentleness as she folded her arms. "I'm sure Jesus will enjoy this a great deal."

After the other Wise Men, the shepherds, and the kings had come to the manger, the angels sang "Silent Night," and when the scene was over everyone went quietly back to the circle where Judy Smith was sitting. Judy Nelson and Rosella hurried over to sit near her. "Did you like it?" Rosella asked. Judy Smith smiled and nodded and then she turned to the leader who was sitting beside her. "I wish I could be an angel too," she said. And before the morning was over, Judy joined with the others in their playing. What a different class this had been, not alone because of Judy's visit, but because the leader had recognized and respected the children's point of view!

SOCIAL SPIRIT

"A teacher should be friendly. She should try to understand every child and should respect each one for what he is—she should not show favoritism. She should be firm, but always just." What better advice could a teacher find as she strives to create an environment in which every child feels comfortable and secure! A good leader will be aware of a child's sensitivity to his status within a group. She will realize that everything that takes place within the classroom will have an influence for good or ill upon a child's personality. What she says, the tone of her voice, her smile, her fairminded attitudes—everything that is done in a child's presence, even though it is not intended specifically for him, affects his social development. She will use care in never threatening a child's feeling of security by allowing him to be humiliated or embarrassed or laughed at by others. On the other hand, she will endeavor to build up gradually within each child a confidence, in order that he will not suffer from social fears. A leader must feel secure before she will be able to help children feel secure.

Far and away the most important single factor in determining a leader's success with children will be her ability to manage them in a group. Unless she has the capacity to maintain a courteous respect and a kind consideration within a classroom, she cannot hope to encourage creative thinking. One of the first things children notice about a new teacher is whether she can keep order. There seem always to be a few children in a group who test a teacher's authority and "try her out," seeing for themselves just how far they can go without restriction. She will strive to make a class so interesting, by challenging the children's thinking, that they will have neither time nor inclination to take advantage of her or each other. A leader who is too lenient at the outset is likely to discover through unfortunate experiences the necessity of orderliness and strong guidance if she is to avoid behavior problems. She will realize that children cannot think amidst confusion and will recognize the wisdom of waiting and of having the entire group wait until each of its members is ready to coöperate before she proceeds. She may find it helpful to remind a few children kindly that the entire group is having to wait because of them.

The emotional and social maturity of a leader will determine her stability to a great degree as she works with children, for a calm, cheerful person generally handles an unexpected situation graciously, as she keeps a proper perspective on the problem at hand. A good leader may very well look upon her class as a gardener views his flower garden, knowing that to plant seeds is not enough—that it is essential, too, to tend and care for each one. All teaching, and particularly the teaching of creative dramatics, requires patience, tolerance, understanding, and a delicate touch.

ATTITUDES AND APPRECIATIONS

If creative dramatics were simply an activity carried on by children in their own way, there would be no real need for an adult leader to work with them. In fact, many children do spend hours creating plays without adult supervision, and they gain much from the experience, even though their creations generally remain at a certain level of playing. However, since creative dramatics can be an art which deals directly with a child's heart and mind, it requires sensitive leadership to keep the standard of playing on a high level that encourages individual growth. If a leader is to appeal to a child's finer self, she will of necessity be a person of high ideals, for her worthy attitudes and appreciations will go far in influencing a child's attitudes and appreciations.

John Merrill and Martha Fleming, in emphasizing the importance of a leader's character, point out that ". . . The teacher of dramatic work should be distinguished by the qualities which mark the man or woman of good breeding. His manners should be the expression of a delicate courtesy which comes from real kindness of heart and which has its basis in a true consideration for others. The finest ideals of truth, righteousness, justice, and sincerity of spirit must motivate his every act, because, from the very nature of the work and the special fascination of dramatics for the children, they will tend to imitate this leader."[4]

When a leader has worthy appreciations for literature, for beauty, and for humanity, she is able to awaken similar appreciations within a child. For this reason a leader will measure her sense of values with extreme care, and she will constantly reach out for new experiences to strengthen her cultural and aesthetic appreciations. She will heed the wisdom of the ancient Persian poet who said, "If thou hast two pennies, spend one for bread. With the other, buy hyacinths for thy soul." A strong awareness on the part of the leader generally results in more accurate and sensitive observations on the part of each child, and rich experiences in living provide a child with a background from which he draws constantly as he expresses himself.

An ideal leader will have a genuine love for good literature. She will be familiar with many of the finest traditional stories for children and will be vitally interested in finding worthy modern stories

---

[4] John Merrill and Martha Fleming, *Play-making and Plays*, The Macmillan Company, 1930.

and verse to share with boys and girls. Her genuine zest and appreciation for the best in children's literature will lead to a strong desire to open to children the greatness of the treasure house of literature. Children have a genuine respect for a person who is ready with a good story at a moment's notice, and a good leader will be a good storyteller; that is, she will be able to tell stories so that they live for children.

In introducing children to literature, a leader will realize the importance of having them participate in a variety of experiences where many characters of different kinds meet together. Thus, as a child vicariously experiences honesty and dishonesty, kindness and selfishness, honor and dishonor, and other exemplifications of right and wrong through fine literature, he is better able to form his own sense of values and to develop discriminating attitudes in his living.

SENSE OF HUMOR

"A good teacher will laugh with children." Wherever there are happy, healthy children, there will be spontaneous laughter, and one of the finest indications of an understanding leader will be her ability to laugh with them. Laughter contributes greatly to the friendly and relaxed atmosphere that is essential for creative thinking. A leader who has a ready smile and a warm sense of humor inspires confidence in others, and a child grows with a person who can laugh readily with him—one who makes it comfortable for him to laugh without embarrassment.

Laughter is universally understood. When a leader laughs with children, they know at once that she understands their viewpoint and that she appreciates their sense of humor and their special joy in nonsense and in clowning. One of the friendliest ways for a leader to acknowledge to children that she too makes mistakes is for her to smile and to laugh readily at herself when she has been mistaken about something. When children laugh heartily, they are completely relaxed, and during such moments a leader may gain rare insight into a child's personality that he may not reveal when he is completely on guard. A leader with a fine appreciation for good wholesome fun will be able to help children develop discriminating appreciations for genuine humor and, thus, lift them above a taste for mere buffoonery. Above all, she will see that children do not offend others by laughing at them, but that everyone has a good time laughing together.

VOICE AND SPEECH

"A teacher should have a pleasant speaking voice." If a leader realized the degree to which her voice and speech affect her listeners, she would use great care both in what she says and how she says it. When a leader's voice is quiet, mellow, and low-pitched, it tends to have a pleasing effect on the children with whom she works. If, on the other hand, her voice is loud, rasping, or high-pitched, it tends to irritate her listeners. A monotone which is lifeless and dull is especially uninteresting to boys and girls, for they are unusually sensitive to sound. A leader who is aware of the ineffectiveness of her voice should improve its quality through careful and continuous training.

Since children readily reflect the speech of someone they admire, a leader will strive to set a worthy example by speaking with ease and grace and by using a refined vocabulary. An ideal leader will honor language as an art and will realize that beauty and vividness of expression on her part are the very best stimuli toward an appreciation and desire for good speech on the part of the children.

TRAINING REQUIREMENTS

Good leadership is the most important single factor governing the quality of success in a creative dramatics program. What children learn and the way in which they grow is determined almost entirely by the kind of person the leader is and how she succeeds in getting children to put forth their best efforts. Since leadership is of primary concern, one may inquire into the amount of training an adult should have before she becomes a qualified leader in this field. There are many possible avenues of leadership that enter into this consideration.

It is understandable that a mother who has had no formal training in creative dramatics may very well guide her children constructively and have a wonderful time playing "The Three Bears" or other stories with them at home. Or, with sincere enthusiasm for creative play, she may lead a group of Camp Fire Girls or neighborhood children into jolly experiences in which they make up plays and create original scenes that are worthy and satisfying.

Librarians who have a strong appreciation for children's literature and an excellent understanding of children may feel confident enough to go ahead with dramatic play activity in connection with story-telling programs. Even so, they usually begin by making a careful study of creative dramatics in study groups, or by working closely with a handbook and proceeding slowly.

Many classroom teachers have become outstanding leaders by introducing creative dramatics gradually and proceeding cautiously until they have gained confidence in leadership and experience in working creatively.

Religious instructors, leisure-time volunteers, social workers, and recreational leaders have found that concentrated work-shop courses, or a few weeks of intensive study in this field under a qualified professional leader, have given them sufficient understanding of the philosophy and technique of creative drama to enable them to proceed with children's groups with notable degrees of success.

Therapists, realizing the tremendous power of creative dramatics in rehabilitating emotionally disturbed children, have realized the necessity for specialized training before attempting to use creative dramatics for therapeutic treatment. A carefully trained leader will find creative dramatics invaluable in helping children who are suffering from physical handicaps, emotional tensions, and social fears, but an untrained person should be warned against the danger of using this medium for curative purposes unless she has a psychological background which justifies her working for such purposes.

The young student who is desirous of becoming a specialist in creative dramatics should know that the future is challenging and is bright with opportunities. The need for outstanding creative dramatics leaders in the fields of education, recreation, social work, and religion is being felt everywhere across our country. There is an ever-increasing demand for people qualified to fill this need in both school and community programs. The request for trained leaders to introduce creative dramatics into youth programs in European countries is urgent just now, since the rehabilitation of war-sick children cannot be delayed.

A leader will be rewarded a hundredfold for the time and effort spent in thorough preparation, but she must recognize from the outset that there is no short-cut way of becoming an artist-teacher, the ideal for which every professional leader strives. She will find that a sound and liberal educational background, including a thorough knowledge of children's literature and a working knowledge of child psychology, will be the first phase of her preparation. At the same time, she will avail herself of first-hand experiences in working with boys and girls in many different situations. General teaching experience has proved invaluable to leaders who have later become specialists in this field.

Training and study in drama and speech will enable a leader to guide children with a skill and an artistry that she will not be able to achieve without availing herself of this relevant background. Just as a teacher with a knowledge and an appreciation of music is better able to guide children into composing songs and melodies than one who lacks these things, so a teacher with a knowledge and appreciation of drama will be better able to guide children into creating plays which are thrilling and satisfying because of their artistic standards.

LOOKING TO THE FUTURE

It is true that many leaders will have a special flair for creative dramatics, but sincerity, enthusiasm, and common sense will go a long way in helping a person who is willing to try to work creatively with children. A leader may not often reach the depths nor the heights she dreams of, but through a sincerity of purpose she can accomplish far more than she may realize by helping a group of boys and girls to have good wholesome fun playing together.

If a leader has faith in what she is doing, she will grow immeasurably along with the children, and with her make-believe heart, creative dramatics can take her and the children wherever they choose to go—to the mountains of Tibet, to King Arthur's Round Table, to Banbury Cross, or up to the moon in a shoebox. A mother, a teacher, any adult leader who really cares for children and who guides them slowly but surely into an appreciation of their cultural heritage, will be doing far more than she may ever realize to build future patrons in the fine art of living. People the world over need to strengthen their cultural and spiritual values if world understanding is to become a reality, for cultural forces are far more unifying than political ones. When a child's thinking has grown beyond a mere interest in material living into a broader world of ideas, of truth, and of beauty, his entire life will become richer and happier, and he will be more tolerant.

Since drama has been a cultural force for over two thousand years, and since the play spirit is deep and fundamental in all children, it would seem practical for leaders wherever they might be to introduce creative dramatics, in order that children might understand each other better. Creative dramatics does not lead children into a make-believe world but rather helps them to see the world around them and to discover the magic that is real and deep within each one. It teaches children to listen as well as to hear, to see as well as to look, and to speak as well as to talk. Through creative dramatics parents, teachers, and community leaders can help the children of today understand the world of tomorrow. If we can laugh and talk together—if we can play and work together —then we can live together.

Appendix A

MATERIAL FOR DRAMATIZATION

> Books are the gateway to the world.
> —STEFAN ZWEIG

I. POETRY LIST

The use of rhythmic verse which is strong in character, feeling, and action has been found most successful in creative dramatics programs. The following poems have been chosen for these qualities and may be used for creative dramatics, dramatic play, or as motivation material.

Poetry, perhaps more than any other thematic material, provides a challenge to the children's imaginations, for often only the mere skeleton of a story plot may be given. Still more frequently, a poem may only set the mood which will lead to the subsequent development of a story by the children. The poem, "Some One," provides an excellent example of this type of stimulating, thought-provoking material.

In using appropriate poetry as motivation for a story, the leader may dynamically reach the children's minds and imaginations and coördinate the thinking of the group. The atmosphere thus created makes for smooth transition into story presentation.

The following verses have been categorized according to subject matter. Since most of the categories are the same as those in the story list, poems may be easily found for use in conjunction with stories of similar types, that is, for setting a mood and enriching an experience. There has been no attempt made to organize the poems into age groups, since so many are suitable for all ages. The numbers after the poem titles refer to their sources, as listed in the bibliography immediately following.

IN THE BEGINNING

LONG, LONG AGO, un.: 7, 13
CRADLE HYMN, Martin Luther: 1, 13, 19, 21
A CHRISTMAS FOLK SONG, L. W. Reese: 1
ALL THINGS BRIGHT AND BEAUTIFUL, Cecil Frances Alexander:
    4, 19
BUTTERCUPS AND DAISIES, Mary Howitt: 11

SKY SONGS

Clouds
    CLOUDS, Helen Wing: 9
    MORNING CLOUDS, Nellie B. Miller: 9
    CLOUDS, Norman Ault: 11
    AUTUMN RACES, Emilie Blackmore Stapp: 9
Wind
    THE MERRY WIND, Mary M. Dodge: 22
    THE WIND (WHO HAS SEEN THE WIND?), Christina Rossetti:
        1, 4, 7, 8, 9, 11, 19, 21
    WINDY NIGHTS, Robert Louis Stevenson: 4
    THE WIND, Robert Louis Stevenson: 4, 9, 11, 13, 19, 21
    BLOW WIND, BLOW, un.: 12
    TAKE CARE, Rose Waldo: 9
Moon
    THE MOON'S THE NORTH WIND'S COOKIE, Vachel Lindsay: 1,
        17, 19, 21

A STORY IN THE SNOW, Pearl R. Crouch: 13
SNOWMAN, un.: 9
FOG, Carl Sandburg: 1, 19

It's Spring!

WHO LIKES THE RAIN?, Clara B. Bates: 4, 8, 9, 12
RAIN IN THE NIGHT, Amelia J. Burr: 18
KITE TALES, Rose Waldo: 9
LITTLE WIND, Kate Greenaway: 21
MUD, Polly C. Boyden: 8, 13
CROCUS, Sarah J. Day: 13
BABY SEED SONG, Edith Nesbit: 7, 11, 13, 18
LITTLE SNAIL, Hilda Conkling: 13
WOULD YOU LIKE TO SEE GOATS DANCE ON STILTS? un.: 12
AT THE WEDDING OF MISS JENNY WREN, un.: 12
THE BLUEBIRD, Emily H. Miller: 4, 13
THE BUILDING OF THE NEST, Margaret Sangster: 11
SKIPPING ROPES, Dorothy Aldis: 5
THE SECRET, un.: 8, 24
JONATHAN BING DANCES FOR SPRING, Beatrice C. Brown: 8
A COMPARISON, John Farrar: 1, 13
APRIL AND MAY, Anne Robinson: 21
THE UMBRELLA BRIGADE, Laura Richards: 21
SINGING, Robert Louis Stevenson: 21
DAFFODOWNDILLY, A. A. Milne: 25

Summertime

GRASSHOPPER GREEN, un.: 1, 4, 8, 9, 13, 24
BELONGING TO SUMMER, Mildred D. Shacklett: 9
SUMMER WISH, John Farrar: 9
THE BUTTERBEAN TENT, Elizabeth M. Roberts: 19, 21
OVER IN THE MEADOW, Olive H. Wadsworth: 12
BAREFOOT DAYS, Rachel Field: 7, 14, 23
A SUMMER MORNING, Rachel Field: 21
CANTICLE, William Griffith: 11

MUMPS, Elizabeth M. Roberts: 1, 13
SATURDAY TOWELS, Lysbeth B. Borie: 1, 24
THE SOUNDS IN THE MORNING, Eleanor Farjeon: 1
WYNKEN, BLYNKEN, AND NOD, Eugene Field: 1, 4, 7, 8, 11,
    12, 13
FUN IN A GARRET, Emma C. Dowd: 9, 21
MIX A PANCAKE, Christina Rossetti: 9, 11, 21
HUSH-A-BYE BABY, un.: 1, 11
MUD PIE SHOP, Anne M. Halladay: 7
THE TEA PARTY, Kate Greenaway: 7, 13
I LIKE HOUSECLEANING, Dorothy B. Thompson: 7
THE SPRINKLER, Dorothy Aldis: 7
THE SHINY LITTLE HOUSE, Nancy M. Hayes: 21
BREAD MAKING, E. L. King: 23
MONDAY MORNING, Helen Wing: 9

BOYS AND GIRLS JUST MY AGE

MISS MUFFET: 1, 19
LITTLE BOY BLUE: 1, 19
LITTLE BO PEEP: 1, 11
JACK AND JILL: 1, 19
MARY'S LAMB, Sara J. Hale: 1, 9, 11, 19
MISTRESS MARY: 1, 19

ALL KINDS OF ANIMALS

THE CAT AND THE FIDDLE: 1
TWO WRENS: 1
THREE LITTLE KITTENS, Eliza Lee Follen: 1, 9, 21, 19
PUSSY CAT, PUSSY CAT: 1
THE OWL AND THE PUSSYCAT, Edward Lear: 1, 4, 8, 9, 13, 14,
    19, 23, 24
CAT, Mary B. Miller: 19, 21, 24
CAT, Dorothy W. Baruch: 1, 21
THE LITTLE TURTLE, Vachel Lindsay: 7, 8, 9, 18, 21, 24

THE WOODPECKER, E. M. Roberts: 7, 8, 9, 13, 14, 23, 24
MRS. PECK PIGEON, Eleanor Farjeon: 1, 7, 21, 24
MY DOG, Tom Robinson: 7
THE SQUIRREL (WHISKY FRISKY), un.: 1, 7, 9, 21, 24
MR. RABBIT, Dixie Willson: 8
THE SEA GULL, Leroy F. Jackson: 9, 24
WHITE BUTTERFLIES, Algernon C. Swinburne: 24
THE CHICKENS, un.: 1, 8, 24
BAREBACK RIDER, Dorothy Aldis: 24
ELEPHANTS, Dorothy Aldis: 24
SPIDER WEBS, James S. Tippett: 1, 24
THE CITY MOUSE, Christina Rossetti: 4, 7, 11, 13, 19, 21, 24
THE DUCK, Edith King: 9, 11, 19, 23
THE EGG, Laura E. Richards: 13
FUZZY WUZZY, CREEPY CRAWLY, Lillian Schulz: 21
THE TIRED CATERPILLAR, un.: 24
WILD BEASTS, Evaleen Stein: 1, 24
OVER IN THE MEADOW, Olive A. Wadsworth: 9, 12
IN THE BARNYARD, Dorothy Aldis: 24
THE ANIMAL STORE, Rachel Field: 1, 8, 14, 23, 24
HOW CREATURES MOVE, un.: 7, 9
UNDER THE TENT OF THE SKY, Rowena B. Bennett: 24

THINGS THAT GO

Trains
THE STATION, Kitty Parsons: 15
ENGINE, James S. Tippett: 1, 21
TRAINS, James S. Tippett: 9, 21
Boats
BOATS, Rowena B. Bennett: 9
SHIPS, Nancy B. Turner: 21
FERRY-BOATS, James S. Tippett: 7, 9, 21
I SAW A SHIP A-SAILING, un.: 1, 4, 13, 23
FREIGHT BOATS, James S. Tippett: 7, 9, 13

WHERE GO THE BOATS, Robert Louis Stevenson: 4, 8, 19, 21
TUGS, James S. Tippett: 9
Airplanes
UP IN THE AIR, James S. Tippett: 1, 21
AIRPLANES, Muriel Shulz: 7
THE AIRPLANE, Annette Wynne: 9
THE ZEPPELIN, Rowena B. Bennett: 9
Miscellaneous
TRUCKS, James S. Tippett: 1, 9
ROADS, Rachel Field: 1, 7, 14, 19, 23
STOP-GO, Dorothy Baruch: 21

OUR OWN COUNTRY AND FAR-OFF LANDS

AN INDIAN LULLABY, un.: 1
INDIAN CHILDREN, Annette Wynne: 9, 13, 14, 21, 23
THE ROAD TO CHINA, Olive Beaupre Miller: 13
THE LITTLE TOY LAND OF THE DUTCH, un.: 13
OTHER CHILDREN, Helen Wing: 9
ABOU BEN ADHEM, Leigh Hunt: 19, 20
WRAGGLE TAGGLE GYPSIES, un.: 2, 19
KING JOHN AND THE ABBOT OF CANTERBURY, un.: 1, 2, 16, 20
ROBIN HOOD AND LITTLE JOHN, un.: 1, 19
SONG OF SHERWOOD, Alfred Noyes: 11, 14, 16, 18, 23
YOUNG LOCHINVAR, Sir Walter Scott: 2, 16, 19
PAUL REVERE'S RIDE, Henry Wadsworth Longfellow: 1, 11, 20
THE ADMIRAL'S GHOST, Alfred Noyes: 1
GET UP AND BAR THE DOOR, un.: 2
THE GLOVE AND THE LIONS, Leigh Hunt: 20
THE KING AND THE MILLER OF MANSFIELD, un.: 20

THE MAGIC SPELL

HAVE YOU WATCHED THE FAIRIES?, Rose Fyleman: 6, 7, 18
THE CHILD AND THE FAIRIES, un.: 4
TWENTY FOOLISH FAIRIES, Nancy B. Turner: 21

250   *Creative Dramatics in Home, School, and Community*

JONATHAN BING, Beatrice C. Brown: 1, 14, 23
JONATHAN BING'S MANNERS, Beatrice C. Brown: 23
DOOR BELLS, Eugene Field: 14, 23
SKATING, Herbert Asquith: 1, 19
BUNDLES, John Farrar: 9
THE CLOCK SHOP, Hugh Chesterman: 9
THE SUNDAY MORNING FISHERMAN, Dorothy Aldis: 3
THE COBBLER, Eleanor Chaffee: 7
THE BALLOON MAN, Rose Fyleman: 6, 7, 9, 21
MERRY-GO-ROUND, Dorothy Baruch: 19, 21
MERRY-GO-ROUND, Marguerite Gode: 7
CIRCUS PARADE, James S. Tippett: 24
CIRCUS, Eleanor Farjeon: 1, 7, 13, 14, 21, 23, 24
I'LL BE A CLOWN, Mary C. Davies: 23
WHEN EVERYBODY, Dorothy Aldis: 3
THE ORCHESTRA, Olive Beaupre Miller: 12
FISHING, Vivian Gouled: 7
PEOPLE, Lois Lenski: 7
THE ROMP, Nancy B. Turner: 7
THE DUEL, Eugene Field: 1, 8, 9, 11, 19, 23, 24
HANDS, Dorothy Aldis: 5, 21
FEET, Dorothy Aldis: 5, 21
SEA FEVER, John Masefield: 1, 13, 14, 18, 19
ROBINSON CRUSOE, Charles E. Carryl: 11, 13
MUD CAKES, Mildred D. Shacklett: 9
ON THE BEACH, Emilie Blackmore Stapp: 9
THE OLD MARKET WOMAN, (Nursery Rhyme): 2
MARKET SQUARE, A. A. Milne: 25
THE ENCHANTED SHIRT, John Hay: 20

POETRY BIBLIOGRAPHY

1. *Anthology of Children's Literature,* Edna Johnson, Carrie Scott, and Evelyn Sickels, Houghton Mifflin Company.
2. *Ballads and Ballad-Plays,* John Hampden, Thomas Nelson and Sons, Ltd.

3. *Before Things Happen,* Dorothy Aldis, G. P. Putnam's Sons.
4. *Children's First Book of Poetry,* Emilie Kip Baker, American Book Company.
5. *Everything and Anything,* Dorothy Aldis, G. P. Putnam's Sons.
6. *Fairies and Chimneys,* Rose Fyleman, Doubleday and Company.
7. *For a Child,* Wilma McFarland, The Westminster Press.
8. *The Golden Book of Poetry,* Jane Werner, Simon and Schuster.
9. *The Golden Flute,* Alice Hubbard and Adeline Babbitt, The John Day Company.
10. *Heigh Ho for Hallowe'en,* Elizabeth Sechrist, Macrae Smith Company.
11. *Home Book of Verse for Young Folks,* Burton E. Stevenson, Henry Holt and Company.
12. *My Book House, in the Nursery,* Olive Beaupre Miller, The Bookhouse for Children.
13. *My Poetry Book,* Grace T. Huffard and Laura M. Carlisle, The John Winston Company.
14. *One Hundred Best Poems for Boys and Girls,* Marjorie Barrows, Whitman Publishing Company.
15. *Poems for the Children's Hour,* Milton Bradley Company.
16. *Rainbow Gold,* Sara Teasdale, The Macmillan Company.
17. *The Saint Nicholas Book of Verse,* Mary B. Skinner and Joseph O. Skinner, Century Company.
18. *Silver Pennies,* Blanche J. Thompson, The Macmillan Company.
19. *Story and Verse for Children,* Miriam Blanton Huber, The Macmillan Company.
20. *Story-Telling Poems,* Frances J. Olcott, Houghton Mifflin Company.
21. *Sung Under the Silver Umbrella,* Literature Committee of the Association for Childhood Education, The Macmillan Company.
22. *The Topaz Story Book,* Ada M. Skinner and Eleanor L. Skinner, Duffield and Company.

23. *Two Hundred Best Poems for Boys and Girls,* Marjorie Barrows, Whitman Publishing Company.
24. *Under the Tent of the Sky,* John E. Brewton, The Macmillan Company.
25. *When We Were Very Young,* A. A. Milne, E. P. Dutton & Company.
26. *Words and Music,* Halvor L. Harley, Halvor L. Harley.

II. STORY LIST

In compiling a list of stories for use in creative dramatics, we have attempted to select material which is outstanding in action and feeling, which provides opportunities for imaginative thinking, and which appeals strongly to children. Most of the stories are not new but are traditional and classic in children's literature. They have been found most successful in actual use with creative drama groups.

A few of the stories, among the finest in children's literature, may incorporate minor incidents which are unsuitable for playing. In such cases, the leader must use discriminatory taste and judgment in the presentations, deleting the material or substituting appropriate action in its place when necessary. For example, in the story of "The Three Billy Goats Gruff," the plot might end with the Troll being pushed into the river, instead of his meeting the horrible fate described in the original version.

It has been our desire to include in this list as great a variety of subject-matter and style as possible, in order that these stories may bring to mind still others. The list is necessarily only a cross-section of the excellent and abundant material suitable for creative dramatics use.

The stories have been categorized according to subject-matter to facilitate reference and selection. Within the categories, stories for each age group may be found together; however, these divisions are by no means rigid, for the consideration of individual or group differences in maturity, interests, and environment may determine the choice of more or less complex material. The numbers after the story titles refer to their sources, as listed in the bibliography immediately following.

IN THE BEGINNING

LET'S GO TO NAZARETH (7-8) 7

Let's go to Nazareth and visit Tobiah and his family. Tobiah, who is just seven years old, can show us much about the way of living when Jesus was a boy. (All seven stories are good for dramatization.)

JESUS, THE STORY OF (7-14) 38

These short stories about Jesus' works on earth help us to understand more about His life and the people who lived in His time. Many beautiful and exciting stories can be played effectively.

JOSEPH AND THE COAT OF MANY COLORS (7-14) 7, 8: Vol. V, 30

What a wonderful gift is a coat of many colors! Joseph never would have guessed that his prized possession would one day lead him to be sold as a slave to the Ishmaelite merchants.

THE BABY IN THE BULRUSHES (7-14) 7, 24, 30

What frail hope Moses' mother must have had when she placed her son in the water-proof basket to protect him from the Egyptian king's decree of death. What do you suppose happened to the child in the basket-boat?

THE COMING OF THE MAGI AND THE FLIGHT INTO EGYPT (7-14) 7, 30

The story of God's gift to the world and the real meaning of Christmas is one that can be played by all age groups. There are many good children's versions of this story. Joseph's and Mary's flight into Egypt goes hand in hand with the story of the coming of Christ.

NOAH'S ARK (7-14) 7, 8: Vol. I, 24, 30

The first and most famous ship was Noah's ark. What kinds of animals and birds do you suppose Noah took with him on this ship during the great flood?

A STAR SHONE (9-14) 69

These stories tell of Jesus' birth, the way he grew, and the things he did as a man. They show us in a beautiful way the fundamentals of truth and love which He taught.

THE GOOD SAMARITAN (9-14) 7, 24, 30

How can one prove himself a worthy neighbor? Let's follow the good Samaritan on his travels, and I'm sure that we shall find the answer.

WHERE LOVE IS THERE GOD IS ALSO (12-14) 8: Vol. IV, 86

Martin was a poor Russian cobbler. He was unhappy and bitter, until a very strange thing happened to him. As he read his Bible one night, he heard a voice saying that Christ would visit him the next day. Many people did come on the morrow, yet surely not one of them was He. But then it was that Martin learned a wonderful truth.

THE TIME OF THE YEAR

THE LITTLE PINK ROSE (5-6) 72

Why do you suppose the Little Pink Rose wouldn't let in the wind and the rain when they knocked on her door? Perhaps she didn't know that one day she would be the "prettiest little pink rose in the whole garden!"

THE LAMB THAT WENT TO FAIRYLAND (5-6) 58, 81

Would you like to know why tiny white lambs with woodeny legs and little black noses always skip and dance in the meadows in the spring? A fairy queen and her dancing fairies can tell you the secret.

OUT OF THE NEST (5-6) 48

A little bird just learning to fly has many problems—particularly if he's a curious little bird who peeps over the edge of his nest to see who is saying, "Kerchunk!" What a surprise it would be for anyone to fall right in the middle of a frog chorus rehearsal!

THE THREE LITTLE BUTTERFLY BROTHERS (5-6) 31
Three little butterflies, one white, one red, and one yellow, were caught in the rain. They tried to find shelter, but the flowers were very unkind and wouldn't let them in. The sun, at last, took pity on them, and what do you think he did?

THE LITTLE ISLAND (5-6) 41
Come with us and see the seasons change on the Little Island. We'll see lobsters and seals and gulls, and perhaps the kitten will have faith when we tell him our secret.

RED MITTENS (5-6) 61
Mommie knit Joe a beautiful pair of red mittens, and when the snow came they kept his fingers nice and warm. But then he lost them. None of his animal friends could find them until Cow helped, and what a joke it was when she found them!

THE WINTER NOISY BOOK (5-6) 88
Come with Muffin and me outside to listen to the winter sounds. It's always such fun to listen with Muffin!

THE WIND AND THE SUN (5-6) 5, 12, 13, 24, 72, 73
Who is the stronger, the wind or the sun? They argued and argued, and finally agreed to have a contest to decide the matter!

THE SNOWDROP (5-6) 31
Wouldn't it be lonely to be a little flower living in a bulb house deep in the ground, waiting for spring to come? The little Snowdrop was so anxious that she just couldn't wait until the snow went away.

WHY THE EVERGREEN KEEPS ITS LEAVES IN WINTER (5-6) 31, 35
The kind frost king forbade the north wind to blow the leaves off all the trees for a very special reason. Could the little bird with the broken wing have had something to do with it?

WHY THE BEAR SLEEPS ALL WINTER (7-8) 26

Do you know why bears sleep all winter? It all started long ago when Brothers Rabbit, Frog, Squirrel, Mole, and Fox played a clever trick on mean old Brother Bear.

THE SNOW MAIDEN (7-8) 8: Vol. II, 24

Ivan and Marie, two Russian peasants, had always wanted a child. They finally made a little snow maiden, and what a surprise they had when she came to life! Of course a snow child must be very careful, or else a dreadful thing might happen.

THE TWELVE MONTHS (7-8) 5, 31

Little Marushka saw twelve men sitting about a fire on top of a high mountain. These men were, of all things, the months of the year, and they helped Marushka solve her problems and find happiness.

THE THREE GOLDEN APPLES (9-12) 83

Hercules, in search of the three golden apples in the garden of the Hesperides, was not in the least afraid when he heard they were guarded by a hundred-headed monster. His adventures with the Old Man of the Sea and the Giant Atlas were only part of his search.

A MIDSUMMER NIGHT'S DREAM (12-14) 65, 76

Do you think the dreams that you dream in the summertime are very different from those of other times of the year? If you do, you will understand this strange and wonderful story.

TODAY'S A SPECIAL DAY

ASK MR. BEAR (5-6) 24, 73, 81

It's hard to find a nice present to give Mama on her birthday or on Mothers' Day. If you should happen to meet Mr. Bear, why don't you ask him what to give her?

MRS. MALLABY'S BIRTHDAY (5-6) 50

If you were living all alone and were exactly one hundred years old, it would be very nice to have all your friends remember your birthday. Of course, the very nicest thing of all would be to have a cuddly little kitten, because, .as Mrs. Mallaby said, "It can be your very own."

THE CHRISTMAS CAKE (5-6) 48

Have you ever made a Christmas cake? Well then, let's make one now, and before you know it, " 'Tis just the right time for the baker to bake the nice brown sugary Christmas cake!"

THE WHITE EASTER RABBIT (5-6) 47

"Just how can I become an Easter Rabbit?" wondered the little bunny. He asked all his animal friends, but no one would listen. Then a little fairy helped him!

A SURPRISE FOR MRS. BUNNY (5-6) 75

Do you know how Easter eggs came to be? Eight little bunnies, who wanted to give their mother an extra special birthday present, can tell you.

EASTER HAT AND EASTER BUNNY (5-6) 49

One morning, Mrs. Goose received an invitation to the Easter Bunny's Saturday breakfast, so she went right down and bought a new hat. That poor hat didn't last very long, however, with Mrs. Goose's appetite!

THE COUNTRY BUNNY AND THE LITTLE GOLD SHOES (5-6) 19

If you are wise and kind and swift, the Grandfather Bunny might choose you for the fifth Easter Bunny, even if you are a Country Bunny. If you are especially brave, you might even be able to wear the gold shoes!

TWINKLING FEET'S HALLOWE'EN (5-6) 83

What an awful thing it would be to lose your laugh—especially if you were a little elfin like Twinkling Feet. None of the other pixies nor Jack O'Lantern nor even Jolly Little Witch could help him, for some people say you can never find anything you've lost on Hallowe'en.

THE LITTLE PUMPKIN (5-6) 83

If you were a pretty little pumpkin, wouldn't you love to be made into a Jack O'Lantern? One little pumpkin thought he wouldn't like it at all, until it really happened!

THE DISCONTENTED PUMPKIN (5-6) 83

After Jack Frost visited Farmer Crane's field, all the pumpkins turned a beautiful color. One pumpkin was very proud—too proud just to be made into a pie! Perhaps if he hadn't been so proud, the awful thing wouldn't have happened.

GIFTS FOR THE FIRST BIRTHDAY (5-8) 25

The Christ Child was given gifts that we have heard about for many years, but did you know of the gifts from the nightingale, the fir tree, and the robin? Their gifts remain for all the world to enjoy.

THE LITTLE FIR TREE (5-8) 72

If you were a little fir tree watching all of your big brothers and sisters being taken away to new and wonderful places, wouldn't you be sad that you were too little to go along? One little fir tree was, until someone thought he was just the right size for a Christmas Tree.

GIFT OF THE EARTH (7-8) 29

Three little chiquitas prayed very hard for a doll on Christmas, and their prayers were answered in a very strange way. What do you suppose happened one sad day when a stranger came to take away their new doll?

A TURKEY FOR THE STUFFING (7-8) 83

Who ever heard of a Thanksgiving dinner of stuffing without a turkey? When you're poor, you have to make the best of it, unless, of course, you should meet a nice boat-captain.

THE CONJURE WIVES (7-8) 33

Just keep on stirring your enchanted brew, Witches! You don't know it now, but something fearful is going to happen if that "knock-knock-knocking" keeps on at your door!

THE CHRISTMAS CUCKOO (9-12) 31

If a cuckoo gave you the choice of having a green leaf from the Merry Tree or a leaf of pure gold, which would you choose? Spare took the first, and Scrub took the latter, and who do you suppose became the richer?

IN CLEAN HAY (9-12) 36

This beautiful Yuletide story of four Polish children and their puppet show is an enriching experience, for in it lies the true spirit of Christmas.

THE TWO ALMS (9-12) 83

Many rich travelers passed a poor blind beggar-lady on a snowy Thanksgiving Day. One man finally gave her a gold piece by mistake—but that wasn't all he did for her!

ARCHIE AND THE APRIL FOOLS (9-12) 25

There's a giraffe in the back yard! Don't you believe me? Of course it is April Fools' Day, but don't be too sure this is a joke!

THE CHRISTMAS CAROL (9-14) 16

Can you believe that there was ever a man who didn't believe in Christmas? Ebenezer Scrooge didn't for a long time, until a tiny little boy helped him learn the real spirit of Christmas.

THE CHRISTMAS APPLE (9-14) 80: Ch. IV

Even an apple can be a very wonderful present, if it is all you have to give. A German clockmaker learned this truth when he had to sell his beautiful gift, planned for the Christ Child, to pay a doctor bill.

WHY THE CHIMES RANG (9-14) 12, 87

A gift far richer than jewels or even a king's crown made the chimes ring in the great church. Do you know what the beautiful, simple gift was?

THE JUGGLER OF NOTRE DAME (9-14) 85

A poor little juggler, taken into a monastery by kind monks, gave the Virgin the only gift he had. As the monks were about to stop him, a miracle happened!

THE PEDDLER OF BALLAGHADEREEN (9-14) 25, 85

There is surely no finer story to tell on Saint Patrick's Day than that of the kind peddler of Ballaghadereen, and how his goodness was rewarded.

THE CURIOUS BIRTHDAY (9-14) 40

Frederic, the pirates' apprentice, overthrew pirate life on what he believed was his twenty-first birthday. His many adventures with the Pirates of Penzance provide thrills galore!

BOYS AND GIRLS JUST MY AGE

THE POPPY SEED CAKES (5-6) 24

If you were a little boy like Andrewshek from the old country, would you rather have poppy seed cakes or fluffy green goose feather pillows to go on your jumpy feather bed? Well, it all depends on the greedy green goose!

BILLY'S HAIRCUT (5-6) 71

Did you know that everybody's hair grows just a teeny bit longer every single day? And what do you do when the time comes when your mother says that your hair is just a teeny bit too long? Why, of course, you take a trip to the barber shop, just as Billy did.

GROCERIES (5-6) 71

Hello, Mr. Grocer! I have only a few pennies, so what shall I buy? Don't you like being a grocer man? You say you are getting tired? Well, let's change places for a day. May I bring along my friends?

HERE COMES DADDY (5-6) 59

When *will* Daddy come home? Peter and his cat, Finnigan, waited and watched. All kinds of people came and went, but no Daddy yet!

THE RATCATCHER (THE PIED PIPER), (5-8) 60

Hamlin is a sleepy town now, for the Pied Piper has played the rats and even the children right out of it! He must play very enchanting tunes. Why, we might even follow him, too!

THE CAP THAT MOTHER MADE (5-8) 8: Vol. II, 24

No wonder Anders would not trade his cap even for a king's crown, for nothing is really as wonderful as a hat made by your own mother!

PELLE'S NEW SUIT (7-8) 24

Everyone loves new clothes, but a new suit is ever so much nicer if you have to work for it. That is just why Pelle's was one of the nicest suits anyone ever had.

HANSEL AND GRETEL (7-8) 8: Vol. III, 27, 31, 73, 89

When Hansel and Gretel saw a beautiful little house in the woods made of sugarplums and gingerbread children, they couldn't resist taking a wee little nibble. That was the start of their fearful adventure with the wicked witch who lived in the enchanted cottage.

THE PRINCESS WHO COULD NOT CRY (7-8) 58

Some people never laugh, but have you ever heard of anyone who couldn't cry? A little princess in a far-off land couldn't, though the whole kingdom tried to make her shed a single tear. A little peasant girl finally found the way!

WHITTINGTON AND HIS CAT (9-12) 8: Vol. II, 12, 23, 78, 89

Who would have thought that a little cat would bring riches beyond imagination to poor little Dick? His hard life working in the kitchen under a cruel cook was suddenly at an end!

TOM SAWYER (9-12) 73, 82

It may be hard to whitewash a fence, but if you think it's fun, then it is! Let's all help Tom paint his fence, and then join him on some of his many adventures.

PENROD (9-12) 52

Penrod Schofield was just like Billy who lives down the street. Along with his friend Sam and his dog Duke, he jumped from one prank to another. Being called a "little gentleman" was considered an insult to Penrod, for he was just that kind of a boy!

CAPTAINS COURAGEOUS (9-14) 10

Harvey, a self-satisfied American boy, fell off a liner bound for Europe and was picked up by a fishing schooner. What a world full of lessons he learned during his travels!

THE ADVENTURES OF HUCKLEBERRY FINN (9-14) 2

Do you know Tom Sawyer's friend, Huck Finn, who found "civilized living pretty rough, because it's so dismal regular?" Huck was a lot like the boys next door, and, best of all, he's just their age!

LITTLE WOMEN (12-14) 8: Vol. VI, 44, 73

Wouldn't you like to be part of the March family, as Meg, Jo, Beth, or Amy? Perhaps we could spend Christmas with them, or we might even be there when some very exciting things happen to the Marches.

THE PRINCE AND THE PAUPER (12-14) 55

Isn't it amazing how two boys can look so much alike, yet be from such different surroundings? What do you suppose would happen if the prince and the pauper traded places?

ABRAHAM LINCOLN (12-14) 1

Do you think it's odd for boys to spend time reading instead of playing ball? Some of Abe Lincoln's friends thought so. I wonder what they thought when he became president!

ALL KINDS OF ANIMALS

THE TURTLE WHO COULDN'T STOP TALKING (5-6) 8: Vol. I, 24, 47

Have you ever met an animal who never stopped talking or never listened to what anyone else had to say? If you have, he was probably a lot like the slow, pokey turtle!

GEORGE AND ANGELA (5-6) 81

If two little mice named George and Angela decided to do exactly as they pleased, where do you think they would hide? I must tell you that Angela was never very original, and George was "a bit of a pickle," so you can be sure they really got into trouble.

SNIPPY AND SNAPPY (5-6) 68

Two little fieldmice followed a knitting ball into a very strange land called a house. Imagine their surprise when they found that the flowers on the rug didn't smell at all, and that they couldn't even hide under them.

THE HARE THAT RAN AWAY (5-6) 5, 13

Can you imagine how shocked all the animals in the forest were when they heard that the earth was falling in? King Lion wasn't quite so sure it was true and went off to find the rabbit who started the rumor.

THE TURKEY'S NEST (5-6) 48

"They may go to the East and go to the West, but they'll never be able to find my nest," said the sly old turkey hen. And do you know that not one of the animals ever could find her nest, though in the end she did give them a fine surprise.

THE THREE BEARS (5-6) 5, 12, 23, 24, 26, 27, 73, 89

What do you suppose the three bears were doing while Goldilocks ate up all of Little Bear's porridge, broke his chair, and fell fast asleep in his bed? I can think of many things, can't you?

THE TALE OF PETER RABBIT (5-6) 8: Vol. I, 12, 27

Camomile tea isn't much fun to drink—especially when your three little sisters are having bread and milk and blackberries for dinner. But camomile tea is just the thing for naughty little rabbits who trespass into Mr. McGregor's garden.

LITTLE LAMB (5-6) 42

Neither the merchant nor the tailor nor the weaver nor the shepherd could help Little Lamb when he found his coat was falling off. Black Sheep told him a secret, though, that made him happy again!

THE RUNAWAY BUNNY (5-6) 63

Once a little bunny wanted to run away from home. He and Mother Bunny talked for a long time about many things, and after they had *done* all these things, (in their heads, of course), the little bunny changed his mind.

THE THREE LITTLE PIGS (5-6) 6, 12, 23, 89

"I'll huff, and I'll puff, and I'll blow your house down," howled the wolf. Do you think we can build a house strong enough to fool him?

MONKEY SEE, MONKEY DO (5-6) 46

Lucky for the cap peddler that "monkeys see, monkeys do!" But it was certainly a joke on the monkeys.

THE THREE BILLY GOATS GRUFF (5-6) 6, 12, 22, 26, 27, 47, 73, 89

My, how sly those three Billy Goats Gruff were, and what a trick they played on the mean old troll. He really must have been surprised when he landed in the middle of the river!

THE FIRE IN THE KITCHEN (5-6) 49

What a surprise Mrs. Squirrel got when Mrs. Goose threw a pitcher of cold lemonade at her new red dress. Do you know why she did it? The reason was pretty silly!

THE LOST APRON POCKET (5-6) 49

Mrs. Goose made herself a nice new apron with a lovely little pocket. Mr. Pig came to tea, and after he left, Mrs. Goose looked and looked, but her apron pocket was gone! What do you suppose had happened?

THE LITTLE DUCKLING TRIES HIS VOICE (5-6) 81

Sometimes it is hard to find a voice that is your very own. The Little Duckling tried on many different voices, but for a long time he just couldn't find one to suit him.

MRS. GOOSE'S RUBBERS (5-6) 59

Poor Mrs. Goose lost her rubbers, just when it was about to rain. She searched high and low and asked all her friends, but still no rubbers! Then she just gave up, got ready to go out, and opened her umbrella. Guess what!

CASEY JOINS THE CIRCUS (5-6) 24

What could a little puppy dog like Casey do in a circus? Certainly all the rest of the animals didn't know. Casey found out at last, when Peter the baby elephant ran away.

THE TAR BABY (5-8) 8: Vol. III, 73

One summer a great drought came to the country, and Brother Fox was the only animal wise and ambitious enough to find water. To guard his well from sly Brother Rabbit, he made a Tar Baby. Just when he thought Brother Rabbit was trapped—well, that little rabbit's a clever one, you know!

THE LITTLE RABBIT WHO WANTED RED WINGS (5-8) 8: Vol. I, 47

It isn't always wise to wish you could look like someone else. A little white rabbit discovered this when he wished he had red wings just like a little bird. In the wink of an eye, he had them, and then his troubles began!

THE UGLY DUCKLING (5-8) 5, 8: Vol. VI, 12, 24, 27, 73, 89

"It does not matter in the least having been born in a duckyard, if only you come out of a swan's egg!" But who would ever have guessed that the Ugly Duckling would one day become a beautiful swan?

TIGGER'S BREAKFAST (7-8) 34

Winnie the Pooh, who lived with a donkey, a pig, and a kangaroo, found that Tigger didn't like honey or haycorns or even Eyore's thistles for breakfast. But Kanga's Extract of Malt was quite another matter.

HOW THE CAMEL GOT HIS HUMP (7-8) 5, 39

Do you know when a humph is a hump? Perhaps the lazy old camel can tell you, for he has one!

THE RAREST ANIMAL OF ALL (7-8) 5

To the deepest jungles of Africa went lovable Dr. Doolittle, to cure the monkeys of a terrible disease. The rarest animal of all that he met was the Pushmipullya, who, believe it or not, had two heads!

THE BREMEN TOWN MUSICIANS (THE TRAVELING MUSICIANS) (7-8) 5, 12, 27, 73, 89

A runaway donkey, dog, cat, and rooster set off to become musicians in the town of Bremen. Instead, they had a marvelous adventure and captured the house of some robbers in a most mysterious manner.

THE ELEPHANT'S CHILD (7-8) 39, 73

Some people just don't know what's good for them! But you will see what a "vantage" it was for the elephant's child to get a nice long trunk, thanks to the crocodile, instead of having just a "mear smear" nose.

LIVING IN W'ALES (7-8) 81

This story starts out with W'ales, but if you pay attention, you'll see it ends with whales. You'd think that being swallowed by a whale would be a pretty scary adventure, but it wasn't at all for a little girl and an Alsatian dog.

THE ADVENTURES OF THE LITTLE FIELD MOUSE (7-8) 35

A little field mouse chased a pretty, shiny acorn down a hole. When he reached the bottom, he was made prisoner by a tiny Red Man who knew what the acorn held!

PETER AND THE WOLF (7-8) 5

What a merry chase Peter had catching the ferocious wolf. But what would have happened if it hadn't been for all of Peter's animal friends and, of course, the hunters?

GUBRAND ON THE HILLSIDE (7-12) 5, 89

Gubrand went to town to sell a cow and, instead, traded her for a horse, the horse for a pig, and went on trading until he had neither a thing nor an animal to bring home. So sure was he of his wife's loyalty that he bet a friend his last hundred dollars that she wouldn't be angry!

THINGS THAT GO

FERRY BOATS (5-6) 4

Do you like to ride ferry boats? I do, too! Especially when we hear that "jingle, jangle, here's a tangle when some get off and some get on."

THE BIG BLACK ENGINE (5-6) 4

"Choo choo, puff puff," goes the engine. "Ding dong, ding dong," sings another shiny black engine. But the best sound of all is the whistle!

CHOO CHOO, THE STORY OF A LITTLE ENGINE WHO RAN AWAY (5-6) 15

When a little train like Choo Choo runs away, that is real cause for alarm. She had many adventures, but when she was found, she was so happy that she let out a tiny "toot" with her last breath of steam.

CLEAR THE TRACK FOR MICHAEL'S MAGIC TRAIN (5-6) 17

Allll Aboarrrrrrrd! Clear the track for Michael's magic train!

You all know that a magic train is better than any other kind of a train, because you may be the conductor, the brakeman, the fireman, or just anyone on the train you'd like to be.

How the Automobiles Got Cured (5-6) 4

Have you ever seen a green-white-black-blue automobile? Well, no one else had either, until the day when Mr. White, Mr. Green, Mr. Black, and Mr. Blue had a terrible accident.

How the Road Was Built (5-6) 24

Ned lived in the country, where there were no real roads at all. He told the farmer and the cowboy that he would love to have a smooth road so he could ride his bicycle. Then the surveyors came, and, sure enough, they began the building of the road.

The Little Engine (5-6) 8: Vol. I, 47

A farmer who had some fine wheat asked all the engines he saw to haul it to market. These engines were all so lazy, though, that they refused. Then one little engine said, "I think I can!"

The Red Gasoline Pump (5-6) 24

What is more beautiful than a brand new red gasoline pump? And what fun it is to fill the tanks of taxis, trucks, Fords, and all sorts of cars.

The Tugboat (5-6) 24

Jo Anna was a happy, peppy tugboat, for she helped ferries and freighters and liners and barges and tankers. She and her captain were certainly busy people.

Bill and His Steam Shovel (5-6) 59

A man named Bill had a big red steamshovel. A fine steamshovel man he was, but he grew awfully tired of digging the same old things. Then, one day, he had the chance to dig a wonderful new swimming pool!

OUR COUNTRY AND THE FAR-OFF LANDS

Why Wild Roses Have Thorns (5-6) 5

Nanahboozoo was a great Indian magician who could make him-

self as tall as a tree or as little as a turtle. It was to him that the
wild roses came for help when the rabbits ate their brothers and
sisters.

How Glooscap Found the Summer (7-8) 5
Have you ever heard of a whale who carries Indians on her back
or smokes a peace pipe? Blob was that kind of a whale, and she
carried her friend, Glooscap, far across the sea on his journey to
find Summer.

The Poor Turkey Girl (7-8) 5
What would you think of a flock of turkeys who could change
old clothes into beautiful new ones and even make beautiful jewels?
The little Turkey Girl thought it was wonderful, until she forgot her
turkey friends!

The Wonderful Pear Tree (7-8) 77
Boys and girls in China enjoy hearing their grandmothers tell
stories just as we do. One of their favorite tales is about a pear tree
that sprung up from seeds planted by an old farmer. A selfish fruit
peddler could not understand why the pear tree had grown so
suddenly, nor did he know why the tree was so wonderful. See if
you can tell!

The Tongue-Cut Sparrow (7-8) 8: Vol. II, 12
When the Tongue-Cut Sparrow and his family bow their heads
down to the ground, you will know they are welcoming you into
their humble dwelling. When they bring boiled rice, fish, and cress,
and dance a sparrow dance, you will know that they are honoring
you with gracious and ancient Japanese customs. But what could
be in the magic chests they offer us?

The Mountain of Jade (The Red Dragon Kite) (7-8) 14
An old Chinese sculptor, who lived at the Hill of Dawn, made
wonderful forms from the clay that he found on the hillside. One
morning when the Maker of Forms looked into the pool of clear-no-
color water, he saw the reflections of a horde of dragons. He cre-

ated a hundred such creatures to frighten the evil spirits, and keep them away from the beautiful Mountain of Jade.

THE KING AND THE MAGIC STICK (THE FIRST CHINESE FLUTE) (7-8) 79

"At least five thousand years ago, there lived in China a great and powerful king." Visitors from far-off lands journeyed to the royal palace to honor the king by bringing wonderful presents. One day, when the king was presented with a very unusual gift, he exclaimed, "That is the most beautiful present I have ever received!"

PAUL BUNYAN (7-12) 5, 24, 73

Some people don't believe that there ever was a woodsman so huge that men could use his frying pan for a skating rink. Paul Bunyan, however, was just such a man, and he and his giant blue ox, Babe, had many fabulous adventures in the North woods.

MACBETH (7-12) 76

What could be more fearful than meeting three old witches cackling over their mysterious brew on a lonely Scottish heath? Who knows what they have to tell of the future?

THE NÜRNBERG STOVE (9-12) 8: Vol. IV, 51

August and his nine brothers and sisters were very poor, and their one delight was the sumptuous stove, Hirschvogel, which kept them warm in the bitterly cold winter. One tragic day, August's father sold the stove, and August felt there was nothing to do but to go with it. He hid inside and traveled many miles until he reached—well, it was a magnificent surprise!

THE GIRL WHO COULD THINK (9-12) 24

Lotus Blossom and Moon Flower loved to go to parties, even after they were married and should have settled down. One day, as they were on their way to a party, their disapproving mother-in-law ordered them to bring home fire and wind wrapped in paper, or else never to return. How do you suppose they solved the problem?

THE NIGHTINGALE (9-12) 5

"The Emperor of Japan's nightingale is very poor compared to the Emperor of China's," for the Chinese nightingale has a heart of gold and a beautiful song that never dies. Do you know the great mystery about this bird?

CERES AND PROSERPINE (9-12) 5, 12

Who would ever have guessed that Proserpine's picking flowers would lead her to a terrible adventure in the underworld palace of Pluto? Many of the Greek gods take part in this exciting tale.

ARION AND THE DOLPHIN (9-12) 5

Arion sang so beautifully that he charmed both men and beasts. It was his fine voice that even saved his life and restored his wealth to him.

ARACHNE (9-12) 5, 31

It was not wise for Arachne to boast that she could weave more skillfully than Athena herself. She did just that, and she challenged the goddess to a contest. Today Arachne is weaving still, but, because of Athena's wrath, she is no longer a beautiful maiden!

ATALANTA'S RACE (9-12) 5

It is a rare thing to find a maiden who can outrun any man in the country. Atalanta was so fleet-footed, however, that she vowed she would marry no one but the man who could win a race with her. The goddess Aphrodite then took a hand in her fate!

ODIN'S SEARCH FOR WISDOM (9-12) 5, 12

A deep well of clear water was the source of Odin's wisdom. This new-found knowledge led him to a contest with Vafthrudner, the wisest of the Norse giants. The battle of wits lasted long, and no one could guess who would win.

THE QUEST FOR THE HAMMER (9-12) 5, 6, 8: Vol. IV

The secret of Thor's power to make thunder was his hammer, Miolnir. It came to pass that the giant Thrym stole Miolnir, and, to recover his power, Thor played a most unusual trick on the giant!

BALDER AND THE MISTLETOE (9-12) 5, 12

Everyone would certainly believe that mistletoe is the most harmless of plants. The evil god, Loki, however, made use of its seeming innocence to bring the greatest of harm to the gentlest of gods, Balder.

THE OLD MAN OF THE GOURD (9-12) 5

Did you ever hear of anyone's climbing into a gourd? One old man did and found a magnificent rock crystal palace inside—for this was the gourd of a shen! Then the old man began learning how to be a shen himself, which was no easy task.

THE KNIGHTS OF THE SILVER SHIELD (9-14) 8: Vol. IV, 12

The knights of a certain castle all carried magic silver shields which recorded their brave deeds, and well you may wonder how this could be! At first the shields were dull, but as the knights won glory, their shields grew brighter and brighter. On winning the greatest of all battles, a knight's shield glowed with a golden star. Sir Roland "won his star" without even raising his sword!

THE BELL OF ATRI (9-14) 28

The first bell in the town of Atri was called the Bell of Justice, for all who had grievances could ring the bell and call a council to solve their problems. Who would ever have guessed that even an old horse would know this!

THE RED LION BECOMES DANGEROUS (9-14) 32

The Red Lion Inn with its blazing fire and fine food gave shelter to six boys just returning from their long skating trip in Amsterdam. Watch out for the two men in the corner, boys, for a robbery is about to take place!

THE WINNING OF KINGHOOD (9-14) 6, 9, 12, 35

Do you know how Arthur became king and of the events leading to his being chosen? Come with me down the road of long ago, and we'll watch the contest of the knights as they try to pull a magic sword from a rock.

PROLOGUE TO THE ADVENTURES OF ROBIN HOOD (9-14) 45

Jesting Will Stutley, a member of Robin Hood's carefree band, tells us of Robin Hood's adventures with the king's foresters and of how he gathered his band. Shall we follow jolly Will into Sherwood Forest?

ROBIN HOOD AND THE TINKER (9-14) 6, 9

Do you know of the adventures and consequences that befell the Tinker when he tried to arrest Robin Hood? Why, here comes the Sheriff of Nottingham. Perhaps he will tell us!

THE PRINCESS AND THE VAGABOND (12-14) 85

This story tells of the taming of an Irish shrew. Who could believe that a vagabond could tame a haughty princess and marry her after all!

SIEGFRIED (12-14) 56, 70

Wotan, King of the Gods; the fair maiden Brunhilde; Siegfried the Brave; and Mime the dwarf all take part in this great adventure. Let's relive the days of the Norse gods with them!

CARMEN (12-14) 56, 70

As rich and bright as Carmen, the gypsy, is this exciting story laid in a brilliant Spanish setting. Blow the bugles! Enter the Torcadors!

THE BARBER OF SEVILLE (12-14) 56, 70

Do you know why barber shops have red and white poles in front of their shops? I know of no better place to find out than in the story of Figaro, the Barber of Seville.

TREASURE ISLAND (12-14) 5, 84

What a thrill it would be to take part in an adventure with pirates, or even to be one of the crew on an old sailing ship. As for landing on the coast of Treasure Island with Jim Hawkins, that would be the most exciting adventure of all!

THE MAGIC SPELL

THE GOLDEN GOOSE (5-6) 5, 60, 89

What would you think if you saw a long line of people stuck fast to each other, as well as to a boy holding a golden goose? It sounds pretty funny to me, and it looked funny even to the princess who couldn't laugh.

THE GINGERBREAD BOY (5-6) 5, 6, 8: Vol. I, 73

A little gingerbread boy ran and ran and ran away from everybody—that is, until the fox began chasing him!

SNOW WHITE AND ROSE RED (7-8) 5, 8: Vol. II, 12, 27, 73, 89

Why did two lovely sisters befriend a mean, long-bearded little dwarf, and what happened to the friendly, lumbering bear that finally caught him? Snow White and Rose Red can tell you, especially since, can you believe it, Snow White married one of them.

HOW TO TELL CORN FAIRIES IF YOU SEE 'EM (7-8) 81

Let's follow the Corn Fairy King right up this sunbeam and listen to the corn fairies singing, "Pla-sizzy, pla-sizzy, softer than an eye wink, softer even than a Nebraska baby's thumb."

THE REAL PRINCESS (THE PRINCESS ON THE PEA) (7-8) 5, 6, 12, 27, 73, 89

Did you know that real princesses are very sensitive? Why, they can even feel a tiny pea hidden under twenty mattresses and twenty feather beds. This test helped discover the true identity of a little ragged girl.

PINOCCHIO'S FIRST PRANKS (7-8) 5, 73

Fairy tales can be long, but so can a certain puppet's nose. It all started with a very ordinary looking piece of wood, but wait until it walks, talks, and sings—and look, too, at the mischief it brings!

THE HILLMAN AND THE HOUSEWIFE (7-8) 31

Never ever, ever try to deceive the fairies! A selfish housewife found that their magic can be as bad as it usually is good, as she tried to use her bewitched kettle.

THE WONDERFUL POT (7-8) 8: Vol. III, 26

A poor little boy sold his cow, the family's last possession, for an old three-legged pot. Can you imagine his mother's sorrow? But wait, there seems to be something magic about this pot!

THE NUTCRACKER AND SUGARDOLLY STORIES (7-8) 8: Vol. II, 25, 26

A little old peddler and his wife were on their way to market when they saw a magic garden with sugarplums and giant nut trees and sugar flowers. Against the warnings of the enchanted birds, the man and his wife took a nut and an egg. When the nut was cracked and the egg hatched, you'll never guess what came out of them!

THE SLEEPING BEAUTY (7-8) 6, 8: Vol. III, 27, 89

A needle prick isn't usually very dangerous, but to the little Princess Rosamond, it meant a hundred years' sleep. Do you know what was the magic greater than death which finally awakened her?

WISHING WISHES (7-8) 48

If you ever meet your fairy godmother, she is liable to give you three wishes. Your wishes will very likely come true, too, unless you're late, as Billy was.

THE ELVES AND THE SHOEMAKER (7-8) 6, 8: Vol. I, 12, 27, 31, 72, 73, 89

What could be more fun than making suits of tiny clothes for the shoemaker's elfin helpers? Or perhaps you'd rather be one of the sprightly elves who made a storeful of brand new shoes!

THE JOLLY TAILOR WHO BECAME KING (7-8) 5

Nittechka was so thin that noodles were the only food he could eat! He was a fine tailor, however, and one day he became king, after sewing up a hole in the sky over the kingdom.

THE HUT IN THE FOREST (7-8) 5

What would you think if you found a little hut in the forest where there lived an old man whose hen, cock, and brindled cow talked to you? A little girl's kindness to these strange animals led her to a magic adventure.

THE NUTCRACKER AND THE MOUSE KING (7-8) 5

A nutcracker headed a battle against the Mouse King and his army. Marie, who was watching, brought the battle to an end and disenchanted the nutcracker. Could it all have been just a dream?

THE LAD WHO WENT TO THE NORTH WIND (7-8) 5, 22, 73, 89

The North Wind gave a poor lad a magic cloth, a ram, and a stick. These were stolen by an inn-keeper, who found that the stick's magic was not as pleasant as that of the other gifts!

JACK AND THE BEANSTALK (7-8) 5, 8: Vol. II, 12, 23, 27, 60, 73, 89

Let's climb up the beanstalk with Jack and walk across the clouds to the Giant's castle. But don't forget, when you hear, "Fee, Fi, Fo, Fum," you'd better hide!

SNOW WHITE AND THE SEVEN DWARFS (7-8) 24, 73, 89

Mirror, mirror, on the wall, tell me what you see? Is it Snow White, Happy, the wicked queen, or whomever else you'd like us to be?

THE PLAIN PRINCESS (7-8) 54

Sometimes the best magic of all is the kind you work yourself. Princess Esmeralda, who had everything she could possibly want but was very, very plain, discovered this. It was then that she began to change most remarkably!

THE DANCING TEA KETTLE (7-8) 21

It is surprising to see a tea kettle dance, but it is even stranger to see it walk a tight rope! It isn't very wise to boil water in this particular kettle, for you never can tell what might happen!

PETER PAN (7-8) 53

Peter Pan, the elfin boy who never grew up, had many wonderful adventures with the Darling children. One of the most exciting was their encounter with the cruel Captain Hook!

WHY THE SEA IS SALT (7-8) 8: Vol. III, 12, 24, 35, 89

What a wonderful thing is a magic mill which can grind out anything you might ask for. Of course, one must know how to stop as well as to start it, as many people discovered.

RUMPELSTILTSKIN (TOM TIT TOT) (7-8) 12, 23, 24, 27, 89

How would you like to spin a roomful of straw into gold? Perhaps you wouldn't have to, if you could guess the name of a strange little man!

THE FIVE HUNDRED HATS OF BARTHOLOMEW CUBBINS (7-8) 5

It "happened to happen" that a little boy had a new hat on his head every time he took one off. So let's have it happen again to see what went on in the Kingdom of Didd.

OLD PIPES AND THE DRYAD (7-12) 12, 57

Did you know that the kiss of a dryad can make you ten years younger? Old Pipes, who played the cattle down from the hills, received several of these magic kisses from a grateful dryad. And my, oh my, wasn't the Echo Dwarf angry!

TWELVE DANCING PRINCESSES (7-12) 8: Vol. II, 60, 89

What could have been the reason that the shoes of twelve beautiful princesses were always worn out when they awoke in the morning? Star Gazer, a poor little shepherd, found their secret, with the aid of his magic laurel trees.

BOOTS AND HIS BROTHERS (7-12) 8: Vol. II, 12, 22, 73, 78, 89

Curiosity is sometimes a very fine thing, as little Boots discovered. When he went searching after strange noises and to see why rivers run, he learned the secrets that won him half a kingdom and the hand of a princess.

THE THREE WISHES (7-12) 8: Vol. III, 24, 27
If a beautiful fairy gave you three wishes, what would you wish for? Riches, a beautiful new house, or jewels? A poor old man and his wife thought of wishing for all of these, but they were so foolish that they wasted every one of their wishes.

THE TINDER BOX (7-12) 5, 73, 89
A witch and three dogs with most amazing eyes, plus a magic tinder box, changed a common soldier into a prince of fortune. What do you suppose happened when he almost lost the magic box?

MANY MOONS (7-12) 5
Do you know what the moon is made of? Is it molten copper, or green cheese, or gold? We must find the answer for the sake of Princess Lenore! Perhaps we should ask the court jester, or even the Royal Wizard.

PANDORA (7-12) 5, 12, 24, 73
Not many people can resist taking a tiny peek when someone says, "Don't open that box!" Pandora certainly couldn't, and she found that her curiosity led to real trouble!

CINDERELLA (7-12) 5, 6, 12, 24, 27, 73, 89
Who could ever believe that a poor, ragged little girl would one day become more beautiful than a fairy princess and marry a real prince! Of course, a fairy godmother can make almost anything happen.

THE PRINCESS ON THE GLASS HILL (7-12) 5, 8: Vol. III, 22, 73, 89
A princess sat on top of a glass hill holding three golden apples in her lap. All the bravest knights in the kingdom tried to ride up the slippery hill to fetch the apples, and thus win the hand of the princess. It wasn't a knight at all who finally succeeded!

LONG, BROAD, AND SHARPSIGHT (7-12) 5, 6, 20
If you had three friends such as a certain prince had, all your troubles would be solved. One friend, called Long, could stretch

himself to any height. The second, called Broad, could stretch himself to any width. And the third, called Sharpsight, could see for hundreds of miles and could smash rocks at a glance!

KING MIDAS AND THE GOLDEN TOUCH (7-12) 12, 24, 89

Wouldn't it be fun to have a magic touch that turned everything into gold? Perhaps it would be for a while, until you might try to eat or pick a fragile flower!

THE SORCERER'S APPRENTICE (7-12) 5

"Lif! Luf! Laf! Broom fetch water from the river!" Thus spoke the Sorcerer's apprentice, in the words he had heard his master use. The Broom obeyed him in the wink of an eye, but it was quite another matter to make it stop.

TOM THUMB (9-12) 5, 8: Vol. II, 12, 23, 73, 89

Take a good look at your thumb. Now, just imagine having a little son that size! Tom Thumb was no bigger, and he was so delicate that almost anything in the world could have harmed him. Just the same, he became a noble knight in King Arthur's Court.

ALADDIN AND THE WONDERFUL LAMP (9-12) 5, 73, 89

Aladdin, the son of a poor tailor, met his evil magic uncle. Through him, Aladdin found the fabulous enchanted lamp and learned the secret of the monstrous genie who lived inside.

HOW TILL GOT HIS NAME EULENSPIEGEL (9-14) 5, 78

Can't you just see merry Till, dressed in a black gown covered with green stars, and wearing a pointed cap with ears and bells on it? In this strange garb, he told fortunes from a magic straw mirror frame at the fair.

THE MIRACULOUS PITCHER (THE STRANGE VISITOR) (9-14) 12, 13, 23, 31

Can you imagine how wonderful it would be to have a milk pitcher which could never be emptied? A poor couple was given this gift in return for their great kindness to a stranger, who was really Mercury, the fleet-footed god.

THE LEGEND OF SLEEPY HOLLOW (12-14) 62, 67

How would you feel if one dark night you should see a headless horseman galloping through Sleepy Hollow? It would be a very frightening experience, I assure you!

RIP VAN WINKLE (12-14) 62, 73

Imagine awakening from a nap to find that everything and everyone around you has changed! That is just what happened to Rip Van Winkle, who took more than a nap!

JUST FOR FUN

THE MERRY-GO-ROUND AND THE GRIGGSES (5-6) 24, 81

All six of the Griggs children saved their pennies until they had enough to ride on the circus merry-go-round. They certainly didn't expect the wonderful surprise the kind merry-go-round gave them!

THE WORKMEN BUILD THE HOUSE (5-6) 4

Have you ever helped build a house? Well, then, let's build one right now—a nice, big, bright, new house!

THE INDOOR NOISY BOOK (5-6) 37

The little dog Muffin has a cold and must stay in bed, but he has fun listening. Who could the visitor be who walks so softly?

THE SEASHORE NOISY BOOK (5-6) 64

Muffin has never been to the sea before, so you can imagine his surprise at all the new noises he hears and sights he sees. The biggest noise and funniest sight of all, however, is Muffin himself!

TWO LITTLE SHOES (5-6) 81

Do you know how it is to feel like an old shoe? Well, just imagine how it would feel to be Sally Lou's two little scuffed shoes that were put aside for a shiny new pair of strap slippers!

GINGHAM LENA (5-6) 81

Along the highway, past the schoolhouse and the Church of Blooming Valley, frisks a little gingham dog looking for a blue-eyed doll with orange wool hair and a smudgy face. Perhaps if he looks behind a pink bonnet in the blackberry patch, he might find her.

COME MEET THE CLOWNS (5-6) 18

Heigh ho! Who doesn't love a circus? Why, look! Here come clowns of every sort—tall, thin Ga-Ga; short, fat Bumpo; sad-faced Droopie; and Baggo, who has to be pumped up with air.

SHHHH—BANG, A WHISPERING BOOK (5-8) 66

sh—for in this town, everyone is oh, so very quiet. They just whisper. All of a sudden, in comes a visitor WITH A BANG!

MR. AND MRS. VINEGAR (7-8) 5, 6, 12, 23, 26, 73, 89

Living in a vinegar bottle is really rather silly, but Mr. Vinegar was even sillier. One morning, he started out with forty gold pieces and bought and traded all the rest of the day. And my, what a sound cudgelling Mrs. Vinegar gave him!

AND TO THINK THAT I SAW IT ON MULBERRY STREET (7-12) 3

You're never quite sure what you'll greet going down Mulberry Street. For in this wonderful tale, you can "turn a minnow into a whale!"

THE EMPEROR'S NEW CLOTHES (7-12) 8 Vol. V, 12, 13, 24, 27, 73, 78, 89

What do you think of two rogues who deceived a whole kingdom? Weavers of magic cloth, indeed! Even the Emperor dared not admit he couldn't see the cloth at all.

THE LITTLE WOMAN WHO WANTED NOISE (7-12) 43

The country always sounds very quiet in comparison with the city hustle-bustle. The Little Woman couldn't stand the country quiet, until she heard a noise that was, to her, "delicious," and better than machines or animals. The answer even rhymes with noise!

THE SQUIRE'S BRIDE (9-14) 6, 8: Vol. IV, 22, 78, 89

When the miserly old Squire wanted something, he was used to having his way. And so it was when he decided to marry. What a hilarious trick the neighbor's daughter played on him—a trick which cured him from ever courting again!

THE UNCOMMON COMMON SAILOR (9-14) 40

The captain of Her Majesty's Ship Pinafore, anchored at Portsmouth Bay, was the pompous Sir Joseph. Little Buttercup was, of course, one of his favorite passengers, but his crew made life very difficult for him.

THE OLD WOMAN AND THE TRAMP (9-14) 6

Who ever heard of making broth out of a nail? A witty tramp persuaded a stingy old woman that it could be done. She thought it would be a fine trick, but little did she think that she'd have to bare her cupboard in the bargain!

DON QUIXOTE (12-14) 8: Vol. V, 12

Have you ever heard of such a strange old man as Don Quixote, who actually believed he was a knight-errant back in the days of chivalrous adventure? In truth, he had read so many tales of knighthood that he knew just how to proceed. He donned his great-grandfather's suit of armour, equipped himself with a steed and a squire, and launched himself on the great and fantastic adventures of "The Valorous and Witty Knight-Errant, Don Quixote of La Manche."

STORY BIBLIOGRAPHY

1. *Abraham Lincoln,* Ingri and Edgar Parin d' Aulaire, Doubleday and Company.
2. *The Adventures of Huckleberry Finn,* Mark Twain, Harper & Brothers.
3. *And to Think That I Saw It on Mulberry Street,* T. S. Geisel, Vanguard Press, Inc.

4. *Another Here and Now Story Book,* Lucy S. Mitchell, E. P. Dutton and Company.
5. *Anthology of Children's Literature,* Edna Johnson, Carrie Scott, and Evelyn Sickels, Houghton Mifflin Company.
6. *Bag o' Tales,* Effie Power, E. P. Dutton & Company.
7. *Bible Stories,* Rev. Jesse L. Hurlbut, D.D., The John C. Winston Company.
8. *The Book House,* Six Volumes, Olive Beaupre Miller, The Book House for Children.
9. *The Book of King Arthur,* Howard Pyle, Charles Scribner's Sons.
10. *Captains Courageous,* Rudyard Kipling, Doubleday and Company.
11. *The Children's Homer, The Adventures of Odysseus* and *The Tale of Troy,* Padraic Colum, The Macmillan Company.
12. *Children's Literature,* C. M. Curry and E. E. Clippinger, Rand McNally and Company.
13. *Children's Stories to Read or Tell for Pleasure and Understanding,* Alice I. Hazeltine, Abingdon-Cokesbury Press.
14. *Ching Li and The Dragons,* A. W. Howard, The Macmillan Company.
15. *Choo Choo, The Story of a Little Engine Who Ran Away,* Virginia Lee Burton, Houghton Mifflin Company.
16. *The Christmas Carol,* Charles Dickens, E. P. Dutton and Company, The Macmillan Company.
17. *Clear the Track for Michael's Magic Train,* Louis Slobodkin, The Macmillan Company.
18. *Come Meet the Clowns,* Dorothy Neumann, The Macmillan Company.
19. *The Country Bunny and the Little Gold Shoes,* Du Bose Heyward, Houghton Mifflin Company.
20. *Czechoslovak Fairy Tales,* Parker Fillmore, Harcourt, Brace and Company.

21. *The Dancing Tea Kettle,* Yoshiko Uchida, Harcourt, Brace and Company.
22. *East o' the Sun and West o' the Moon,* Gudrun Thorne-Thomsen, Row, Peterson and Company.
23. *English Fairy Tales,* Joseph Jacobs, G. P. Putnam's Sons.
24. *Favorite Stories Old and New,* Sidonie M. Gruenberg, Doubleday and Company.
25. *Feasts and Frolics,* Phyllis R. Fenner, Alfred A. Knopf.
26. *Firelight Stories,* Carolyn S. Bailey, Milton Bradley Company.
27. *Folk and Fairy Tales,* Childcraft III, Field Enterprises, Inc.
28. *From Long Ago and Many Lands,* Sophia B. Fahs, Beacon Press.
29. *Gift of the Earth,* Pachita Crespi, Charles Scribner's Sons.
30. *The Golden Book of Bible Stories,* C. M. Sheldon, Grosset and Dunlap, Inc.
31. *Good Stories for Great Holidays,* Frances Jenkins Olcott, Houghton Mifflin Company.
32. *Hans Brinker,* M. M. Dodge, Harper & Brothers.
33. *Heigh Ho for Hallowe'en,* Elizabeth H. Sechrist, Macrae Smith Company.
34. *The House at Pooh Corner,* A. A. Milne, E. P. Dutton & Company.
35. *How to Tell Stories to Children,* Sara Cone Bryant, Houghton Mifflin Company.
36. *In Clean Hay,* E. P. Kelly, The Macmillan Company.
37. *Indoor Noisy Book,* Margaret W. Brown, William R. Scott, Inc.
38. *Jesus, The Story of,* New Testament, The Macmillan Company.
39. *Just So Stories,* Rudyard Kipling, Doubleday and Company.
40. *The Last Pirate,* Louis Untermeyer, Harcourt, Brace and Company.
41. *The Little Island,* Golden McDonald, Doubleday and Company.
42. *Little Lamb,* Dahris Martin, Harper & Brothers.

43. *The Little Woman Who Wanted Noise,* Valentine Teal, Rand McNally and Company.
44. *Little Women,* Louisa May Alcott, Grosset and Dunlap, Inc.
45. *Merry Adventures of Robin Hood of Great Renown in Nottinghamshire,* Howard Pyle, Charles Scribner's Sons.
46. *Monkey See, Monkey Do,* Ruth Tooze, Grosset and Dunlap, Inc.
47. *More Friends and Neighbors* (2), W. S. Gray and M. H. Arbuthnot, Scott Publications, Inc.
48. *More Mother Stories,* Vachel Lindsay, Milton Bradley Company.
49. *Mrs. Goose and the Three Ducks,* Miriam Potter, Frederick A. Stokes and Company.
50. *Mrs. Mallaby's Birthday,* Helen E. Gilbert, Rand McNally and Company.
51. *The Nürnberg Stove,* Louisa de la (Ouida) Ramee, J. B. Lippincott Company.
52. *Penrod,* Booth Tarkington, Grosset and Dunlap, Inc.
53. *Peter Pan,* Sir James M. Barrie, edited by Frederick Perkins, Silver Burdett Company.
54. *The Plain Princess,* Phyllis McGinley, J. B. Lippincott Company.
55. *The Prince and The Pauper,* Mark Twain, Harper & Brothers.
56. *The Prize Song,* Henriette Weber, Oxford University Press.
57. *The Queen's Museum and Other Fanciful Tales,* Frank R. Stockton, Charles Scribner's Sons.
58. *The Rainbow Cat,* Rose Fyleman, Doubleday and Company.
59. *Read to Me Story Book,* Child Study Association of America, The Thomas Y. Crowell Company.
60. *Red Fairy Book,* Andrew Lang, Longmans, Green and Company.
61. *Red Mittens,* Laura Bannon, Houghton Mifflin Company.
62. *Rip Van Winkle and the Legend of Sleepy Hollow,* Washington Irving, The Macmillan Company.

63. *The Runaway Bunny,* Margaret W. Brown, Harper & Brothers.
64. *The Seashore Noisy Book,* Margaret W. Brown, William R. Scott, Inc.
65. *Shakespeare Story-Book,* Mary MacLeod, A. S. Barnes and Company.
66. *Shhhh—Bang, A Whispering Book,* Margaret W. Brown, Harper & Brothers.
67. *The Sketchbook,* Washington Irving, J. B. Lippincott Company.
68. *Snippy and Snappy,* Wanda Gag, Coward-McCann, Inc.
69. *A Star Shone,* Robbie Trent, Harper & Brothers.
70. *Stories from Great Metropolitan Operas,* Helen Dike, Random House.
71. *Stories to Begin On,* Rhoda W. Bacmeister, Dutton and Company.
72. *Stories to Tell to Children,* Sara Cone Bryant, Houghton Mifflin Company.
73. *Story and Verse for Children,* Miriam Blanton Huber, The Macmillan Company.
74. *Story of Ulysses,* M. Clarke, American Book Company.
75. *A Surprise for Mrs. Bunny,* Charlotte Steiner, Grosset and Dunlap, Inc.
76. *Tales from Shakespeare,* Charles and Mary Ann Lamb, The Macmillan Company.
77. *Tales of a Chinese Grandmother,* Frances Carpenter, Doubleday and Company, Inc.
78. *Tales of Many Lands,* Alice Schneider, Citadel Press.
79. *Tales of Olden Days, Kinscella Readers,* Hazel Gertrude Kinscella, The University Publishing Company.
80. *This Way to Christmas,* Ruth Sawyer, Harper & Brothers.
81. *Told Under the Magic Umbrella,* Literature Committee of the Association for Childhood Education, The Macmillan Company.
82. *Tom Sawyer,* Samuel L. Clemens, Harper & Brothers.

83. *The Topaz Story Book,* Ada M. Skinner, Eleanor L. Skinner, Duffield and Company.
84. *Treasure Island,* Robert Louis Stevenson, Rand McNally Company.
85. *The Way of the Storyteller,* Ruth Sawyer, Viking Press.
86. *Where Love Is and What Men Live By,* Count Lyof Nikolaye-vitch, Thomas Y. Crowell Company.
87. *Why the Chimes Rang,* Raymond MacDonald Alden, Bobbs-Merrill Company.
88. *The Winter Noisy Book,* Margaret W. Brown, William R. Scott, Inc.
89. *A World of Stories for Children,* Barrett Clark and M. Jagendorf, Bobbs-Merrill Company.

Appendix B

DRAMATIC PLAY AND PANTOMIMES

We have included suggestions for rhythmic and dramatic play for young children and pantomimes for older children. These lists are by no means complete and are intended primarily for the purpose of stimulating the imagination of the leader so that she may in turn stimulate the imaginations of the children.

RHYTHMIC AND DRAMATIC PLAY

Helping Mother at Home
  Washing dishes
  Making beds
  Sweeping and vacuuming
  Dusting furniture
  Making cookies
  Cutting cookies
  Baking cookies
  Frosting cookies
  Setting the table
  Eating cookies and drinking milk
  Planning Surprises
Helping Father at Home
  Raking leaves
  Pushing a heavy wheelbarrow

Mowing the lawn
Cutting hedges
Watering flowers
Hoeing the garden
Washing the car
Going for a ride in the car

Going to the Park

Riding a bus to the park
Riding on a merry-go-round
Playing on teeter-totters
Swinging in park swings
Pushing each other in swings
Wading in the pool
Rolling on the grass
Buying ice cream cones
Walking to the bus
Riding home at the end of the day

Going to the Forest

Hiking up a hill
Carrying heavy duffle
Making camp
Making a bonfire
Being animals and birds frolicking in the forest
Being animals and birds fearing campers when they come near
Being raindrops dancing in a deeply wooded forest
Being sunbeams dancing in the forest when the raindrops dance
away
Being autumn leaves scurrying and dancing among the trees
Being elves and fairies dancing in the forest
Being campers picnicking in the forest
Being campers hiking down the hill

Going to the Zoo

Riding on a bus to the zoo
Skipping across the lawn to animal cages

Riding around the ring on shetland ponies
Riding around the ring on high-stepping horses
Being elephants eating hay, eating peanuts, and drinking water
Being monkeys playing and chattering in an outdoor cage
Being lions pacing back and forth in iron cages
Being polar bears swimming and playing in a deep pool
Being kangaroos hopping and leaping in an outdoor pen
Being peacocks strutting along a winding path
Being parrots talking together in a large indoor cage
Being swans swimming in a pool

Going to the Rodeo

Arriving at the grandstand
Being cowboys playing in a rodeo band
Being cowboys riding into the arena in a grand parade
Being cowboys whirling lariats over heads and roping steers
Being work-horses pulling heavy loads in a pulling contest
Being prize-winning horses parading in a ring while being led
   by proud owners
Being race-horses galloping around the track
Being Indians dancing ceremonial dances

Going to a Railroad Station

Being passenger trains waiting for passengers
Being conductors taking tickets
Being passengers boarding the trains
Being passenger trains steaming away to special places
Being freight trains chugging into the station
Being trainmen unloading freight cars
Being trainmen loading cars with freight
Being freight trains clanging and puffing their way out of the
   station
Being freight trains climbing up steep mountains

Going to a Service Station

Being service station attendants sweeping and cleaning the station

Being cars chugging into the station
Being attendants washing cars
Being cars coming into station for gasoline and oil
Being attendants servicing a large trailer-truck
Being attendants servicing a school bus that is carrying children
Being attendants putting air into bicycle tires

Building a House

Being steamshovels digging a basement
Being bulldozers pushing dirt and trees
Being trucks bringing loads of brick and lumber
Being carpenters sawing boards
Being masons mixing cement
Being masons wheeling heavy wheelbarrows
Being carpenters hammering boards
Being painters painting the house
Being gardeners making a lawn
Being gardeners planting shrubs, trees, and flowers

Being in a Parade

Being in a band playing instruments
Being drum majors and majorettes
Being policemen parading with drums
Being policemen parading on horses
Being policemen parading on motorcycles
Being policemen parading in motor cars
Being soldiers and sailors parading on Independence Day
Being clowns parading in a circus parade
Being circus animals parading in a circus ring
Being airplanes flying in formation over a city

Going to a Farm

Being farmers driving cows and sheep to pasture
Being cows and sheep grazing in a deep meadow
Being farmers riding after horses and driving them into the
    barnyard
Being frisky young colts galloping in the pasture

Being farmers hauling hay into the barn
Being teams of horses pulling heavy hayracks full of hay
Being farmers plowing a large field with tractors and plows
Being farmers feeding chickens, ducks, and turkeys
Being chickens, ducks, turkeys and geese in the chickenyard
Being farmers eating a hearty dinner

PANTOMIMES

Large Action

Pantomiming sports, such as skiing, tennis, golf, basketball, boxing, fencing, swimming, fishing

Pantomiming occupations, such as that of a farmer, clerk, fisherman, tailor, shoemaker, woodsman, gardener, janitor, carpenter, truck driver, waiter

Pantomiming professions, such as that of a doctor, minister, musician, teacher, nurse, beauty operator, engineer, stenographer

Pantomiming modes of travel, such as hiking, riding a horse, riding in a buggy, bicycling, motorcycling, riding on a bus, riding on a train, riding on a boat, riding on a plane

Pantomiming characterizations of historical figures, such as Christopher Columbus, William Penn, George Washington, Daniel Boone, Benjamin Franklin

Pantomiming characterizations of national sport figures, such as Babe Ruth, Joe Louis

Pantomiming characterizations of holiday figures, such as Hallowe'en witches, ghosts, cats, goblins, Thanksgiving turkeys, pilgrims, Indians, Santa Claus, shepherds, wise men, angels, carolers

Pantomiming characterizations from favorite stories, such as Long John Silver, Jim Hawkins, Tom Sawyer, Huck Finn, Aunt Polly, Cinderella, Fairy Godmother, Rumpelstiltskin, Mary Poppins

Small Action

Pantomiming daily habits of washing, brushing teeth, combing hair, eating a meal, and dressing

Pantomiming daily activities, such as writing a letter, opening a letter, reading a letter, reading a book, reading a newspaper

Pantomiming activity concerned with washing and drying dishes and setting a table

Pantomiming activity concerned with making a cake, measuring the ingredients, breaking eggs, beating eggs, stirring batter, pouring batter into pans, and putting cake into oven.

Pantomiming activity concerned with harvesting fruit, such as picking apples, cherries, peaches, plums, pears, grapes, and raspberries

Pantomiming activity concerned with building a house, such as measuring, sawing, reading blueprints, hammering, using a plane, sanding, painting

Working in Pairs

Two boys carrying on a friendly telephone conversation

A young girl buying bus fare from the driver as she boards a bus

A daughter marking the hem in a new dress for her mother

A grandfather getting a haircut from an inexperienced barber

A young boy taking an accordion lesson from a famous instructor

A policeman signalling for a woman to return to the curb after she has started to cross the street against a traffic light

A father teaching his son how to drive a new car

A nurse bringing a glass of water to a patient in a hospital

A young girl having her fortune told by a gypsy

A grandmother receiving a special delivery letter

Emotional Experience in Groups

A carnival is in town. A gay crowd walks down the midway. They watch eager barkers inviting the crowds to ride on merry-go-rounds, ferris wheels, roller coasters, and to see colossal side-shows.

A family of six hunt pheasant in a large corn field. Everyone becomes anxious when it is learned that their hunting dog has disappeared. Each one looks for the dog. At last he is found. He has been shot and is badly wounded.

Neighbors in a small community decorate a Christmas tree for a small boy. The child has just returned from a hospital. He has been in a cast for three months as a result of an automobile accident.

Young teen-agers enjoy ice cream sodas after a victorious football game.

A teacher loses her diamond ring while she is chaperoning a school picnic. The news spreads quickly. Everyone searches for the ring. At last it is found.

Vacationers at a summer resort stroll casually along a hotel veranda. They suddenly recognize a famous radio celebrity.

A party of campers are sleeping in sleeping bags out in the open near a mountain stream. They are suddenly awakened in the middle of the night by a weird noise. Two of the bravest boys investigate.

Situations in Groups

A party of six foreign travelers enter a dining room in a large hotel. They are served breakfast by a waiter.

Four shrewd individuals play a game of cards in an observation car on a passenger train.

A group of neighbors watch a funny television show.

Boy Scouts see Old Faithful in Yellowstone Park for the first time.

Camp Fire girls enjoy a taffy-pull after an evening of ice skating.

At a family reunion, sixteen members decide to pose for a family portrait. The photographer has considerable difficulty with his camera and with the relatives. Finally, after several trials, he gets one satisfactory picture.

Appendix C

BIBLIOGRAPHY

We have included the best books that are available in the field of creative dramatics. We have listed others that are largely concerned with child psychology and child growth and development. Others have been selected because of the interpretation they present of the philosophy of creative teaching.

Books in various fields have been suggested either for background material or for the practical technique they present in a specific area. The reader will be interested in discovering through related reading that the technique in releasing a child's creative activity is fundamentally the same in all fields.

We have categorized the books in the hope that specific reading material may be located more readily, but it should be understood that the divisions are flexible. For instance, parents will find many books listed under the Education division that will be of specific help to them, whereas teachers and educators will find valuable suggestions listed under divisions other than their specific field.

HOME

Bacmeister, Rhoda W., *Caring For the Run-About Child,* E. P. Dutton & Company, 1937.

Bacmeister, Rhoda, W., *Growing Together,* D. Appleton-Century Company, 1947.

Baruch, Dorothy W., *Parents Can Be People,* D. Appleton-Century Company, 1944.

Benedict, Agnes E., and Franklin, Adele, *The Happy Home,* Appleton-Century-Crofts, 1948.

Coleman, Satis N., *Creative Music in the Home,* The John Day Company, 1939.

Garrison, Charlotte G., and Sheehy, Emma D., *At Home With Children,* Henry Holt and Company, 1943.

Grossman, Jean Schick, *Life With Family,* Appleton-Century-Crofts, 1948.

Gruenberg, Sidonie M., *We, the Parents,* Harper & Brothers, 1939.

Millgate, Irvine H., and Millgate, Rachel, W., *Let's Live At Home,* Harper & Brothers, 1949.

EDUCATION

Adams, Fay, *Educating America's Children,* The Ronald Press, 1946.

Association for Supervision and Curriculum Development, 1950 Yearbook, *Fostering Mental Health in Our Schools,* National Education Association, 1950.

Ausubel, David P., "Problems of Adolescent Adjustment," *The Bulletin,* National Association of Secondary-School Principals, January, 1950, pp. 1 ff.

Averill, Lawrence A., *The Psychology of the Elementary-School Child,* Longmans, Green and Company, 1949.

Baruch, Dorothy W., *New Ways in Discipline,* McGraw-Hill Book Company, 1949.

Caswell, Hollis L., and Foshay, A. Wellesley, *Education in the Elementary School,* American Book Company, 2d ed., 1950.

Cole, Luella, and Morgan, John J. B., *Psychology of Childhood and Adolescence,* Rinehart and Company, 1947.

Dale, Edgar, *Audio-Visual Methods in Teaching,* The Dryden Press, 1946.

Dewey, John, *Experience and Education,* The Macmillan Company, 1938.

Dixon, Clarice M., *High, Wide and Deep,* The John Day Company, 1938.

Forest, Ilse, *Early Years at School,* McGraw-Hill Book Company, 1949.

Frank, Mary and Lawrence K., *How to Help Your Child in School,* The Viking Press, 1950.

Gesell, Arnold, *The First Five Years of Life,* Harper & Brothers, 1940.

Gesell, Arnold, and Ilg, Frances L., *Infant and Child in the Culture of Today,* Harper & Brothers, 1943.

Gesell, Arnold, and Ilg, Frances L., *The Child From Five to Ten,* Harper & Brothers, 1946.

Griswold, Frederic H., *Creative Power,* David McKay Company, 1939.

Hartman, Gertrude, and Shumaker, Ann, (Eds.), Progressive Education Association, *Creative Expression*, The John Day Company, 1932.

Lane, Robert H., *The Teacher in the Modern Elementary School*, Houghton Mifflin Company, 1941.

Lee, Jonathan, and Lee, Doris M., *The Child and His Curriculum*, Appleton-Century-Crofts, 2d ed., 1950.

Lowenfeld, Viktor, *The Nature of Creative Activity*, Harcourt, Brace and Company, 1939.

Lowenfeld, Viktor, *Creative and Mental Growth*, The Macmillan Company, 1947.

Mearns, Hughes, *Creative Youth*, Doubleday, Doran & Company, 1928.

Mearns, Hughes, *Creative Power*, Doubleday, Doran & Company, 1935.

Mearns, Hughes, *The Creative Adult*, Doubleday, Doran & Company, 1940.

National Elementary Principal, Twenty Third Yearbook, *Creative Schools*, National Education Association, 1944.

Poston, Richard W., *Small Town Renaissance*, Harper & Brothers, 1950.

Pratt, Caroline, *I Learn From Children*, Simon and Schuster, 1948.

Pressey, Sidney L., and Robinson, Francis P., *Psychology and the New Education*, Harper & Brothers, rev. ed., 1944.

Read, Katherine H., *The Nursery School*, W. B. Saunders Company, 1950.

Redl, Fritz, *Understanding Children's Behavior*, Bureau of Publications, Teachers College, Columbia University, 1949.

Slavson, Samuel R., *Creative Group Education*, Association Press, 1937.

Torgerson, Theodore L., *Studying Children*, The Dryden Press, 1949.

Washburn, Ruth W., *Children Know Their Friends*, William Morrow and Company, 1949.

Weber, Julia, *My Country School Diary*, Harper & Brothers, 1946.

Weill, Blanche C., *Through Children's Eyes*, Island Workshop Press, 1940.

ART

Cole, Natalie R., *The Arts in the Classroom*, The John Day Company, 1942.

D'Amico, Victor E., *Creative Teaching in Art*, International Textbook Company, 1942.

Dewey, John, *Art As Experience*, Minton Balch and Company, 1934.
Dunnett, Ruth, *Art and Child Personality*, London, Methuen, 1948.
Edman, Irwin, *The World, the Arts and the Artist*, W. W. Norton and Company, 1928.
Gregg, Harold, *Art for the Schools of America*, International Textbook Company, 2d ed., 1947.
Hartman, Gertrude, (Ed.), *Creative Expression Through Art, A Symposium* . . . The Progressive Education Association.
Perrine, Van Dearing, *Let the Child Draw,* Frederick A. Stokes Company, 1936.
Shaw, Ruth F., *Finger Painting*, Little, Brown, and Company, 1934.
Tomlinson, Reginald R., and Holme, C. G. (Ed.), *Picture Making by Children*, The Studio Publications, 1934.
Tomlinson, Reginald R., *Children as Artists*, The King Penguin Books, 1944.
Zaidenberg, Arthur, *Your Child Is An Artist*, Grosset and Dunlap, 1949.

DRAMA AND SPEECH

Alekseev, Konstantin S. (Stanislavsky, Constantin, Pseud.), *Building A Character*, Theatre Arts Books, 1949.
Barton, Lucy, *Historic Costume for the Stage*, Walter H. Baker Company, 1935.
Brown, Corrine, *Creative Drama in the Lower School*, D. Appleton and Company, 1929.
Brown, Ivor, *Shakespeare*, Doubleday and Company, 1949.
Burger, Isabel B., *Creative Play Acting*, A. S. Barnes, 1950.
Cheney, Sheldon, *The Theatre: 3000 Years of Drama, Acting, and Stagecraft*, Longmans, Green and Company, 1930.
Childs, Jessica, *Building Character Through Dramatization*, Row Peterson and Company, 1934.
Clark, Barrett H., and Freedley, George (Eds.), *A History of Modern Drama*, D. Appleton-Century Company, 1947.
Fisher, Caroline E., and Robertson, Hazel G., *Children and the Theatre*, Stanford University Press, 1940.
Freedley, George, and Reeves, John A., *A History of the Theatre*, Crown Publishers, 1941.
Gassner, John, *Producing the Play*, The Dryden Press, 1941.
Hill, Frank E., *To Meet Will Shakespeare*, Dodd, Mead & Company, 1949.

Hughes, Glenn, *The Story of the Theatre*, Samuel French, 1928.

Merrill, John, and Fleming, Martha, *Play-Making and Plays*, The Macmillan Company, 1930.

Nicoll, Allardyce, *The Development of the Theatre*, Harcourt, Brace and Company, 3d rev. ed., 1946.

Ommanney, Katharine A., and Ommanney, Pierce C., *The Stage and the School*, Harper & Brothers, 2d rev. ed., 1950.

Pardoe, T. Earl, *Pantomimes for Stage and Study*, D. Appleton-Century Company, 1931.

Rasmussen, Carrie, *Speech Methods in the Elementary School*, The Ronald Press Company, 1949.

Ward, Winifred L., *Creative Dramatics for the Upper Grades and Junior High School*, D. Appleton-Century Company, 1930.

Ward, Winifred L., *Theatre for Children*, D. Appleton-Century Company, 1939.

Ward, Winifred L., *Playmaking with Children*, D. Appleton-Century Company, 1947.

Webster, Margaret, *Shakespeare Without Tears*, Whittlesey House, McGraw-Hill Book Company, 1942.

MUSIC AND RHYTHMS

Coleman, Satis N., *Creative Music for Children*, G. P. Putnam's Sons, 1922.

Dixon, Clarice M., *The Power of Dance*, The John Day Company, 1938.

H'Doubler, Margaret N., *Dance: A Creative Art Experience*, F. S. Crofts and Company, 1940.

Driver, Ann, *Music and Movement*, Oxford University Press, 1936.

Fox, Lillian M., and Hopkins, L. Thomas, *Creative School Music*, Silver Burdett Company, 1936.

Krone, Beatrice P., *Music in the New School*, Neil A. Kjos Music Company, rev. ed., 1941.

Myers, Louise K., *Teaching Children Music in the Elementary School*, Prentice Hall, 1950.

Pitts, Lilla B., *The Music Curriculum in a Changing World*, Silver Burdett Company, 1944.

Pitts, Lilla B., and Tipton, Gladys (Eds.), *A Library of RCA Victor Records for Elementary Schools: Basic Rhythms Program*, Radio Corporation of America, RCA Victor Division, 1947.

Sheehy, Emma D., *There's Music in Children,* Henry Holt and Company, 1946.

Thompson, Carl O., and Nordholm, Harriet, *Keys To Teaching Elementary School Music,* Paul A. Schmitt Music Company, 1949.

Waterman, Elizabeth, *A. B. C. of Rhythmic Training,* Clayton F. Summy Co., rev. ed., 1927.

Waterman, Elizabeth, *The Rhythm Book,* A. S. Barnes and Company, 1936.

RELIGION

Carrier, Blanche, *How Shall I Learn to Teach Religion,* Harper & Brothers, 1930.

Chaplin, Dora P., *Children and Religion,* Charles Scribner's Sons, 1948.

Chave, Ernest J., *A Functional Approach to Religious Education,* University of Chicago Press, 1947.

Hoag, Frank V., *It's Fun to Teach,* Morehouse-Gorham Company, 1949.

Kunkel, Fritz, *Character, Growth, Education,* J. B. Lippincott Company, 1938.

Kunkel, Fritz, *In Search of Maturity,* Charles Scribner's Sons, 1943.

Ligon, Ernest M., *A Greater Generation,* The Macmillan Company, 1948.

Manwell, Elizabeth M., and Fahs, Sophia L., *Consider the Children— How They Grow,* The Beacon Press, 1946.

Munkres, Alberta, *Primary Methods in the Church School,* Abingdon Press, rev. ed., 1930.

Shields, Elizabeth M., *Happy Times in Our Church,* John Knox Press, 1940.

Wieman, Regina W., *The Family Lives Its Religion,* Harper & Brothers, 1941.

CHILDREN'S LITERATURE

Arbuthnot, May H., *Children and Books,* Scott, Foresman, 1947.

Becker, May L., *Adventures in Reading,* J. B. Lippincott, rev. ed., 1946.

Duff, Annis, *Bequest of Wings,* The Viking Press, 1940.

Eaton, Anne T., *Reading with Children,* The Viking Press, 1940.

Eaton, Anne T., *Treasure for the Taking,* The Viking Press, 1946.

Hartman, Gertrude, *Medieval Days and Ways,* The Macmillan Company, 1937.

Hazard, Paul, *Books, Children, and Men,* The Horn Book, 3d ed., 1947.

Hollowell, Lillian (Ed.), *A Book of Children's Literature,* Farrar & Rinehart, 2d ed., 1950.

Huber, Miriam, B., *Story and Verse for Children,* The Macmillan Company, 1940.

Johnson, Edna, Scott, Carrie E., and Sickels, Evelyn R., (Comps.), *Anthology of Children's Literature,* Houghton Mifflin Company, 2d ed., 1948.

Moore, Anne C., *My Roads to Childhood,* Doubleday, Doran & Company, 1939.

Sawyer, Ruth, *The Way of the Storyteller,* The Viking Press, 1947.

Shedlock, Marie L., *The Art of the Story-teller,* D. Appleton-Century Company, rev. ed., 1936.

SOCIAL WORK

Allen, Frederick H., *Psychotherapy with Children,* W. W. Norton Company, 1942.

Axline, Virginia M., *Play Therapy,* Houghton Mifflin Company, 1947.

Gillies, Emily P., "Crosses and Knives," *Childhood Education,* May, 1946, pp. 435 ff.; April, 1947, pp. 382 ff.

Gillies, Emily P., "Therapy Dramatics for the Public Schoolroom," *The Nervous Child,* July, 1948, pp. 328 ff.

Haas, Robert B. (Ed.), *Psychodrama and Sociodrama in American Education,* Beacon House, 1949.

Hamilton, Gordon, *Psychotherapy in Child Guidance,* Columbia University Press, 1947.

Hogue, Helen G., *Untying Apron Strings,* Character Associates, 1936.

Jackson, Lydia, and Todd, Kathleen M., *Child Treatment and the Therapy of Play,* The Ronald Press Company, 2d ed., 1950.

Jersild, Arthur T., *Child Psychology,* Prentice-Hall, 3d ed., 1947.

Lewis, Nolan D. C. (Ed.), *Modern Trends in Child Psychiatry,* International Universities Press, 1945.

Moreno, Jacob L., "Mental Catharsis and the Psychodrama," *Sociometry,* July, 1940, pp. 209 ff.

Moreno, Jacob L., *Psychodrama,* Beacon House, 1946.

RECREATION

Butler, George D., *Introduction to Community Recreation,* McGraw-Hill Book Company, rev. 2d ed., 1949.

Canadian Youth Commission, *Youth and Recreation,* (Report No. 6), The Ryerson Press, 1946.

Cox, Doris E., and Weismann, Barbara W., *Creative Hands,* John Wiley and Sons, 1945.

Dank, Michael C., *Creative Crafts in Wood,* The Manual Arts Press, 1945.

Fitzgerald, Gerald B., *Community Organization for Recreation,* A. S. Barnes, 1950.

Harbin, Elvin O., *The Fun Encyclopedia,* Abingdon Cokesbury Press, 1940.

Jones, Anna M., *Leisure Time Education,* Harper & Brothers, 1946.

Lambert, Clara, *School's Out,* Harper & Brothers, 1944.

Meyer, Harold D., and Brightbill, Charles K., *Community Recreation,* D. C. Heath and Company, 1948.

Mitchell, Elmer D., and Mason, Bernard S., *The Theory of Play,* A. S. Barnes, rev. & enl. ed., 1948.

Mulac, Margaret E., *Playleaders' Manual,* Harper & Brothers, 1941.

Wrenn, Charles G., and Harley, D. L., *Time on their Hands,* American Council on Education, 1941.

Index